HARRY S. TRUMAN
The 'Little' Man From Missouri

BY
JOHN HOLLISTER HEDLEY

BARRON'S
WOODBURY, NEW YORK

remembering Hugo

All inquiries should be addressed to:
Barron's Educational Series, Inc.
113 Crossways Park Drive
Woodbury, New York 11797

Library of Congress Card No. 76-54969

International Standard Book No. 0-8120-5136-X

Library of Congress Cataloging in Publication Data

Hedley, John Hollister.
  Harry S. Truman, the 'little' man from Missouri.

  (Shapers of history series)
  Bibliography: p.
  Includes index.
  SUMMARY: A biography of the thirty-third president who helped end World War II and established
several programs to aid European recovery.
  1. Truman, Harry S., Pres. U.S., 1884-1972.
  2. Presidents — United States — Biography.
  3. United States — Politics and government — 1945-
1953. 4. United States — Foreign relations — 1945-
1953. [1. Truman, Harry S., Pres. U.S., 1884-1972.
  2. Presidents.   3. United States — Politics and
government — 1945-1953] I. Title.
E814.H38   973.918'092'4   [B]   76-54969
ISBN 0-8120-5136-X

Contents

Editor's Foreword

It is highly appropriate that John Hedley's study of the life of Harry S. Truman should appear at this time. Truman has only recently become the subject of an increasing volume of scholarly revision and the object of public interest and esteem. Even if Harry S. Truman had done nothing of importance as president, the fact that he presided over the nation's government during the last days of World War II and the beginning years of the Cold War would probably have earned him a significant place in history. Since he was a major factor in the evolution of U.S. policy in the postwar world and a proponent of major domestic programs, his reputation is insured. The chapter entitled "The Verdict of History" provides a comprehensive and important analysis of the changes in interpretations of Truman's presidency and the reasons for such changes.

John Hedley has drawn upon extensive research at the Truman library as well as a variety of more recent sources to give the reader a short and impartial analysis of the former president's career and of this extremely important period in the nation's history. As the author of several articles on U.S. policy toward Russia, Hedley is able to discuss this very significant subject with insight and skill. The selections from Truman's own speeches provided in the appendix give the reader not only the flavor of Truman's thoughts but an opportunity to judge and interpret their importance for him or herself.

John Hedley taught political science at the Universities of Missouri and Tulsa before joining government service. An earlier career in journalism makes this an especially well-written and understandable book. Hedley is currently on the staff of the U.S. Central Intelligence Agency.

I. E. Cadenhead, Jr.

Author's Preface

The reader should know what is in store. This book is not intended to be an exhaustive account of Harry Truman's life and presidency. It is a concise, specialized biography aimed at introducing the reader to the man and to the actions that form the essence of his imprint on history. The emphasis, then, is on Truman's role in international affairs. It is hoped that a feeling for his character and his times comes through as well.

The author is grateful for much help along the way: to the late President Truman and to the former director of the Truman Library, Dr. Philip C. Brooks, for their interest, inspiration, and cordial cooperation when my research began; to David Baad and to Henria and Charles Campbell, close friends who helped with constant encouragement, and to Marilyn Free for her typing and David Free for his reading of the manuscript.

A special debt of gratitude is owed to Ed Cadenhead, my editor, for his help in making this idea into a reality. Above all I appreciate my wife, Liz, and my daughters, Andrea and Allison, for their indispensable patience and understanding.

John Hollister Hedley

Centreville, Virginia

Acknowledgments

The author thanks the following for permission to quote from the works indicated: Alfred A. Steinberg for Alfred A. Steinberg, *The Man from Missouri* (© 1962); the Truman family for Harry S. Truman, *Memoirs* Volumes I and II (© 1955); Eric Sevareid for his column, "An Unknown Side of Truman" (© 1964); Coward, McCann & Geoghegan, Inc., Len Giovannitti and Fred Freed, *The Decision to Drop the Bomb* (© 1965); Farrar, Straus & Giroux, Inc., William Hillman, *Mr. President* (© 1952); Funk and Wagnalls, Arthur Krock, *Memoirs: Sixty Years on the Firing Line* (© 1968); Harcourt Brace Jovanovich, Inc., Clinton Rossiter, *The American Presidency* (© 1956); Houghton Mifflin Company, Winston Churchill, *Triumph and Tragedy* (© 1953); Little, Brown and Company in association with The Atlantic Monthly Press, Samuel Eliot Morison, *The Two-Ocean War* (© 1963); Macmillan Publishing Co., Inc., Cabell Phillips, *The Truman Presidency* (© 1969); M. Evans and Company, Inc., Charles L. Mee, Jr., *Meeting at Potsdam* (© 1975); and William Morrow and Company, Inc., Margaret Truman, *Harry S. Truman* (© 1973).

as well as the following:

From *HST* by David Thompson. Copyright © 1973 by Grosset & Dunlap, Inc. Reprinted by permission of Grosset & Dunlap, Inc.

From *The Berlin Blockade: A Study in Cold War Politics* by W. Phillips Davison. Copyright © 1958 by the Rand Corporation. Reprinted by permission of Princeton University Press.

1 A World at War

It is hard to imagine a challenge like the one Harry Truman faced when fate thrust him into the presidency on April 12, 1945. It came less than twelve weeks after his inauguration as vice-president in the shadow of the unprecedented fourth inauguration of Franklin Delano Roosevelt, the towering figure of the times and the dominant force in American politics for twelve years as the country's chief executive. During most of the brief period Truman was vice-president, Roosevelt had been away from Washington and much of the time was out of the country. President Roosevelt's sudden death had a tremendous impact on a nation still locked in the most awful war in history. An end to that war was only near enough at hand for specter of enormous postwar problems to be coming into view.

World War II was a monumental epoch of bloodshed and destruction that was changing the country and the world. Most of the world was caught up in it. No less than two dozen nations were directly involved in fighting which raged on three continents. It engulfed Europe and Asia. It included Africa, reached across the Middle East, and extended into the subcontinent of South Asia. The military machine of the Axis powers — Nazi Germany, Japan, and Italy, along with their associates, Bulgaria, Finland, Hungary, and Romania — pit more than 20 million men under arms against the Allied powers — principally the United States, the Soviet Union, China, Great Britain, and France, but including 12 other countries, which together raised armed forces numbering nearly 47 million. Before the fighting ended, 29 other countries had declared war on the Axis powers. It was a war so vast that few corners of the world escaped being engulfed by it. There were none that did not feel its effects.

The sinking of American ships by German submarines had led to an undeclared state of naval warfare with Germany, but World War II began for the U.S. — officially and in the sense of a unified national war effort — when on Sunday, December 7, 1941, Japan declared war on the U.S. and attacked the naval base at Pearl Harbor, Hawaii. The surprise assault killed more than 3000 Americans and destroyed or damaged nearly 200 airplanes and 15 ships, including eight battleships. By that time Germany already had taken over Austria, Czechoslovakia, Poland, Norway, Denmark, the Netherlands, Belgium, Luxembourg, and France; had invaded Russia; and was bombing Britain. Four days following Pearl Harbor, after which Congress had reciprocated Japan's declaration of war, Germany and Italy declared war on the U.S.

World War II is estimated to have caused the death of as many as 60 million people. In less than four years, it was to cost America one million casualties, including nearly 300,000 battle deaths (about six-and-a-half times the number of Americans killed in Vietnam over a 12-year period). From a population not even two-thirds the size of that recorded in the 1970 census, 15 million Americans served in the armed forces during World War II. The war effort cost the federal government $321 billion, and financing it caused a 530 percent increase in the national debt between 1941 and 1945.

With its unprecedented magnitude, World War II had far-reaching effects in America. It put a sudden premium on manpower after years of unemployment. War industries raised the work force by several million. Many women took jobs outside the home, millions of persons moved from rural areas to jobs in cities, and some two million blacks obtained work in defense plants. The country's productive effort was prodigious in the extreme. U.S. industry turned out 6500 ships, more than 85,000 tanks, and nearly 300,000 planes. America's productivity soared to such astronomical levels that by the beginning of 1944, it was double that of all the enemy countries combined.

Producing new types of weapons was an effort of the highest priority, as American scientists and engineers matched wits with their German counterparts. Scientific ingenuity was applied to the refinement of radar and sonar and to the development of countless devices such as improved bombsites and radio-directed proximity fuses. The most dramatic race in this deadly competition was the secret one to develop an atomic bomb. American physicists had learned in 1939 of experiments in Germany demonstrating the possibility of nuclear fission that could release energy in an explosive weapon of unprecedented power. Six months before Pearl Harbor, the U.S. Office of Scientific Research and Development was created. It was assigned joint responsibility with the War Department in the top-secret undertaking, known as the Manhattan Project, to build an atomic bomb. Two billion dollars was spent on plants and laboratories in a four-year race against time and enemy efforts before the first workable nuclear weapon was tested and readied for use.

During this time, the U.S. was doubling the output of its factories. American wages and living standards during World War II were rising higher than ever. Although it was a rare household that was not touched at least indirectly by the personal tragedies of war, most American families were benefiting economically. Personal incomes were a third greater than goods and services, which were made scarce by the country's war footing and the diversion of resources and production to meet military needs. During the war years, much of the excess purchasing power that was building up was drained off into purchases of war bonds and savings stamps. But pressures were building up that inevitably would overheat the economy and contribute to the dislocations of reconverting to peacetime and the return of millions of servicemen.

The direction of the economy in this colossal war effort, the conduct of international diplomacy with wartime allies, and the exercise of responsibility for determining the strategy and battle plans for massive military campaigns enhanced the pre-eminence of President Roosevelt. The revolutionary changes he introduced in leading the country from the depths of a depression did not, of course, make him revered by all his countrymen. And during the war there were debates over the way it should be waged. There were unending disputes over government controls — of prices, war production, and the allocation of war supplies and scarce consumer commodities. Yet the war, emphasizing the President's role as commander in chief and bestowing unprecedented powers on the office, made Franklin Roosevelt all the more indisputably the nation's leader.

Senator Truman

Until after the war buildup began, Harry Truman had no national prominence at all. For six years he had been just another midwestern senator, although in his first term he had distinguished himself as a hard worker. He was one of those freshmen congressmen who favorably impress the congressional leadership by coming to the Capitol not looking for the limelight but ready to work and eager to learn.

Truman usually got to his office at 7 a.m., returned home for dinner at 7 p.m., and had no taste for Washington society.[1] He kept quiet, did his homework, and learned a great deal from his two very favorable major committee assignments — to the Appropriations and the Interstate Commerce committees. (Only two others in the Senate, the Finance and the Foreign Relations committees, had equal or superior rank; long service in the Senate was generally a prerequisite for membership on any of them.)

Truman's work on the Appropriations Committee brought him directly in contact with America's rather frantic, eleventh-hour effort to arm and equip itself as the shadows of war were rapidly being cast more ominously across the horizon. During the six years of his first term, Truman never missed a meeting of the committee, perusing every federal expenditure. When he began his second term as senator in January, 1941, the country was undertaking a crash program to develop by leaps and bounds the military preparedness it was sadly lacking. It was decided that the nation needed a two-ocean navy, and must train and arm a million men a year for the next five years.

U.S. defense expenditures would soar beyond $25 billion in the first few months of 1941. Washington was swarming with people seeking contracts that were being hastily negotiated for the enormous, almost overnight expansion of military installations, equipment, munitions, and supplies. Money was being force-fed into this monumental buildup, but the early results showed confusion, waste, and a questionable return on the dollars expended.

Truman saw lobbyists seeking the inside track for purchases, contracts, and plant locations. He heard rumors of huge fees paid to them by big businesses that were cornering defense industries in certain large cities while thousands of small shops and factories were being forced out of work.

Machinery, in short supply, was being bought away from small businesses. When the machines were moved, workers had to follow, which meant greater concentrations of population and housing problems — of shortages in the cities to which workers moved and of vacant housing in the communities they left.

Truman suspected that certain contractors, manufacturers, and others were lining their pockets with inordinate wealth and that the taxpayers were getting less than their money's worth. He decided to look into the situation on his own. The month he was sworn in for his second Senate term, he got into his own car and began driving. He covered 30,000 miles from Washington through Maryland, then down to Florida, across to Texas, north through Oklahoma to Nebraska, and back across Wisconsin and Michigan. He visited military installations and defense plants throughout the trip without letting any of them know who he was.[2]

Firsthand observations turned Truman's suspicions into conviction. Upon his return to Washington, he explained to Senate leaders that he had no witch hunt in mind, and was not after publicity. After all, he had just been re-elected to a six-year term. But someone should be looking into the use of the vast sums being spent of defense. On February 10, 1941, he made a speech — to an almost empty Senate chamber — expressing his belief that things were going from bad to worse and that the national defense program was suffering. He introduced a resolution calling for the creation of a special investigating committee. It was a fateful move. A similar appeal had been made in the House of Representatives by a congressman who despised the Roosevelt administration. To keep that sworn enemy out of business, Jimmy Byrnes, influential senator from South Carolina and one of Roosevelt's chief spokesmen in the Senate, lent support to Truman's suggestion and the resolution was enacted. As its author, Truman was made chairman of a seven-member Special Committee to Investigate the National Defense Program. Byrnes, as head of the Senate's Audit and Control Committee, voted the grand sum of $10,000 (later negotiated by Truman up to $15,000) to conduct the investigation.[3] It was a budget calculated to keep the investigation on a scale that would not cause embarrassment to the administration.

Chairing a headline-making investigating committee can carry a congressman to fame, but getting a committee and its chairmanship in the first place is a major exercise in political finesse. It is not a simple feat just to obtain the right kind of committee. There must be a valid and dramatic subject for inquiry. The member of the House or Senate who would launch the investigation must sell the leadership on the idea. It is no small accomplishment to do this without having some prejudiced senior member nip it in the bud or preempt the chairmanship for himself. If the would-be chairman makes it this far, he is only at the beginning of the minefield he must cross when the committee comes into being and its work begins. He must continuously judge its direction, set the speed, and run the committee's affairs with a certain sense of showmanship and a large measure of managerial skill.

Determined not to let his committee be used for either a smear or a whitewash, Truman directed it strictly to the issue of how the war effort was being supported. Truman's avid interest in history took him to the Library of Congress, where he borrowed the only copy of the hearings of the Civil War Committee on the Conduct of the War. He studied closely its yellowed pages, and vowed not to visit upon Roosevelt the almost disastrous detraction and presumptuous meddling that a Republican Congress had imposed upon Abraham Lincoln from 1863 to 1865. Truman

remembered from his reading of history that Robert E. Lee
had considered that committee worth two divisions to the
Confederate cause. And Truman saw to it that his committee resisted any temptation to try to tell the President and the
generals how to run the war. He stuck to what he saw as the
business at hand: how defense contracts were being
awarded and fulfilled; how the country's economic and
manpower resources were being utilized; and how the responsible agencies of government — a bureaucracy that
mushroomed after the attack on Pearl Harbor — were doing
their job.[4] There was no desire and no time to range further
afield. The committee had plenty to do in digging out facts
and suggesting remedies before the problems it unearthed
did irreparable damage.

Three weeks before the Japanese attack on Pearl Harbor
which, followed by the declaration of war on the U.S. by
Germany and Italy, brought America into world war, the
Truman Committee issued a report, ''Concerning Priorities
and the Utilization of Existing Manufacturing Facilities.''
The Congressional Digest published the report three
months later and, in doing so, inadvertently illustrated the
fact that Harry Truman's name was still not widely known
and well established. In a paragraph introducing the report,
the journal explained to its readers that the Special Committee to Investigate the National Defense Program was being
referred to as ''the Truman Committee'' because its chairman was Harry S. Truman of *Indiana*.[5]

For three and a half years the Truman Committee was a
model of integrity, thoroughness, and conscientious fact-
finding. Persistently and impartially, the committee focused a spotlight on the construction of army camps and
defense plants. It investigated shortages of strategic materials and parts. It looked into the shipbuilding program, the
new aviation industry, and the conversion of the auto industry to war production. The committee gained a full measure

of respect and all the financing it needed. It did not seek headlines, but it made them with startling disclosures and constructive recommendations.

The job of chairing the Special Committee Investigating the National Defense Program completely dominated Truman's second Senate term — a term he was not to complete. The Truman Committee lifted him out of obscurity, and set him up for the vice-presidency. But it was not merely a matter of luck. It was an exceptionally good job. It was clear throughout the country that the committee's work materially advanced America's belated drive to be prepared for war and then its phenomenal productive effort in support of the fighting. The Truman Committee exposed scores of crooked contractors and influence peddlers. It brought about notable reforms in government contract procedures and in the administration of wartime economic controls. By the summer of 1944, it had issued forty-four studies and reports, and saved the government $15 billion.

By the summer of 1944, the Truman Committee also had brought its chairman a flattering degree of national recognition. It had sealed for Harry Truman the admiration of his fellow senators, and had won him new respect with Washington officialdom, beginning at the White House. Truman had gained enough political weight to help get his man from St. Louis, Bob Hannegan, the chairmanship of the Democratic National Committee. And when Hannegan offered Truman's name for Roosevelt's consideration as a running mate, the President is said to have rubbed his chin reflectively and said, ''Yes . . . yes . . . I put him in charge of that war investigating committee, didn't I?''[6]

An Opening on the Ticket

The Democratic National Convention at Chicago in 1944 was eventful only because trouble was brewing over the question of who would be Roosevelt's running mate. The inside track obviously belonged to Henry A. Wallace, the incumbent vice-president. But trouble had long been brewing around him. Wallace, a left-wing liberal from Iowa, was a close associate of Roosevelt who had been a member of his administration from its beginning. Wallace served as secretary of agriculture for eight years before he became the vice-president in 1940. At the 1940 national convention, Roosevelt had dictated his selection, pure and simple. He had made the nomination of Wallace a "must", a fact that did not sit well with all Democrats.

Wallace did not sit well with all Democrats, either. Despite the fact that he had the President's confidence, he was distrusted by the politicians, feared by the business community, and hated throughout much of the South. He was disliked by the Senate, over which he presided as vice-president. To no small number of Democrats, the prospect that the White House might one day be occupied by the moody, erratic, and unpredictable Wallace, with his penchant for occult philosophies and applied altruism, was intolerable.

Another who had an inside track, or at least convinced himself and a number of others that he did, was James F. Byrnes, former senator from South Carolina, former supreme court justice and, at the same time of the 1944 convention, director of the Office of War Mobilization. Roosevelt may never have given Byrnes an unequivocal endorsement, but with Wallace's weaknesses and at least intimations of presidential interest in a bid by Byrnes, the South Carolinian began to think seriously about it. Less than a week before the convention was to open, he announced his candidacy.

On the day he announced it, he telephoned Harry Truman, who was at home in Independence, Missouri, packing the family Chrysler to drive his wife, Bess, and daughter, Margaret, to Chicago for the convention. Byrnes said the President had given him the "go" sign and asked Truman to nominate him for vice-president.[7] Truman replied that if that was what the President wanted, he would be glad to do it. After the call from Byrnes, Truman went to Chicago where, as chairman of the Missouri delegation and its member on the Resolutions Committee, he was due to arrive before the convention formally opened on Wednesday, July 19.

Although his own name had been mentioned often during recent months as a vice-presidential possibility, Truman never took it seriously. The day before Byrnes called, Truman had reiterated that he had no intention of seeking the nomination. For one thing, he was happy in the Senate. He had succeeded there far beyond his fondest dreams. He knew a good thing when he saw it, and wanted nothing more than another term or two in the Senate. For another thing, Truman knew that getting the vice-presidential nomination would require Roosevelt's endorsement, and he did not expect he would qualify. Truman's star had taken a recent and rapid rise in Washington, but he still was an outsider at the White House. He had reason to believe he had ruffled the administration's feathers with some of the Truman Committee disclosures. He had given outspoken backing to Senator Alben Barkley a few months earlier when the majority leader resigned over a dispute with Roosevelt. From a practical standpoint, Truman didn't think much of his own chances, and didn't much care.

Upon his arrival in Chicago, Truman found himself in the awkward position of trying to speak up for a man — Byrnes — whom the party leadership and the President were not going to support. What Truman didn't know was that well before the convention, key party leaders had met with the

President and finally got across to him their message that Wallace would cost more votes than almost any other candidate for the second spot on the ticket. And Byrnes' name turned out to be one that was quickly dismissed as an alternative. The party professionals feared that as a southerner Byrnes would cost vital black votes in the cities of the north, and that his renunciation of the Roman Catholic faith would cost Catholic votes everywhere. Truman, it seemed, turned out to be the man with the fewest handicaps and some real advantages. In addition to the good record he had made with the Truman Committee, he came from a border state, stood well with labor, and had voted for Roosevelt's New Deal legislation. The President really had nothing much against him. And Hannegan, owing his present preeminence as national chairman to Truman, was determined to champion his benefactor with or without his blessing.

The President opted to sit out the convention. His own renomination was a foregone conclusion, and convention officials arranged for him to make his acceptance speech by radio. As for the choice of a vice-presidential candidate, Roosevelt — apparently convinced at last that Wallace's renomination could be a serious mistake — communicated with the convention by writing to the national chairman who was on the scene in Chicago. There were two presidential letters, and they rocked the convention like well-timed bombs. The first was released before the formal proceedings began. As state delegations were swarming into Chicago, Hannegan called a press conference to make public a letter from the President disavowing any intention to dictate the choice of a running mate, and leaving Wallace's fate to the delegates.

In the letter, Wallace was warmly described as a "personal friend" for whose nomination the President would vote if he were a delegate. But Roosevelt then went on to say that "obviously the convention must do the deciding."[8] The President thereby notified his party that nominating Wallace was not a condition of his own willingness to accept the presidential nomination. It was at best a lukewarm endorsement of his vice-president. In effect, it challenged the party to do what Roosevelt would not permit the convention to do four years earlier — to produce a candidate of its own choosing. The letter made the nomination of a vice-president the only business of the 1944 convention, and set a fast-moving drama in motion.

Although most observers believed that Roosevelt had done Wallace in, the vice-president still had strong backing for staying on the ticket. Wallace, for his part, was determined to fight to the finish. On the other hand, before Byrnes could really get into the fight, whatever hopes he held were dashed once and for all by Sidney Hillman, chairman of the political action committee of the Congress of Industrial Organizations. The CIO was a potent force at the convention. When Hillman let it be known that his branch of labor would not accept Byrnes, that fact added to the South Carolinian's other liabilities killed his chances. On the first day of the convention, Byrnes withdrew his name.

With Byrnes out of the picture, the anti-Wallace people began a scramble to unite behind someone who could block him. They were assured of enough votes to do it, provided they could crystalize this diffused strength behind someone Roosevelt would not veto, and do it within the next 24 hours. Wallace was picking up some votes he was not expected to have, and it was clear that too much shifting on a candidate to challenge him might improve the chance of his renomination. Connecticut's delegates voted to give their 18 votes to Wallace; a caucus of Georgia delegates seemed to assure 26 votes to him, and word came that

Mississippi would cast 20 votes for the incumbent vice-president. His backers were becoming almost evangelical as they sought to make the selection a showdown between the "right-center" and "left" groupings of the party.

Truman for Vice-President

In the hours before Governor Robert Kerr of Oklahoma delivered the convention's keynote speech, knowledge that Hannegan, the national chairman, was actively boosting Truman's candidacy spread to party leaders and influential delegates. At the same time, the growing intensity of the contest for vice-president was prompting repeated appeals by delegation leaders for further word on the President's stand. One of those seeking it was Truman himself, who was still resisting the pressure being put on him by Hannegan and other Democratic leaders. It was not until the afternoon before he was to be nominated that a stunned Truman finally was convinced. Hannegan invited him to his hotel room, and put in a long-distance call to the President. When the connection was made, Truman sat on one of the twin beds, and Hannegan, with the phone, sat on the other. Because Roosevelt always talked on the telephone in such a strong voice that it was necessary for the listener to hold the receiver away from his ear to avoid being deafened, Truman was able to hear both ends of the conversation.

"Bob," Roosevelt said to Hannegan, "have you got that fellow lined up yet?"

"No," Hannegan replied. "He is the contrariest Missouri mule I've ever dealt with."

"Well you tell him," Truman heard the President say, "if he wants to break up the Democratic party in the middle of a war, that's his responsibility."

With that, Roosevelt banged down the phone.

After a few moments of silence and pacing the room, Truman finally said, "Well, if that is the situation, I'll have to say yes, but why the hell didn't he tell me in the first place?"[9]

The night the convention nominated Roosevelt to seek his fourth term as President, Hannegan made public the second letter written him by Roosevelt, and its impact was as great as the first one that threw open the race for vice-president. This presidential letter said:

"Dear Bob:

You have written me about Harry Truman and Bill Douglas. I should, of course, be very glad to run with either of them and believe that either one of them would bring real strength to the ticket." [10]

However much the President personally preferred Wallace, the release of this second letter was to be decisive for many delegates who did not. Supreme Court Justice William O. Douglas — the "Bill" in Roosevelt's letter — was a liberal too close in outlook to Wallace to be regarded favorably by those seeking an alternative. So the second Roosevelt letter helped give momentum to a movement toward Truman, although the avalanche did not occur until the second ballot. On the first ballot, coming on the third and last day of the hectic convention, the votes were scattered among sixteen candidates, most of them favorite sons. Wallace led Truman at the end of the first ballot, 429 to 319, but each contender was considerably short of the 589 votes needed to win the nomination. When the swing to the Missouri senator came during the second round of voting, it came quickly. Twenty-five minutes after the second ballot began, Truman's nomination was formally announced. The senator described by some as Roosevelt's second choice for second place was proclaimed the party's nominee with

1100 votes, compared to 66 for Vice-President Wallace and 4 for Justice Douglas.

Pulled to the microphone, Truman responded to demands that he address the crowd:

"You don't know how very much I appreciate the very great honor which has come to the State of Missouri," he said in a halting, shy manner. "It is also a great responsibility which I am perfectly willing to assume.

"Nine years and five months ago I came to the Senate. I expect to continue the efforts I have made there to help shorten the war and to win the peace under the great leader, Franklin D. Roosevelt.

"I don't know what else I can say, except that I accept this great honor with all humility. I thank you."[11] It was the shortest speech of the day, and for that fact alone it was applauded appreciatively by a convention that adjourned a moment later.

The 1944 convention and Truman's nomination revealed cracks in the coalition of diverse interests Roosevelt had molded together and led to victory in 1932, 1936, and 1940. By 1944, big-city political organizations, the largely rural South, and an increasingly potent organized labor — key components of Roosevelt's successful political front — were at odds. Roosevelt, after a period of doubt and dispute, was forced to concede by the time of the convention that his campaign strength was not great enough to carry the controversial Wallace and to write into the party platform specific measures favored by his vice-president, some of the more orthodox New Dealers, and the CIO. Dissidence among the party's power blocs was growing, and the force of Roosevelt's personality and presidential leadership clearly carried less weight than in years past. He could no longer dictate to the convention. He was forced to demand less, give the party freer rein, and find compromises by which the warring groups he assembled twelve years earlier could be held together for one more successful campaign for him and his party.

The 1944 strategy was successful even though Truman's nomination, on the face of it, was a rebuff to CIO leaders who organized Wallace's bid for renomination. They considered Truman at least a tolerable substitute, and he was the only candidate acceptable both to CIO leaders and to the South, their chief opposition. As a result, the CIO was able to prevent the nomination for vice-president of a candidate of whom it disapproved, while the party group opposed to CIO domination was permitted to have its first choice among Wallace's competitors. Truman's nomination was the outcome. Its political significance lay in the fact that it kept a significant segment of labor in active sponsorship of the ticket and in political harness with the southerners who came to Chicago determined to reassert their position in the party.

Truman was not without labor support, despite the attention devoted to the CIO's preference for Wallace and the fact that the maverick United Mine Workers had endorsed the Republican ticket even before the Democratic convention began. The CIO's rival American Federation of Labor, operating so quietly as to be almost unobserved, was working for Truman, apparently with much effect. On the convention floor were fifty delegates affiliated with the federation who were advised by their leadership to support not Wallace but Truman.

It clearly was no liability to have Truman on the Democratic ticket in the presidential election of 1944. He stood for the investigating committee which, on behalf of the people, effectively exposed the faults of the nation's defense program and got them corrected before they did much harm. Truman did not think of his campaign efforts as being made in his own behalf but in Roosevelt's. He could pledge sincerely his continued support of the President's policies,

which the record showed he had faithfully supported in the
Senate. Truman found that the voters were not inclined to
change leaders during wartime. He also discovered that
running for vice-president was a breeze in comparison with
the campaigns he had waged to win his Senate seat. "The
campaign of 1944," Truman said, "was the easiest in
which I had ever participated."[12] The results were decisive.
Roosevelt and Truman topped the Republican ticket by
more than 3.5 million votes.

The Brief Introduction

On a snowy Saturday, January 20, 1945, Harry Truman
stood beside Roosevelt on the south portico of the White
House for the third wartime inauguration in America's
history (the first had been Madison's; the second,
Lincoln's). Two days later, Roosevelt sailed for the
U.S.S.R. where, at the town of Yalta on the Black Sea, he
had another of his wartime conferences with Prime Minister
Winston Churchill of Britain and Premier Josef Stalin of the
U.S.S.R. The President would be in Washington for a total
of no more than thirty days during the time Harry Truman
would serve the second shortest tenure as vice-president in
America's history — only eighty-two days.

Roosevelt's journey to Yalta limited severely Truman's
opportunity for closer contact with him after becoming
vice-president. More than a month elapsed before
Roosevelt returned. He sent a message from shipboard on
the homeward cruise, seeking Truman's counsel about a
presidential appearance before a joint session of Congress
to report on the results of the Yalta conference. Truman
made the arrangements for the address, including the un-
usual feature of providing for the President to speak while
seated in the well of the House chamber, in order to spare

Roosevelt any unnecessary pain from standing with the weight of the steel braces pressing against his crippled legs. Truman had observed expressions of pain on the President's face during the inauguration, and was shocked at his appearance after the long trip to Yalta. His strength seemed spent, and he was plainly a weary man. Immediately after his speech he told Truman he would go away for a rest as soon as possible, remarking that he could be "in trim again" if he could spend two or three weeks at his favorite retreat in Warm Springs, Georgia.[13]

If Roosevelt's mind was on Yalta as his fourth term began, it was because by 1945 he had become almost thoroughly preoccupied with foreign policy — meaning, at that time, the conduct of the war and planning for the postwar world. By then the tide of battle had turned against Germany and Japan, but no one knew how long it would take to conclude the war. Decisive engagements lay ahead. And in the background of the far-flung combat that occupied center stage, America's uneasy relationship with the Soviet Union — never free of suspicion and distrust on either side — was worsening; the outlines of an international organization to guarantee postwar peace and stability were being drafted; and the Manhattan Project was making fateful progress in developing the atomic bomb.

Harry Truman had yet to learn of most of this. While Roosevelt went to Yalta, Truman went back to Capitol Hill to try to fulfill the duties of what must be the most ill-defined office in the world of politics. The U.S. Constitution makes the vice-president the president of the Senate, but neither there nor at the White House is he really a full-fledged member of the club. The vice-president is placed between the executive and legislative branches. As Truman later observed, the vice-president cannot be completely in the know when it comes to the President's policies, and is a sort of fifth wheel in the eyes of the Senate,

where he is looked upon as a presiding officer only and is
hardly ever seriously consulted on legislative matters.[14]

Americans are now more inclined to regard their vice-
president as a sort of President in reserve, standing by to
substitute as the next chief executive. The unprecedented
scandals of Richard Nixon's administration, of course,
made Gerald Ford a substitute President not long after he
became a substitute vice-president. During the preceding
generation there were several dramatic events that helped
establish this outlook, among them Roosevelt's sudden
death in office, the assassination attempt against Truman,
President Eisenhower's serious heart attack, and the murder
of President Kennedy. Before this series of events, people
were less keenly aware of the possibility their President
might not survive his term. Vice-presidents tended to be
regarded as little more than some kind of benign necessity
intended to provide some kind of balance when viewed with
the President. If nothing else, vice-presidents customarily
came from a different part of the country than did the
President; in some instances, they represented different
wings of the party.

There is reason to believe that Roosevelt saw in Truman a
necessary balance to his leadership style. Roosevelt was
every inch the executive leader, the nation's wartime commander in chief. He was not a legislator. By 1945 he had
long since lost his magic touch with Congress. From the
time of his unsuccessful bill in 1937 to ''pack'' the Supreme
Court with additional justices, Roosevelt had faced increasingly formidable congressional opposition. Conservatives
in Congress from both parties were coming together more
and more often to block his New Deal proposals. The war
forced foreign affairs to take precedence over domestic
reforms. There was also a rejuvenation of the Republican
party and a reassertion of congressional authority working
against Roosevelt. Along with this, Henry Wallace as

vice-president had become a liability on Capitol Hill. Truman, having earned a solid reputation in the Senate, and being well liked there as one of their own, would be in a position to help push the President's policies. Having just won considerable status in the party, too, Truman was likely to be listened to by the legislators. So Roosevelt, having compromised on Harry Truman as the vice-presidential candidate for 1944, no doubt had hopes of seeing Truman succeed where Wallace had failed.

The vice-president attends cabinet meetings at the invitation of the President. Truman attended the few that were called during the brief time he was vice-president. He noted that little of real importance was dealt with during Roosevelt's cabinet meetings. They were formal affairs that did not feature open discussion or exchanges of views. The President transacted his business in conferences with individual cabinet members before and after these meetings.

While he was in the Senate and was chairman of the committee investigating the defense program, Truman saw Roosevelt at least once a week about matters that came before the committee. Truman considered their association close, cordial, and interesting, and found that it did not change when he became vice-president. He began attending Roosevelt's meetings with his "Big Four" — the vice-president, the speaker of the House, the majority leader of the Senate, and the majority leader of the House — which focused on the President's legislative interests. But only a few of these "Big Four" meetings were held before Roosevelt left on March 30 to rest at Warm Springs. Truman never saw or spoke with him after that.

Uncertain Times

April, 1945 began on an Easter Sunday. There were rainstorms and high winds in much of the nation; thousands

of persons were homeless as unprecedented floods struck
the South. Food shortages were a lively issue across the
country. In Washington, a Senate committee was holding
hearings on the search for more meat. There had been
derisive laughter from spectators when a spokeman for the
Office of Price Administration told the senators that Americans already had more than they ever did before the war.
The spokesman noted that millions for the first time in their
lives had incomes sufficient to buy meat as a regular part of
their diet and not just a rare "luxury." But Americans
wanted more.

There was a debate underway over a guaranteed annual
wage. The Easter recess was holding up congressional
action on President Roosevelt's bill asking for a draft of
nurses. And the Federal Bureau of Investigation was reporting progress in catching draft dodgers. As in World War I,
those who deliberately avoided a call to serve in America's
armed forces had resorted to all kinds of schemes, from
shooting off a toe or hand to acquiring a criminal record to
keep out of the draft. But the FBI was able to announce as
April began that, of 464,640 cases it had handled in four-
and-a-half years, it had reclaimed enough men for thirteen
full divisions. The Bureau's primary aim was getting the
evaders into the armed services, but it was cracking down
hard on flagrant violations. It had a total of nearly 12,000
convictions, involving sentences adding up to more than
30,000 years in prison and fines totalling more than $1
million.[15]

Newspaper readers on that Easter Sunday were learning
of the impact of disclosures about some of Roosevelt's
Yalta decisions on the U.S. delegation making final preparations for the San Francisco Conference to establish a
United Nations organization. It turned out that one of
Roosevelt's concessions to Stalin in bargaining for Russia's
entry into the war against Japan had been to give the Soviets

three votes in the assembly of the projected world organization. Roosevelt had not mentioned this in his report to Congress and the nation. Only later, when it had come out in the press, was it confirmed.

Congress had been led to believe that the projected assembly would represent the principle of the equality of the nations which the State Department had stressed often, and that President Roosevelt would never yield on this principle. Now there was confusion and division in the delegation, with the U.S.-sponsored conference scheduled to open April 25.

In the corridors of Congress, cynics were asking when the leak of the next Yalta secret would come. And indeed the outlook for the San Francisco Conference was not a bright one. In addition to the voting issue, the preliminaries were hobbled by the question of seating Poland. The communique issued after the Yalta Conference had called for a broadening of the Soviet-installed provisional government of recently liberated Poland to include Polish democratic leaders from within and abroad. Rejection by the U.S. and Britain of Russia's proposal to invite the present Polish regime to San Francisco had stalled the Allied talks in Moscow. And Russia seemed to be treating the U.S. conference all too lightly, having announced that its delegation would be headed by Ambassador Gromyko rather than Foreign Minister Molotov. Some critics in the U.S. believed Roosevelt had been so eager to convince the American people to join this new League of Nations, and so hesitant to discuss difficulties with America's allies during the war, that he had let people overestimate what this new league could do and to underestimate the problems that lay ahead.

Foremost among the difficulties America's civilians were concerned about in April of 1945, however, was the prospect of the most Spartan year of privation and incon-

venience since the war began. It was not only a matter of
shoppers seeing more and more frequent "no meat today"
signs. Butter and sugar were almost as scarce. For many
months the nation had had warnings that food available for
civilian consumption was dwindling. At the beginning of
April, the War Food Administration announced that increasing demands from the armed forces and other countries would mean less meat, butter, sugar, fats, oils, and
canned goods in domestic markets than at any other period
during the war. Clothing was also in short supply, and
campaigns were underway to make patches a mark of patriotism. The ration of shoes was being reduced to a new
low because the sands of Pacific islands and the mud and
snow of Europe's battlefields were consuming shoes at a
rate for which officials were wholly unprepared.

Although food was the civilian's chief worry, there were
many ways in which shortages were felt. With coal and fuel
oil hard to get, people were warned that the next winter their
homes would have to be chillier. Either they must keep
temperatures down to the middle or upper sixties or, if they
want a month of warmth early in the season, shiver with an
empty oil tank or coal bin later on. Gasoline and tires were
in short supply, and passenger car transportation had
reached a state of alarming depletion. According to the
American Automobile Association, only a miracle could
keep millions of vehicles from going off the roads by mid-
year. The nation's stockpile of new cars had disappeared.
The average car was eight years old, and millions of them
were about ready to fall apart. But unlimited supply of war
needs was the first requirement; everything else took second place. No new passenger cars would be manufactured
in 1945. Prospects for new supplies of other consumer
durables, such as washing machines, vacuum cleaners, and
radios, were no less dim than since the war began.

On far-flung battlefronts, the first week of April, 1945, was a momentous one. All but five of the independent nations of the world were engaged in some of the most stupendous battles of history. As the week began, Russia's Red Army swept around western Vienna and had more than two-thirds of the Austrian capital encircled. A U.S. force of 1300 heavy bombers and 850 fighters hit the north German cities of Kiel, Hamburg, and Bremen. In the Pacific, carrier-based U.S. planes dealt a stunning defeat to the Japanese navy, sinking six warships including the super-battleship *Yamato,* two light cruisers, and three destroyers. Monday brought reports that American Marines had landed on Okinawa and that, although Japanese planes sank three U.S. destroyers near the island, there was little resistance on the ground. On Tuesday, General George Patton was reported to be only 135 miles from Germany's capital city of Berlin, and Wednesday it was known he had taken the central German city of Kassel. The news of Thursday morning was that the British had crossed Germany's Weser River south of Bremen. And for breakfast on Friday came word that Russia finally had renounced its neutrality pact with Tokyo and would enter the war against Japan.

The military defeat of Germany was sealed even though there was no surrender; Japan was blockaded by sea and air. But good news from the battlefronts was mixed with warnings from American military leaders against a let-down when victory did come in Europe. General Joseph Stilwell, commander of the Army ground forces, cautioned against expecting that, with Germany soon out of the way, the rest should be easy. He spoke of a desperate struggle ahead, noting that there was no crack in the morale of the Japanese soldier and that the vastness of the Pacific offered no short-cuts to victory. The general pointed out that as the Japanese were pushed back, their supply lines grew shorter and

America's much longer. The U.S. would be shifting from a 3000-mile haul across the Atlantic to a 7000-mile haul across the Pacific. The jump-off, instead of being the east coast with its wealth of port facilities, would be the west coast, where they were few. The Philippine Islands, with one good port, would have to take the place of England with many, and 600 miles of open sea would have to be crossed to reach the mainland, instead of the 26 across the English Channel. Stilwell said it would take more forces to repeat in Japan or on the mainland of Asia what had been accomplished in the case of isolated Japanese garrisons on small islands.[16]

Similarly, General of the Army George C. Marshall appealed to the American people for understanding and support during the redeployment of troops from Europe to Asia that would have to follow the defeat of Germany. He expressed concern that once hostilities ended in Europe, every American fighting man there would have an overwhelming urge to go home, and Americans at home would be hoping their son or husband or fiancé would be the one to return. Yet at that very moment it would be imperative to begin moving units through the Suez and Panama canals to accelerate the campaign in the Pacific. Any delay, Marshall said, any loss of momentum in that campaign would mean the unnecessary loss or mutilation of more young Americans.[17] No military commander could do more than hazard a guess as to when the war in Germany would be over. Even then, many units would need to remain in order to make the victory secure. No one, including the Joint Chiefs of Staff in Washington, the supreme Allied military authority, knew how much more fighting would be necessary in the Pacific to bring about the complete defeat of Japan, or how long it would take.

Altogether, it was not a bright outlook. Although war in Europe was drawing to its grim climax, the continent lay shattered and threatened by wholesale starvation. Japan might mean another year of carnage. A wartime partner, the Soviet Union, was brazenly defying its agreement with the Allies and was installing puppet communist governments in the recaptured countries of Eastern Europe. At home, Americans were restless — impatient under wartime restrictions, yet filled with foreboding that the war's end and reconversion to a peacetime economy would bring on catastrophic depression. It was at this uniquely unsettled time of upheaval abroad and uncertainty at home that Harry Truman abruptly inherited the leadership of the United States.

Truman Becomes President

Many close-hand observers, Truman among them, had in those early days of Franklin Roosevelt's fourth administration noted that twelve eventful years in the White House had taken a toll on the President. Roosevelt looked especially tired following the long Yalta Conference. Whatever talk this may have stirred in private, the thought that he might not have long to live was unthinkable. As Truman noted later, there had always been baseless rumors about Roosevelt. Truman did not want to think about the possibility of Roosevelt's death as President. He told himself that Roosevelt had often demonstrated amazing recuperative powers, and recalled the fact that during the closing days of the 1944 campaign, the President had ridden for four hours in an open car through a driving rain in New York City and had seemed none the worse for it. With Yalta behind him, Roosevelt had had a complete physical examination at the Bethesda Naval Hospital on March 27, three days before leaving for Warm Springs. He was at his vacation cottage there less than two weeks when, at 4:35 in the afternoon of

April 12, while sitting for a portrait, he died instantly of a massive intracerebral hemorrhage.

No one, not even members of his family with him in Warm Springs at the time, had any inkling of what was to happen that fateful day. For the new vice-president, going about his business in the capital, it was a decidedly humdrum day until the thunderbolt struck. Truman worried a little about the misty rain that was falling in Washington as he entered the Capitol building on April 12 for he was to fly to Providence the next day to address Rhode Island Democrats at their Jefferson Day dinner. Truman spent the afternoon presiding over the Senate. A dull, long-winded debate about a water treaty with Mexico droned on, and during it Truman wrote a letter to his mother and sister from his seat at the elevated desk of the president of the Senate. He told them he thought his speech would be on all the radio networks, and that it would be followed by the President, whom he would introduce.

Just after the Senate adjourned at 4:56, Truman headed for the private office of Speaker of the House Sam Rayburn to have a drink. When he arrived, Rayburn told him that Steve Early, the White House press secretary, had called just a moment earlier and left a message for Truman to call immediately. He did, and Early asked him, in a strained voice, to come over as quickly and quietly as possible. Truman did so, still unaware of what had happened. To himself, he guessed that Roosevelt must have returned to Washington to attend the funeral of a good friend, Episcopal Bishop Atwood, for whom Roosevelt was to be an honorary pall bearer. The President, Truman reasoned, must want to go over some matters before going back to Warm Springs.[18]

No sooner had Truman arrived at the White House than he was ushered to Eleanor Roosevelt's second-floor study. There Mrs. Roosevelt, in her graceful, characteristic dignity, told him the shocking news. Placing her arm on his shoulder, she said calmly, "Harry, the President is dead."

For a moment Truman stood stunned, speechless, blinking back tears. Finally, words came. "Is there anything I can do for you?" he asked.

"Is there anything *we* can do for *you*," Mrs. Roosevelt replied, "for you are the one in trouble now."[19]

There was no time for Truman to reflect on the overwhelming event that had occurred. There was no time now for preparation, and no time to waste. Without warning, Truman's presidency had begun. And in its first swift hours, he demonstrated the decisiveness and the down-to-earth quality that would characterize his time in office.

As press secretary Early made the official public announcement of Roosevelt's death, Truman called his wife, Bess, told her the news, and asked her to come to the White House with their daughter, Margaret. He then called the Chief Justice of the Supreme Court, Harlan F. Stone, and asked him to come as soon as possible to administer the oath of office. He assured Mrs. Roosevelt and the other family members there that everything possible would be done for their help and convenience. Truman then decided a cabinet meeting should be called at once, and sent for its members. Truman summoned leaders from the Senate and House of Representatives, then went to the cabinet room to meet the cabinet members as each one came.

Justice Stone arrived a few minutes after 7:00 P.M., and at precisely 7:09, just under two hours after the telephone call that brought him to the White House from Capitol Hill, Truman was sworn in as President of the United States. He stood erectly in the cabinet room crowded with government officials, his wife and daughter at his side. His hand on a Bible and his clear, steel-blue eyes — magnified behind the thick lenses of his glasses — fixed on the chief justice, Truman repeated the simple oath, ". . . and will to the best of my ability, preserve, protect and defend the Constitution of the United States. So help me God.''

Making Decisions

Even before the cabinet meeting that followed had gotten underway, Truman was told that the press wanted to know if the San Francisco Conference on the United Nations, scheduled to begin in less than two weeks, would be convened as scheduled. Without a moment's hesitation, Truman made his first decision as President — yes, the conference to draft a UN charter would be held on April 25 as scheduled. Truman then asked the cabinet members to stay on in their respective posts, and told them his intention to continue the foreign and domestic policies of the Roosevelt administration. Changes were inevitable, but Truman understood the need at this time of crisis to draw on the cabinet members' knowledge and experience with Roosevelt. He would keep an open mind until he had had a chance to work with them. Truman nevertheless left no doubt, with the brief but straightforward remarks in this opening hour of his administration, that he would be the President in his own right. He would take full responsibility for the decisions that had to be made. He wanted advice, and would listen to it. He told the cabinet members they could differ with him, but that all final policy decisions would be his and that once he made the decision he expected their support.[20]

After the meeting, Secretary of War Stimson lingered to tell the new President of the top-secret project to develop a new explosive of almost unbelievable force — the atomic bomb. Truman had guessed that something like this was in the works. As a senator, heading the Committee to Investigate the National Defense Program, he was called on by Stimson and asked not to investigate an extremely sensitive defense project Truman knew was underway at huge installations in the states of Tennessee and Washington. Even many of those working on this so-called Manhattan project, Stimson told him, were unaware of exactly what it was. Truman had directed that the plants be looked into, but he regarded Stimson as a great statesman and patriot and, taking him at his word, he had called off the inquiry. Truman learned nothing of what the secret was until it was divulged to him as President after that first cabinet meeting.

Harry Truman, now the President of the United States, then left the White House and went back to the modest apartment on Connecticut Avenue where he, Bess, and Margaret had lived since coming to Washington ten years earlier. When he returned, he found his wife and daughter sitting in the kitchen of a neighboring apartment, where friends had fixed them something to eat when they returned after Truman was sworn in as President. Truman realized then how hungry he was; he hadn't had a bite to eat since noon. The profound drama of the swearing-in ceremony and the solemn cabinet meeting were behind him. The new President dined late that momentous night on a sandwich made from leftovers at the kitchen table of friends in the apartment next door.

Truman began his first day as President early, a personal habit he would continue. He was up at 6:30 for breakfast and a brisk walk. He drove to the White House at 9:00, stopping on the way to give a ride to an Associated Press reporter he knew.

That first day in the office was, of course, totally unplanned and unorganized. Truman found the oval executive office still filled with the belongings and mementos of the man who had occupied it for so many years. Roosevelt's staff was overwhelmed just making arrangements for the coming funeral, and Truman as yet had no adequate staff of his own.

Problems with Russia

In what was to be a day of phone calls, callers, and many interruptions, Truman's first official business was with Secretary of State Edward R. Stettinius, who began to give the new President a fuller picture of the deepening trouble between the U.S. and the Soviet Union. Relations between the two countries had never been good, and they had rapidly been getting worse. In this first meeting with his secretary of state, and from a background paper provided to the President later that day on principal problems confronting the U.S. in its relations with other countries, Truman learned how dark the picture was. The Soviets were sabotaging Allied agreements and refusing cooperation on nearly every major question the wartime allies were confronting.

Because all its demands had not been met, Moscow was now casting a shadow over the forthcoming San Francisco Conference by downgrading its delegation. In areas that had come under their control in Eastern Europe, the Soviets were refusing to honor the Allied agreement to exchange liberated prisoners of war and civilians. The Russians were not allowing American contact teams even to enter the areas. Dominating the Allied control commissions set up to administer these reoccupied areas, the Soviets were using their military presence for unilateral political interference in conflict with Allied responsibilities agreed to at Yalta. Truman, in fact, was finding out about agreements at Yalta — for which there were no available stenographic or official transcripts — at the same time he was finding out about Soviet violation of them!

The Polish problem was especially far-reaching and severe. The picture the President received — from his briefings and his reading on that first day in office of secret documents including messages between Roosevelt,

Churchill, and Stalin — was a clear one. The American and British governments wanted to see in postwar Poland a government truly representative of the Polish people, a government to be established in keeping with an agreement reached at Yalta.

That agreement had been hammered out by Roosevelt, Churchill, and Stalin from three alternatives to which they devoted more time at Yalta than on any other subject. First there was a Polish government-in-exile that had been established in London early in the war. It was made up of genuine Polish patriots. They were in close touch with the underground resistance movement in Poland, which was adamantly opposed to the puppet government the Soviets had set up in Warsaw and which had opposed the Soviet Red Army as it had moved in and occupied Poland. The exile government had long been recognized by the British and the U.S. as the legitimate government of Poland, although its relations with the British had cooled. A second alternative was the government in Warsaw the Soviet occupation force had already installed, the so-called Lublin or Warsaw provisional government. Neither the exile government in London nor the Warsaw group sponsored by Stalin would win the acceptance of all three powers, so a third alternative became the compromise solution to which Roosevelt, Churchill, and Stalin finally agreed at Yalta. The provisional government already functioning in Warsaw was to be broadened by including certain democratic leaders still in Poland and others living abroad. The new government would then hold free elections as soon as possible, based on universal suffrage and the secret ballot, and including candidates representing all the democratic political parties in Poland.

The Russians now were totally disregarding this Yalta decision. The Soviets refused to allow the U.S. and Britain to send observers into Poland, and Stalin turned a deaf ear to

direct appeals from the allies for cooperation or compromise on the issue. The Russians obviously feared that a
free election would mean the end of the communist control
their military occupation had imposed in Poland. They were
doing everything they could to prevent a more representative government there. Moreover, it was apparent from the
activities of the anti-communist Poles both in Poland and
abroad that this was not merely a problem of political
philosophy but one that seriously threatened civil war. This
had been clear, Truman learned, even at Yalta. He saw
plainly now that the Polish problem was one of the most
complex and urgent ones he faced. In addition to its effect
on America's relations with Russia, it had great impact
upon public opinion in the U.S., with its large population of
Polish origin.

Later in Truman's first day as President there would be a
silver lining to the dark clouds in U.S.-Soviet relations. A
message came from the U.S. ambassador in Moscow,
Averill Harriman, telling of a conversation with Stalin. The
Soviet premier had expressed both deep sorrow at
Roosevelt's death and his desire to establish the same working relationship with the new President. Harriman had
seized the opportunity to propose that the most effective
gesture Stalin could make to demonstrate that desire would
be to send Foreign Minister Molotov to the U.S., first to see
Truman and second to attend the UN conference. Stalin, no
doubt eager to get Molotov's firsthand assessment of the
new President, agreed to arrange for his foreign minister to
visit both Washington and San Francisco.

Pray For Me Now

After meeting with Secretary of State Stettinius, Truman
conferred with the nation's military leaders. Secretary of

War Stimson and Secretary of the Navy James V. Forrestal brought in General Marshall, the army chief of staff; Admiral Ernest J. King, chief of naval operations, Lieutenant Barney M. Giles of the air force, and Admiral William D. Leahy, the wartime chief of staff to the President. They reviewed America's far-flung military operations and gave their new commander in chief a report that was brief and to the point. Germany, they told Truman, would not be finally overcome for another six months at least. Japan, they said, would not be conquered for another year and a half.[21]

Earlier that first morning in office, Truman had asked the secretary of the Senate to arrange a luncheon with congressional leaders of both parties. Now Truman left the White House and drove to Capitol Hill for that luncheon meeting at the Senate office. There the very new President asked the seventeen assembled senators and representatives to arrange a joint session so that he might address the Senate and House in person. He considered it imperative to assure the nation through the Congress that he would continue the policies of the late President, and to appeal for continued bipartisan backing of the war effort. It would not be fitting to do this before Roosevelt's funeral and burial services, which were to be held over the weekend, but Truman wanted to make his first appearance before the Congress as soon as possible thereafter. He suggested that a joint session be scheduled for Monday.

"Harry," said one senator he had long worked with, "you were planning to come whether we liked it or not."

"You know I would have," Truman said, "but I would rather do it with your full and understanding support and welcome."[22]

Leaving the luncheon, the President encountered a long line of page boys and reporters that had gathered outside. He shook hands with each one, asked for their prayers, and described the shock of what had happened to him. "Boys," he said, "if you ever pray, pray for me now. I don't know whether you fellows ever had a load of hay fall on you, but when they told me yesterday what had happened, I felt like the moon, the stars, and all the planets had fallen on me. I've got the most terribly responsible job a man ever had."[23] Before returning to the White House, Truman stopped by for a wistful look into the empty Senate chamber, the surroundings in which he had spent ten active, happy years and had experienced the most exciting adventure he had ever expected to have.

When evening came, after a long afternoon of alternately reading and conferring, Truman picked up some papers to take home to study that night. As he left his desk, a loud buzzer sounded. It was a signal to the secret service men, who appeared to escort him. And it brought home to Truman another reality of his new adventure — the ever-present guards and other restrictions on privacy and personal freedom that he and his family would be forced to accept. The Trumans were in no hurry to take up residence at the White House, wanting to give the Roosevelt family ample time to gather and remove its belongings. But they were conscious of the imposition on their Connecticut Avenue neighbors of having a President among them. Other residents were also unable to come and go as they pleased, being stopped and required to show proper identification in order to enter their own homes. Moreover, Truman needed to be available at all times for messages and official callers, matters not readily handled from the family's apartment. So the Trumans decided it would be easier on their neighborhood if they went to an official residence as soon as they could. The next day, the Truman family moved into Blair House, the government guest residence located diagonally across Pennsylvania Avenue from the White House.

The weekend following Truman's succession to the presidency was occupied mainly by the moving and emotionally draining funeral and burial services for Roosevelt. Truman met the funeral train bearing the body of his predecessor from Georgia. He rode in the funeral procession that wound from Union Station to the White House, where Roosevelt's body lay in state. He squeezed in a few hours of office work before attending the funeral services at four o'clock. That night, Truman and his family boarded the funeral train for the overnight trip to Roosevelt's final resting place on the grounds of his family's estate at Hyde Park, New York.

After the final ceremony, the train left for Washington at noon. Given the press of business awaiting Truman the next day, he devoted as much time as he could on the return trip to working on the speech he would give to the joint session of Congress the next day. He later recalled feeling, when he was back in Washington that night, that an epoch had come to an end. A great leader was gone. Chance had chosen Harry Truman to take his office, and already he was experiencing some of the weight its burdens brought. As he went to bed that night he prayed that he would be equal to the task.

During that initial weekend, the living President was almost overlooked as a grief-stricken nation paid homage to the one who had just died. That weekend Truman telephoned Jesse Jones, head of the Reconstruction Finance Corporation, to tell him "the President" had appointed his executive assistant (a close friend of Truman, John W. Snyder) to be Federal Loan Administrator. "Did he make that appointment before he died?" "No," Truman replied. "He made it just now." Everyone — even himself, Truman admitted — was still thinking of Roosevelt as "the President."

The next day, Truman was being driven along streets filled forty-eight hours earlier with mourners as Roosevelt's body was brought to the White House. Now traffic was

normal as the new President headed for Capitol Hill and his
first address to Congress. Soon after 1 p.m. he took the
rostrum to the customary tribute of a standing ovation by the
packed galleries, the senators and representatives, the
cabinet members, Supreme Court justices, and members of
the diplomatic corps. At this stirring moment, the nervous
new chief executive strode forward and began to speak.
"Mr. Speaker," Truman began. The applause died in time
for the microphones arrayed before him to let the nation
hear the hoarse whisper of Speaker Sam Rayburn. "Just a
minute, Harry," he whispered as he leaned over to the
President, "let me introduce you."

It was a speech, fitting enough in the circumstances, of
reaffirmations and pledges — to wage the war until victory
would be won, to continue the drive begun by his predecessor to improve the lot of the common people, to work for
peace and security. Truman expressed confidence in
America's allies and in its military leaders and their
strategy. He appealed to the legislators and to the people for
patience, understanding, and support.

"I have in my heart a prayer," Truman said at the close.
"As I have assumed my heavy duties, I humbly pray to
Almighty God in the words of King Solomon, 'Give therefore Thy servant an understanding heart to judge Thy
people, that I may discern between good and bad; for who is
able to judge this Thy so great a people?'

"I ask only to be a good and faithful servant of my Lord
and my people."[24]

II Molded in Missouri

Franklin Roosevelt and Harry Truman were born two years and a world apart. Roosevelt was 63 when he died; Truman turned 61 less than a month after succeeding him as President. The contrast between the two was striking, beginning with the paths that led them to the presidency. Roosevelt was born in the East, into wealth and social status, at his family's 1100-acre estate at Hyde Park. Truman's life began — on May 8, 1884 — in a 6½-foot-wide bedroom of a four-room clapboard house that had no number, located on a dirt street that had no name, across from a mule barn outside the rural village of Lamar, Missouri. Roosevelt's family was one of established position and prominence — part of an aristocratic circle of squires who divided their time between Hudson River Valley estates and European resorts. Franklin was a distant cousin of President Theodore Roosevelt. Truman's father aspired to be a mule trader, but was not to fare well at that or any other enterprise. When young Harry moved with his family to Independence at the age of six, it was the fourth place of residence he had known.

Like most men of his generation and circumstances in the American midwest, Truman did not have what are usually thought of as "the advantages." Franklin Roosevelt had private tutors at home and frequent trips abroad; he was sent to the prestigious Groton prep school, then graduated from Harvard and attended Columbia University Law School. Harry Truman got his diploma from Independence High School, and could not afford to go to college. When World

War I came, Harry Truman fought in it; Franklin Roosevelt was appointed assistant secretary of the navy. Roosevelt was elected to the New York Senate at the age of 28, and at 38 was the Democratic Party's candidate for vice-president of the United States. By contrast, Harry Truman at 35 was fresh out of the army, with no idea of how he would earn his livelihood. At 38, Truman was picking up the pieces of an unsuccessful business venture and entering politics for the first time; at 41, he was broke and out of a job. On his fiftieth birthday, Truman wrote that, for him, "retirement in some minor county office was all that was in store."[1] At 50, Franklin Roosevelt, who had become governor of the state of New York at the age of 46, was elected President.

This does not mean that there were no rough spots for Franklin Roosevelt. He struggled for years to regain even limited use of his legs after being stricken with polio when he was 39. He never gave in to the discomfort, if not intense pain, that was with him from that time on. But there was a conspicuous contrast in the backgrounds Truman and his predecessor as President brought to public office. Roosevelt clearly was upper crust and Truman was as common as they come — common in the sense of having no impressive credentials provided by wealth, position, prestige, education, family connections, or what have you.

Harry's boyhood in Independence, Missouri, was distinctive only in the devotion of his time to two activities that were hardly typical of the real-life Tom Sawyers of that small town on the frontier of the great plains. Outside of school, he spent most of his time at the library or practicing the piano. Both pursuits had to do with the discovery that he was severely farsighted and unable to recognize objects close up. Before Harry started to first grade, a Kansas City oculist fitted him with extremely thick-lensed glasses. It was not a great physical handicap, but it set him apart.

In *Plain Speaking,* Merle Miller relates the answer Truman gave many years later when a small boy in a group of children visiting the Truman Library in Independence anxiously asked the former President, "Was you popular when you was a boy?"

"Why, no," Truman replied. "I was never popular. The popular boys were the ones who were good at games and had big, tight fists. I was never like that. Without my glasses I was blind as a bat, and to tell the truth, I was kind of a sissy. If there was any danger of getting into a fight, I always ran. I guess that's why I'm here today."[2] Truman also recounted, much later in his life, something of what it was like to wear glasses from the age of six. "Of course they called me four-eyes and a lot of other things, too. That's hard on a boy. It makes him lonely, and it gives him an inferiority complex, and he has a hard time overcoming it . . . But you can overcome it. You've got to fight for everything you do. You've got to be above those calling you names, and you've got to do more work than they do, but it usually comes out all right in the end."[3]

Wearing glasses kept Harry out of the games of baseball and other activities boys his age spent their time on, but he took up piano. He took lessons briefly from a neighbor and, after showing considerable aptitude, from a teacher in Kansas City who had studied under a renowned European pianist. For years Harry endured the jeers and gibes of other boys to go to piano lessons twice a week with his music roll under his arm. From the time he was ten until the age of 15, Harry got up at five every morning to practice for two hours before school.

As a younger boy, Harry tended to be accident-prone and sickly. He fell out of a chair while combing his hair and broke his collarbone; he swallowed a peach pit and nearly choked to death; he cut off the end of a toe by slamming the

cellar door on it. A bout with diphtheria paralyzed his arms
and legs for several months, during which time his mother
had to push her nine-year-old son around town in a baby
carriage. As a result of his mishaps and illness, and his
avoidance of rough-and-tumble activities, young Harry
spent most of his time inside. He developed a close attach-
ment to home life and a special attentiveness to his mother
and his little sister, Mary Jane. His father, a small, quick-
tempered man nicknamed "Peanuts," was much closer to
Harry's younger brother, Vivian, a more rugged youngster
who loved the outdoors and received most of his father's
attention. Harry's boyhood outings were to the Independence Public Library.

An avid reader at an early age, Truman later traced his
interest in reading about American history and the presidency to a treasured little blackboard his mother gave him,
on the back of which were printed about four or five para-
graphs on every President up to that time. Harry's prize
possession at the age of ten was a four-volume set of
biographies his mother gave him entitled *Great Men and
Famous Women*. By the time he was 12 he had read the
Bible twice from beginning to end. He was always busy
reading, and later claimed to have read all 3000 books in the
Independence Public Library — encyclopedias and all —
by the time he was 14.

Working His Way

The financial fortunes of Harry's father took a serious
tumble about the time Harry earned his high school diploma. John Truman had invested in the Kansas City grain
futures market with some notable success, but once his luck
changed it was not long before it ran out entirely. Mounting
debts forced him to sell the family's house and keep only

enough from the sale for a small down payment on a cheaper one. Harry's high school chum, Charlie Ross, who was the valedictorian of their graduating class, was going to the University of Missouri to study journalism. Harry's mother had her heart set on college for him, too, but the expense made that out of the question.

For a brief time, Truman had hopes that an appointment to the U.S. Military Academy at West Point would enable him to gain a college education anyway. Then a stop at an army recruiting station quickly dashed that hope. He was told that, because of his eyesight, he could not pass the physical exam required for West Point.

Although poor eyesight seems minor enough as a physical limitation, it was a major factor in shaping Truman's life. Having become a bookworm as a boy, in part because of wearing glasses, he became unusually well-read. Problem eyesight and good reading helped determine his career. He probably would have had a military career if the eye exam had not ruled out a West Point appointment, his only hope of going on to college. Despite the fact that his poor eyesight turned out to be a roadblock to formal higher education, Truman's interest in reading gave him an avenue for self-education. It lifted him beyond the kinds of work he might otherwise have been in all his life. Through reading, he developed a range of interests and possessed a background of knowledge that was exceptional for someone who had not gone beyond high school. Reading helped Truman cultivate the capacity for learning that would serve him so well when, much later in life, events thrust him into the presidency.

Wearing glasses was a contributing factor to Truman's piano study. It became significant that this endeavor not only broadened and enriched him culturally, but subjected him — as did his bookishness — to taunts and insults. Harry had to rise above them. His boyhood interests, beyond being worthwhile for their own sake, seemed to foster in him an extra measure of determination. It became a lasting character trait, as did his ability to take the barbs hurled at him in his later political career.

However self-conscious Truman may have been as a schoolboy about wearing glasses, he learned to accept it rather than be defensive about it. Somehow he developed that special kind of bigness that is able to admit to a weakness. When he suddenly gave up piano lessons, for example, it was a shock to his mother and his teacher, both of whom had visions of him as a concert pianist. He had become good at the piano — playing Bach fugues, Beethoven, and Liszt — but he had an even greater talent for facing reality and being honest about it. Truman later said there was only one thing that kept him from being a musician; "I wasn't good enough."[4] Even as a youngster, there was no self-pity in Harry Truman. He was instead developing an honesty, with himself and others, that would also serve him well in politics.

During high school, Harry had a 6:30 a.m. job at a drug store, where he swept, washed windows, and dusted bottles before his school day began. After high school, his family's financial bind made it necessary for him to work full time to help keep his younger brother and sister in school. For a summer he worked six days a week as a time-keeper and paymaster to 400 gandy dancers — unskilled railroad laborers — putting down track for the Santa Fe railroad. They were a rough bunch, and Harry learned then whatever foul language he hadn't heard before. He pumped a hand car between three work camps twice a day to fill out the men's time cards, sometimes eating and staying in their tents with them. Every two weeks he paid them on a Saturday night at a saloon, from where they proceeded to drink up their earnings — about $11 for two weeks — before work began again on Monday.

A better-paying job as a bank clerk brought Harry to Kansas City at about the time his father traded their Kansas City house for a down payment on a farm near Clinton, Missouri. His parents moved there, and Harry was on his own for the first time in his life. He lived at a boarding house, and on Saturdays worked as an usher at a big downtown theater where he could earn extra money and enjoy vaudeville shows free of charge. He found his bank work — making longhand notations all day clearing checks or doing bookkeeping — decidedly dull, but Harry was enjoying life in Kansas City when, at the age of 22, family circumstances changed his course again.

His father had failed again, wiped out this time when a flood washed the crop away at the farm in Clinton. John and Martha Truman moved in with her widowed mother on a farm in Grandview. When Harry's bachelor Uncle Harrison, after whom he was named, decided to leave his farm in Grandview for an easier life in the city, it left more acreage than the elder Truman could handle. He asked Harry to quit his bank job and help manage the farm. Harry did, and if it disappointed him to leave Kansas City, he never mentioned it. For a dozen years, Harry would be up at 4:30 a.m. in the summer and 6:30 in winter to milk cows, feed hogs, and plow fields — with a team of horses or mules, not a tractor. He sowed, reaped, baled hay, and did all the work that had to be done to run a 600-acre farm.

Farm life did not, however, take Harry out of circulation. It was during this time that he regained the attention of Bess Wallace, the girl who had his eye since he first gazed bashfully at her blue eyes and golden curls in Sunday school. Truman joked later that he was so backward that, after that first moment, "I didn't speak to her for five years." But he didn't fail to notice her. He recalled that from the fifth grade until high school graduation they were in the same classes, and that "if I succeeded in carrying her books to school or back home for her, I had a big day.''[5] She did not consider Harry Truman her boyfriend, however, and they had not seen each other in the intervening years since high school. Then one weekend, Harry rode horseback from the Grandview farm to visit his Aunt Ella, who lived across the street from the house in Independence where Bess Wallace and her widowed mother lived with Bess's grandparents. Bess's mother had sent a cake over the day before, and Harry eagerly volunteered to return the clean cake plate. He came back two hours later with a grin that betrayed the beginning of his courtship of Bess Wallace.

More years passed before Bess took Harry seriously, it seems, but they saw each other often. They were different in many ways. She had always been a tomboy, was the town's best woman tennis player, and loved to dance. Harry preferred to talk about history, play the piano for songfests, and go to vaudeville shows and concerts. He prided himself on his refusal to learn to dance. But they liked each other's company. They shared a fondness for joking and teasing, and found a common joy in picnics and outings.

Harry traveled the twenty miles between the farm and Bess's home as often as he could, by horseback, buggy, train, or — after a time — in a secondhand but imposing four-door touring car. He bought the big car, a very expensive model when new, not only to ease his travel problem but to impress Bess's family, which did not quite look upon him as a promising prospect for a husband. Her grandparents were well off financially. They sent Bess to a girls' finishing school, for example, bought her a horse and two greyhounds, and generally provided her a life of ease. Harry, for his part, had no money, no college education, and seemed to lack a future. Mrs. Wallace, who doted on Bess and leaned heavily on her for companionship, found it hard to envision her daughter married to a dirt farmer — even worse, one who did not even own the farm he worked.

His father's death made Harry the head of the house at 30, and his work and responsibility expanded. He not only ran the 600-acre farm, but leased and operated a 300-acre farm his uncle owned. Harry was developing other interests during this period, including a certain taste for politics. This was an area that always had excited the interest of his father, who could never resist a rally or a political argument. With Harry managing the farm, John Truman had indulged his appetite by attaching himself to the Pendergast political machine, which was reaching into rural Jackson County from its operating base in Kansas City.

The last job of his father's life was as a politically appointed road overseer. When his father died, Harry filled the job briefly until his proposal for road improvements provoked an argument and cost him his job. Not long afterward, he was named postmaster of Grandview, a position paying $50 a month, the entire sum of which Truman gave to the woman who assisted him. Soon he began attending the Thursday night meetings of the Kansas City Tenth Ward Democratic Club, which were highly informal occasions for drinking beer and talking about elections and the organization's political problems. Harry would leave right after the meetings, rather than drift with the group to the nearest saloon, as was its custom. He was not quite a part of the crowd that assembled there, but the meetings made him acquaintances of a kind that would figure prominently in his life not much later.

'Captain Harry' Goes to War

America's entry into World War I in April of 1917 proved to be a major development for Harry Truman. Several years earlier, during his days as a bank clerk, he had become a charter member of a 60-man national guard outfit organized in Kansas City. It was an artillery battery, and

Private Truman and his fellow "weekend warriors" paid a quarter each week to drill with it. Harry served two three-year hitches, but after five years of giving up weekend time from the Grandview farm to go to Kansas City for training, he gave up the Guard in 1911. In the spring of 1917, as Kansas City was caught up in the feelings of excitement and patriotism sweeping through the country, Harry ran into some of his National Guard buddies. Several of them had since served with General "Black Jack" Pershing, chasing Pancho Villa at the Mexican border, and had wild tales of their adventures. This chance reunion brought home to Harry the fact that he missed the camaraderie of the old outfit. And he was captivated by the news that, with World War I on, that very outfit — old Battery B of Kansas City — was to be expanded into a new unit, the 2nd Missouri Field Artillery.

It put Truman on the spot when he was asked to join and to help recruit for the new unit. He was torn by the fact that his mother had sizable mortgages to pay off — $25,000 on their farm at Grandview — as well as by his desire to establish his financial independence and marry Bess Wallace. It was not an easy choice, but a sense of patriotic duty tipped the scales. Harry opted to rejoin his old buddies and enter the war. The decision was a shock to the ladies in Truman's life — his mother and sister on the farm, and Bess in Independence — but he won them over. He arranged for his sister, now 28, to run things with the help of farm hands. Bess wanted to get married immediately, but Harry insisted that they wait until after the war. He might come home a cripple, he said, and he didn't want her tied down. But Harry and Bess considered themselves engaged. As he took an aggressive role in rounding up recruits, Truman felt he belonged as never before.[6] In August, the entire unit entered the Army and was designated the 129th Field Artillery, of the 35th Division. In September, it headed for camp at Fort Sill, Oklahoma.

In those days, enlisted men chose their own officers. When the electing was done, Harry — who was hoping to be a sergeant — was surprised to be voted a first lieutenant. His next surprise was to learn, upon reaching Fort Sill, that among his other duties he was to be the regimental canteen officer, assisted by a member of his battery named Eddie Jacobson. Harry didn't know the first thing about merchandising the personal necessities the canteen — an early-day PX — was to make available to the men of the 129th. Fortunately Jacobson had been a salesman and had some notion of how to run a store. Together, Truman and Jacobson collected two dollars from each man. They took the $2200 to Oklahoma City and bought the cigarettes, paper, pens, shaving gear, and other items that were not government issue with which they stocked the canteen. They recruited a clerk from each battery and company, took the novel precaution against stealing of sewing up each clerk's pockets, and opened for business. Truman and Jacobson's canteen stood alone in its success. All the other canteens at Fort Sill showed heavy losses, but the one Truman headed did so well that after only six months he had paid back the $2200 investment and cleared a profit of $15,000.[7]

After Fort Sill, Truman's destination was Europe. Just before shipping out, he spent most of a 24-hour leave in New York at an optometrist's buying three extra pairs of glasses. Then Truman and the rest of the 129th Artillery shipped out, on a boat crammed with several thousand other soldiers, all of them part of the massive, two million-man American Expeditionary Force being rushed to France in the spring of 1918. Truman's unit resumed field training in France, and by late summer was in combat. By that time, he found himself in another dubious post within the 129th, one that presented a tougher challenge than running a canteen.

Battery D of the Second Battalion had become notorious within the 129th Artillery as a rowdy collection of hell-raisers from a tough Irish-Catholic neighborhood in Kansas City. The men of "Dizzy D," as the outfit had come to be called, prided themselves on being "fighting Irish." Their favorite pastimes were drinking, brawling, and playing juvenile pranks. In a few months they had gone through three commanding officers, one of whom had suffered a nervous breakdown and another of whom was thrown out of the army for his failure to control his men. "Dizzy D" enjoyed a well-known and well-deserved reputation for being untamed and unmanageable. And Harry Truman, freshly promoted to captain, was told to take charge of it.

Being in combat had made Truman less nervous than did the prospect of commanding Battery D, he confessed later. His first move was to put responsibility for discipline squarely on his sergeants and corporals, promising to bust them right back into the ranks if they couldn't control the troops. As Truman was trying, with mixed results, to browbeat the battery into line, the turning point came. One night at the front lines, a murderous barrage of German shells began to rain down. Suddenly there was panic; the young toughs of Battery D went to pieces and began to run for their lives. This display of cowardice threw Captain Truman into a rage. Screaming at the top of his lungs, he stopped them in their tracks with a blistering torrent of the vilest four-letter words ever hurled at friend or foe.

"I called 'em everything I knew," Truman said. And it had an astonishing effect. The regiment's Catholic chaplain, who was on the scene, said afterward the Truman's awesome outpouring "took the skin off the ears of those boys."[8] Truman had established himself as the boss of the outfit. Now it was he who earned a reputation. The incident turned them around. After that, the boys of Battery D stood their ground for Captain Harry, as they called him. They dished out their share of artillery rounds during the major American drive through the Argonne Forest and at Verdun, where the war came to an end on November 11, 1918.

Harry Truman did not return as a war hero. He had tasted combat in some of the major battle areas of the war and had some narrow escapes. But there was nothing exceptional about his war record; he won no ribbons for special acts of valor. On the way back home, Truman had time to reflect on what his military service had meant to him. It meant a lot. He had been away from home less than two years but had traveled far, had made many friends, and had had a profound educational experience. In its effect on Truman's life, the army service let the genie out of the bottle. For one thing, it got him off the farm. For another, it showed him and others that he had leadership qualities — that he could command other men effectively and win their respect.

In and Out of A Haberdashery

No aspect of Truman's life was to be so gleefully and unmercifully used against him by political enemies in later years than the fact that he ran a haberdashery and that it failed. His detractors never tired of portraying that ill-fated venture in a way that was meant to suggest that it was the only thing Truman had ever done before becoming President, and that its failure was conclusive proof of being hopelessly inept at managing anything.

The venture began not long after Truman's discharge as an Army major in May, two days before his thirty-fifth birthday. The first thing on his mind as he returned home was to marry Bess Wallace, and nothing else seemed to matter. In June they were wed, despite the fact that her mother still had some misgivings, at the small, red-brick Trinity Episcopal Church where Bess's family were members in Independence. Then the thing that mattered to Harry was how he would support himself and his wife. He had decided he would never take Bess to live on a farm. He could not see himself working for someone else, and was determined to strike out on his own, but had no plans for how he would earn a living. Then in July, soon after he and Bess returned from a brief honeymoon trip and moved in with her mother and grandmother at the house on North Delaware, Truman was in Kansas City and ran into Eddie Jacobson, who had helped him manage the highly successful army canteen.

The two put their heads together and before long had agreed to open a sort of civilian canteen, a men's furnishings store, with Jacobson doing the buying, Truman doing the bookkeeping, and both doing the selling. It was not a far-fetched or unrealistic kind of business venture for Truman to undertake. He did have bookkeeping experience, if nothing else. And in fact there was something else. After all, the rather recent army canteen venture had given Truman and Jacobson experience in a similar kind of endeavor. It showed they could work well together, and that they had the business sense for it to become a highly successful enterprise.

By late fall the firm of Truman and Jacobson was in business, its owners having pooled all their savings and whatever else they could put together to invest in inventory. Truman had sold the stock and equipment on the family farm to raise his share. Times were good, and business went well. Then the Harding administration took office, farm prices plummeted, and in chain reaction, the prices of goods fell dramatically. The recession hit the Midwest especially hard. Truman and Jacobson, who had bought their inventory at the high prices prevailing before the business slump began, were forced to cut retail prices until their profit margin disappeared. The store came to be filled not with paying customers but with old army buddies out of a job who came in to pass the time or to see "Captain Harry" for loans. Truman took out a bank loan to pay creditors, but the recession did not relent. There were small businessmen all around who were in the same plight. In 1922, Harry Truman, 38 years old and deep in debt, joined the ranks of the many other store owners who were forced to close their doors and go out of business.

Two salient facts that his critics omitted when relating this episode in Truman's life include how the business happened to go under and how Truman reacted when it did. The recession that was to be a prelude to the depression had widespread and severe effects. Truman's was hardly the only store going out of business; he was caught in a squeeze that was ruining many small businesses during this period. The common recourse was to go into bankruptcy proceedings, but Truman would not. Truman insisted, instead, on paying off all the debts he and Jacobson had incurred — including the second half of their five-year lease, which their landlord refused to waive. Truman wrote to each creditor, explaining his plan to return what was left from the inventory and deduct its value from total bills, then to make payments on the balance until every debt (the total was $28,000) was paid. His creditors agreed. Truman was still sending them payments ten years later when he was a U.S. senator, and he repaid every cent.

The Pendergast Connection

If a hostile political propagandist could relish anything in Truman's background more than his failure in the haberdashery, it was to be the fact that he got his first political job with the help of a notorious big-city machine. It was true that he did, and he acknowledged it. The fact was, it could not have been otherwise in that particular time and place, if a newcomer wished to enter politics with even the faintest hope of success. In Jackson County, where Kansas City, Missouri, is located, contacting one of the political machines for approval and support was in those days a necessary first step.

The contact came about naturally enough in Truman's case. One of the boys who regularly dropped by the haberdashery was Jim Pendergast. He had been a lieutenant in the 129th Artillery before being transferred to another unit, and Truman had known him at Ft. Sill. Jim's father was Mike Pendergast, whom Truman knew casually from the old Thursday night sessions of the Tenth Ward Democratic Club. The real boss of the so-called Pendergast Machine was Mike's brother, Tom. But Mike had charge of the rural part of Jackson County as well as the Tenth Ward, and Tom would not regard any potential candidate in that area as acceptable without Mike's endorsement.

Truman had plenty of time to think while he stood in the haberdashery devoid of customers, and his thoughts turned to politics. He loved to talk politics, and the boys of the 129th who frequented the store loved to hear Harry hold forth on political subjects. Truman saw that other war veterans were winning political offices in Missouri and elsewhere. He was confident that politics could be a promising career, if only he could break into the field.

It probably was by design that Truman metioned this in the presence of Jim Pendergast, or he may have been saying it to anyone who would listen. There is no reason to think he was keeping a secret of his interest in going into politics. Nor is it out of the question that Jim Pendergast, coming into contact at the haberdashery with Truman and with other veterans who shared a high regard for Truman, could have come up with the idea on his own. In any event, Jim told his father about the availability of Truman — a Baptist, a Mason, a life-long resident of Jackson County, and a war veteran who was well liked by the men who served with him.

Jackson County at that time elected three county commissioners. For some reason they were called judges, even though their duties were administrative — including responsibility for the condition of county roads and buildings and levying taxes — and not judicial in nature. Kansas City proper chose one judge for western Jackson County, and the rural part of the county voted for the eastern judge, each for two-year terms; the entire county elected the presiding judge at large for a four-year term. There was no nominee yet for eastern judge of Jackson County, and this is what Truman had in mind. Mike Pendergast expressed approval. When one Pendergast politician in Independence subsequently told another who their nominee was, the response he got was, "Who the hell is Harry Truman?" It was a question many would ask years later when he became a nominee for vice-president of the United States.

Truman announced his candidacy, and the race was on. Two things became clear from the outset — he was a hard campaigner and a bad speaker. To Truman it was apparent that his first race for public office could be his last. He found himself facing four other candidates — a banker, a road contractor, a road overseer, and a man who once had been an appointed judge in the eastern district. More than that, Tom Pendergast had done some double-dealing behind the scenes that made Truman no more than a token candidate. Tom had struck a bargain with a rival Democratic machine in the county to back their man — the banker — for the eastern judgeship in return for their support of Pendergast's man in the western district. The Pendergast machine was committed to throw its votes to the banker, and Truman's candidacy was a sham.[9] But Truman won anyway. He canvassed for votes from door to door, and appeared at picnics and political meetings throughout the district. He knew a lot of farmers in the county from his years of working a farm there himself. He drew support from his fellow Masons. He had the enthusiastic — perhaps decisive — help of his army buddies from the 129th and the backing of many other war veterans in the area.

Once in office as county judge for the eastern district of Jackson County, Truman plunged into his work. He was as pleased as he could be with his new career, and devoted long hours to the job. He concentrated on reforming the county's shaky fiscal structure and managed, during his two-year term, to help bring improvements in the county's roads and to reduce the county's debt. It was an effort commendable enough to draw rare words of approval on the editorial page of the persistently anti-Pendergast and staunchly pro-Republican *Kansas City Star,* which called attention, on the eve of the next primary election, to the "remarkable showing" the court had made.[10] But Truman had incurred the wrath of the political machine competing with the Pendergasts, whose man had become western district judge as planned. Truman's unexpected win had meant that the Pendergast nominees held two of the three county judgeships. The opposing machine had sworn to prevent Truman's reelection two years later, and succeeded. Pendergast's rival Democrats along with the Ku Klux Klan — the anti-Catholic, anti-Negro hate group was in its heyday in the area — teamed with the Republicans to vote Truman out.

New Directions and Growth

The defeat — the only election Truman would ever lose — coincided closely with the birth of his only child, a daughter named Mary after Truman's sister and Margaret after Bess's mother. The excitement of the event was tempered by Margaret's poor health in infancy. The anxiety of a sickly baby was compounded by the fact that, as Truman turned forty-one the following spring, he was broke and out of a job. He solved his employment problem by selling memberships in the Kansas City Automobile Club. It was a period of general prosperity, and within a year Truman sold more than a thousand memberships and cleared more than twice what his annual salary had been as a judge. He found time for other pursuits as well. He resumed National Guard training, now as a lieutenant colonel, and in so doing renewed his army friendship with captains Harry Vaughn and John Snyder, both of whom would serve him later in the presidency.

During this period Truman also was active in Masons, went to American Legion meetings, made speeches from time to time, and joined an athletic club. He finally learned to swim, using an unorthodox side stroke because he insisted on keeping his glasses on in the water. For a time he continued evening classes at the Kansas City Law School. For two years he carried a heavy schedule, taking eight courses the first year and six the next. He earned grades — ranging from 82 to 96 percent — that averaged 86 for each of the two years.[11] Then he dropped out, attributing the move to the fact that he was besieged every time he came into Kansas City by old buddies from the 129th who would look him up at school for advice and help with their problems.

After abortive flings at being a partner in a banking venture and then the promoter of a savings and loan association, Truman became president of the National Old Trails Association. He traveled in Missouri and a number of other states, urging local governments to see the tourist appeal of their history and to build highways where there were famous trails that had shaped the country's history. But whatever he did during this time out of office, it was obvious that Truman's heart was in politics. He missed it and longed to return. Bess sensed his restlessness, and genial Mike Pendergast and his son Jim were encouraging Harry to get into politics where he belonged.

By the time the 1926 Democratic primaries were approaching, Truman was ready. He called on Boss Tom Pendergast for the first time. During the two years Truman had been out of office, the Democrats had been out of power in Jackson County government. Boss Tom had bested the rival Democratic organization, however, and his power had surged in Kansas City proper. He agreed to back Truman to be presiding judge of Jackson County. With the party now united behind him, Truman won the four-year term by 16,000 votes and became, as he described it, "the key man in the county government." He had the authority to build a record of his own, and dated the real beginning of his political career from this 1926 election.[12]

With characteristic enthusiasm, Truman devoted all his energy to the work at hand. He was determined to provide the honest, economical government he had pledged throughout his campaign. He soon became known in western Missouri by the same reputation he later would establish in the U.S. Senate for diligence and for his rigid, blunt, almost perverse, honesty. He accepted Tom Pendergast's support, but Boss Tom was well aware of Truman's unwavering integrity.

Truman's instructions were to give jobs to Tom Pendergast's friends, but if they failed to get the job done he could fire them. Truman accepted Tom's suggestions for appointments, but he also took him at his word. Within weeks, Truman was firing people right and left. He set up an inspection and audit system. He stopped expense accounts for county road overseers and cut their number from 60 to 16. He appointed a two-man, bipartisan inspection team of engineering consultants to study the county road system and make recommendations. Their report was a devastating indictment of how crooked politics had saddled county residents with almost impassable roads that could scarcely be maintained at any cost. The engineers planned a new system of roads, 225 miles in all, at a cost that could be met only by a bond issue. Against Pendergast's advice, Truman made the bond issue a crusade, and campaigned for it in every corner of the county. To the amazement of Pendergast and the other political experts, Truman's seven-million-dollar bond issue passed, and by a three-fourths majority instead of the required two-thirds.[13]

Truman launched the road-building program by issuing contracts strictly on a low-bid basis. Already his expense cutbacks, firings, and job reductions in county government had caused problems in the Pendergast organization. The low-bid contracts brought things to a head. Angry Pendergast contractors, who had expected to get road-building money as a matter of course, appealed to the boss at a stormy meeting in Tom Pendergast's office which Truman attended. Despite the uproar by the contractors, Truman refused to back down, and after a while Pendergast threw the contractors out.

Pendergast lost a lot of money as a result of Truman's honesty and independence. Truman dotted the roadsides with trees, and decreed that there be a concrete road within two-and-a-half miles of every farm in the county. That called for a lot of concrete, and Tom Pendergast owned a concrete company. In the past, Pendergast's concrete had been used almost exclusively in county paving jobs; in Truman's 225-mile road-building program, only three-fourths of a mile were paved with Pendergast concrete. The program was finished on schedule and gave Jackson County one of the nation's finest highway systems. Again Truman earned praise even from the *Kansas City Star,* which conceded that he was extraordinarily honest and that there was not a suspicion of graft involved in his road program.

Truman's mother maintained that he was too honest for his own good — or hers, at any rate. When a new county road cut off a piece of the Grandview farm that was now hers, Harry refused to pay a cent for it.[14]

Perhaps Tom Pendergast conceded Truman his independence in county affairs because Tom was preoccupied with bigger deals involving strictly the Kansas City urban area. Perhaps he simply had little interest in outlying county affairs. More likely, he felt it was necessary to give up special favors and profits there in order to retain the county patronage, for the power to appoint people to jobs was the backbone of his political organization. But evidently Tom also tolerated Truman because he genuinely admired him for standing up to the organization without fear. Truman was convincing in his argument that it was not only good government but good politics to keep the promises he had made to the voters. Moreover, Pendergast could always point to Truman to refute charges of corruption made against the machine as a whole. When Mike Pendergast died in 1929, Tom turned rural Jackson County, Mike's territory, over to Truman. In 1930, Truman was reelected presiding judge by 55,000 votes.

Once Truman explained his connection with the Pendergast organization to a Kansas City reporter as they were sipping highballs in a tent at a national guard camp in Arkansas.

"Tell me, Harry, if you want to," the reporter had said, "how you, a clean-cut, intelligent public official with unusually progressive ideas, can remain part of a political organization like this? I'm curious." The reporter related that, in his candid, friendly way, Judge Truman — or Colonel Truman, when he was wearing his national guard hat — replied: "I owe my political life to the Pendergast organization. I never would have had an opportunity to

have a career in politics without their support. They have
been loyal friends. I know that the organization has counte-
nanced some things which I believe are wrong. But I do
believe this, and that is that you can get further cleaning up a
political organization from the inside than you can from the
out."[15]

Actually, Truman was in no position to clean up the
organization. He had all he could do to protect himself from
the persistent attacks of Pendergast powers who were also
big contractors. Presiding judges traditionally had served
two terms, and Truman's second would expire at the end of
1934. It looked as if the machine would drop him then.
Truman had helped carve a congressional district for eastern Jackson County in 1933 and entertained thoughts of
running to represent it in Congress in 1934. But Pendergast
would not support him for it. On his fiftieth birthday in
May, 1934, Truman despaired of ever winning the
machine's support for a halfway decent political office. He
thought he had nothing in store but retirement in some
minor county job.

Less than a week later, the sun broke through for Truman
when the third of three men Pendergast had tapped, one by
one, to run for the United States Senate turned down the
offer. The first, a former senator who was 72 years old,
decided he was too old to seek the six-year term. The
second preferred not to risk the safe seat he held in the
House of Representatives. The third considered his chances
too slim to be worth antagonizing the two incumbent congressmen who already had entered the Senate race. One of
the candidates already in the running had the public praise
of President Roosevelt and the backing of the St. Louis
Democratic machine; the other was a seven-term representative loudly boosted by Missouri's Senator Bennett Clark,
son of the late speaker of the House of Representatives.

Two Races to the Senate

Having recently been rejected by Pendergast as a congressional candidate, Truman was absolutely astonished at the opportunity to be supported in the statewide race for the Senate. It exceeded his boldest dreams. Inwardly he jumped at the chance, while being politician enough to play coy in Pendergast's presence and plead that he did not have the necessary money or statewide reputation. Pendergast promised to help him overcome the handicap, and Truman campaigned without letup to make the mind-boggling leap from administrator of Jackson County to a United States Senate nomination.

During the four weeks before the primary, Truman visited 60 of Missouri's 114 counties and made from 6 to 16 speeches a day. He also drew on his acquaintance with county judges all over the state and his familiarity with the ins and outs of the rural county courthouse crowds.

With the New Deal riding high, any Democrat who won the primary would be an odds-on favorite to unseat the mossback Republican, not well-liked in his own party, who was up for reelection. As a result, the primary contest was an unusually spirited one which, for lack of disagreement on issues, degenerated into name-calling and personal attacks. His two opponents branded Truman "Pendergast's office boy," and made as much mileage as they could out of the Pendergast connection. It wasn't enough, and Truman won his first statewide race by a plurality of about 40,000 votes.

The November general election was indeed an easy mark. The Roosevelt name was filled with magic in 1934, and the Democrats won control of Congress in a landslide. Truman won by more than 260,000 votes in Missouri, and became one of 13 new senators destined for Washington, all of them Democrats.

The frankness Truman later became famous for was evident in his first visit to Washington following his election. "I'll do the best I can," he said, "and keep my feet on the ground. That's one of the hardest things for a senator to do, it seems. All this precedence and other hooey accorded a senator isn't very good for the Republic. The association with dressed-up diplomats has turned the heads of more than one senator, I can tell you." Recounting to the Kansas City Elks Club his impressions after his quick trip to the nation's capital Truman said, "My trouble is that I probably won't find a place to live. You see, I have to live on my salary, and a cubbyhole rents for $150 a month there. The ones that are fit to live in run from $250 to $500 a month, and, although it's hard to believe, there are some saphead senators who pay $1500 a month for their apartments."[16] As would later be characteristic of his presidency, Truman's straight-talking quickly drew fire. In a condescending editorial, the *New York Times* castigated Senator-elect "Henry S. Truman" as "just a farmer boy."[17]

Senator-elect Truman was a peculiar mixture of brashness and humility, although those who recall him then remember most vividly the humility, which went beyond modesty almost to the point of apologizing for being there. And as he himself acknowledged, Truman went to the nation's capital under a cloud. Newspaper editorials had type-cast him as a man catapulted from obscurity to the high office of senator by a big-city political boss. Many senators assumed he was simply a Pendergast tool. It was a slur Truman could not easily accept. He knew he had made no promises except on public platforms before the voters. He had earned his way. He had no other way to win confidence and respect than the method he had used all along — honesty and hard work. He dug in and applied himself to the new task at hand.

When the end of his first term approached, Truman's

prospects were looking bleak. Tom Pendergast had pleaded guilty and gone to federal prison on a charge that he had failed to pay income tax on a $430,000 bribe from insurance men. The national publicity focused on Pendergast cast Truman again in the shadow of that connection. When 1940 came, he was dispirited and financially strapped. The Pendergast organization that boosted him before now lay in ruins. The center of political gravity in Missouri had shifted to St. Louis, where Truman had no base.

Then two events stiffened Truman's pride and determination. First, Missouri's wealthy Governor Lloyd Stark, whom Truman despised for having turned on the Pendergasts, announced that he would be a candidate for Truman's Senate seat. Secondly, President Roosevelt, who leaned toward Stark, made a heavy-handed attempt to buy Truman off by offering to appoint him to the Interstate Commerce Commission. That was all Truman needed. "I sent the President word," he said later, "that I would run if I got only one vote — mine."[18]

Stretching his own bank credit to the limit and scrounging a few dollars wherever he could, Truman mounted a ramshackle campaign that was short on almost every essential ingredient, including hope. But Truman's persistent effort paid dividends. As Cabell Phillips described it, there were few big rallies, since they cost money. So Truman went to see the people instead of bringing the people to see him. Ten to 15 hours a day through the broiling summer he popped unheralded into countless barnyards and feed lots, into village stores and restaurants and banks, into county courthouses and city halls. He shook hands by the hundreds, swapped small talk, and asked for votes. "I just wanted to come down and show you folks that I don't have horns and a tail just because I am from Jackson County," he would say, flashing his warm, disarming grin. The people were cordial, and found their senator to be an engaging, straightforward sort of fellow who talked their language and didn't put on airs. Gradually things began looking up in the threadbare Truman camp.[19]

The district attorney from Kansas City who had prosecuted Pendergast threw his hat into the ring, making it a three-way race for the Democratic Senate nomination and splitting the state's Democrats in several directions. Truman then did some decisive horse-trading for the coveted support of Bob Hannegan, the Democratic leader of St. Louis whom Truman later helped make the national committee chairman. Truman promised to back Hannegan's choice for governor if Hannegan would swing his backing to Truman in the last days of the campaign. Truman's outlook was also helped by some of his Senate colleagues, whose speeches for him in Missouri imparted an element of national stature to the struggling campaign.

Perhaps the greatest boon to Truman's bid for reelection to the Senate came from the powerful railroad unions. They were grateful for his work on railroad legislation in the Interstate Commerce Committee, and the word was passed that their friend in Missouri needed help. They gave it. "Truman Clubs" sprang up at every railroad yard in the state. The clubs spread to union halls of the American Federation of Labor and to other labor groups. Money began to come in, and Truman's campaign began to show new muscle. Finally, ten days before the primary, more than half a million copies of a special "Truman Edition" of *Labor*, the railroad brotherhoods' newspaper, flooded the state, reaching not only every union man but thousands of Rural Free Delivery boxholders. Even so, the primary was a photo finish, with Truman winning renomination by a plurality of only 7476 votes.[20]

In many ways, the 1940 campaign was Truman's toughest and most valuable. He won it on his own. There could no longer be any doubt that he was entirely his own man. It

won new respect for him from the Roosevelt administration
and an extra measure of respect from his Senate colleagues.
The 1940 campaign also gave him priceless experience as a
political craftsman. There was no ready-made political organization this time to serve as a base of support. Truman
put the campaign together himself, building the support,
mapping the strategy, choosing the tactics. He forged a
keen sense of the public mind and mood. He developed new
sophistication in the nature and use of political power. He
understood as never before the practice of politics as the art
of the possible, surmounting obstacles by compromising
and accommodating. And on a more practical level, the
1940 campaign established a bond with the working men of
organized labor that would be a source of strength for
Truman for years to come.

The Legacy and the Change

Truman's experience in winning reelection to the Senate,
added to the work he did while there, would serve him well
in the White House. His earlier education had been in the
school of hard knocks, in the training grounds of farm
work, army life, and local politics. Then came ten years of
uncommonly hard work in the Senate. The knowledge he
gained from his good committee assignments gave him an
understanding of government finance and of the appropriations process perhaps unmatched by any President. The
New York Times, which had heaped scorn on him when he
became a senator, observed when Truman became President that no officer of the U.S. government knew more
about the American war effort. On the basis of his direction
of the Truman Committee, Truman had been chosen by the
"well-informed newspaper correspondents in Washington" as the civilian who, next to President Roosevelt him-

self, "knew most about the war."[21] At the time, of course, the war effort was *the* matter of overriding concern. And Truman's current knowledge was built upon a firm foundation — his stubborn, single-minded devotion to "doing right." He had his own hard-headed conception of public service from which he never wavered.

Honesty, for one thing, was ingrained in Harry Truman. He was honest about what he did, and honest about himself. Maybe it was the very simplicity and unpretentiousness of Truman's background that molded his character. He grew up with a simple, unaffected lifestyle and lived by simple truths. There was always hard work, and you always did the best you could at it. There were friends and family; they meant a lot and were to be cherished. There were responsibilities to your work and to other persons, and one did not shirk responsibility.

There were absolute values, instilled in Truman by many homespun influences and reinforced by his Baptist faith and his membership in the Masons. He was dogmatic about these values. In his view, he knew what was right — period — and what was right was not up for discussion. Truman also was always a doer. He was decisive. These qualities, too, had to do with the way he grew up. On a farm such as he lived and worked on for so many years, there is too much to do to spend much time pondering and philosophizing. One simply gets on with it. You do what has to be done. And once the field is planted, there is no second-guessing. One has to be decisive in the military, too, especially when commanding men in combat. Truman was good at it.

Part of Truman's creed of "doing right" was to be unswervingly loyal to friends. His boyhood friend and high school classmate, Charlie Ross, became Truman's trusted aide and presidential press secretary. Harry Vaughn of the 129th Artillery became President Truman's military aide; John Snyder, another long-time army buddy, held several important posts in the Truman administration. Bob Hannegan became postmaster general. And Truman never turned his back on Tom Pendergast, even though others did and it would have been "smart politics" for Truman to do so. When Pendergast died in 1945, Harry Truman — then President of the United States — attended his funeral.

As a political figure and in his personality and appearance, Truman bore no resemblance to the man he succeeded as President. He had none of the exterior greatness that distinguished Roosevelt. Truman's was an inner quality. Truman had none of the sparkling chemistry of charm and grace that made Franklin Roosevelt such a majestic figure. Perhaps it was this stark absence of outer distinction in Truman when compared to Roosevelt that caused people to refer to Truman as a "little" man. It was not only his partisan detractors but people in general who almost invariably tended to think of Truman as smaller in physical stature than he was. In fact he stood about five feet ten inches tall — well above the average height in his day — and weighed between 165 and 170 pounds. With erect posture and a 34-inch waist, he was a trim-looking, vigorous man who in his sixties continued to make exercise a daily ritual and whose brisk, early-morning walks would become a characteristic of his presidential style. But he was utterly lacking in outward signs of stature. Roosevelt was an imposing, dramatic figure who projected an image of being the great "papa" to the American people. Truman described himself as looking "just like any other fifty men whom you meet on the street, " and indeed had an inconspicuous kind of appearance. He was the archetype middle-class, middle-continent American, with steel-rimmed glasses, flatly combed gray hair, and a rather flat but not unpleasant Missouri twang.

Next to the shock of Roosevelt's death, the next most shocking thing to the American people was that this man

Truman was now the President. He was so different, so little known, and seemed so unlikely a successor. But Truman — simple, small-towny, and self-tutored — knew vastly more than anyone supposed he did. He was far better prepared than anyone expected to meet the unexpected challenges that would make the presidency the powerhouse of many nations rather than principally of one.

A sea of change in the course of history was soon to force a fundamental change in the institution of the American presidency. Truman's accidental elevation to the office coincided with this profound historical process. His coming into office did not create the circumstances but coincided with the impact of the new set of pressures, obligations, and mandates they generated. It was Truman's fate that the very nature of the presidential office had to change in order to meet a qualitative change in the nature of its overriding challenges.

The change would have occurred had Roosevelt lived on. It already was in process, but was masked by the fact that Roosevelt, although he had led the nation into war and very largely through it, was above all a domestic leader. His crucial tests and crucial concerns had been domestic. He had done battle with the great depression, and had reshaped the country's social, economic, and political fabric. Roosevelt was extravagantly hailed and condemned as America's great innovator. But it was Truman, who appeared to be the very model of the parochial politician, who would become the innovator in something much larger than a solely national scene. William S. White put it in terms of the pseudo spiritual in which it is said that He — meaning God — has got the whole world in his hands. "It may be tasteless, but it is not at any rate irreverent to say," White wrote, "that as matters turned out the departure from life of the privileged and patrician Roosevelt was to leave the whole world, in secular terms, very largely in the humble, the untried, the abashed but determined hands of the very unpatrician man who was Harry Truman.''[22] It was up to Truman to transform the presidency to meet unprecedented challenges from a world undergoing unprecedented, cataclysmic change. They were challenges that would demand, for the first time in history, the subordination of purely national interest to faraway, competing interests in a broken world maddened in spirit by trials and dangers.

III Taking Command

It was not at a bright moment in history that the reins of national leadership were abruptly placed in Harry Truman's hands. The long night of world war was not over. The dawn of the nuclear age was at hand. The hot war for military supremacy in Europe, the heartland of Western civilization, was ending, but a cold war for political supremacy had begun. This was the message Averell Harriman, the U.S. ambassador in Moscow, had been sending to Washington for several months — that postwar Soviet policy was cynically and single-mindedly aimed at extending Soviet control in Europe as far as it could reach. Wordly sophisticate that Roosevelt was, he either did not foresee or did not face up to the fact that the end of the war would profoundly redistribute world power. It would thrust the U.S. and the Soviet Union face to face across an enormous vacuum where Britain and its old European alliance had been.

Nothing that Truman began grappling with in his first days as President was as unsettling and ominous as this news Harriman brought from Moscow. Harriman travelled to Washington to explain to the new President the chilling evidence that the previous one had ignored. He found that Truman had already done his homework, having read back over the cables and reports exchanged between Harriman and the State Department. This reporting made clear that the wartime alliance of Russia and the West was no more than a marriage of convenience in Moscow's eyes, and that postwar cooperation was seen by the Soviets as a mask they could wear when it suited them. Premier Stalin had first

71

made a pact with Nazi Germany to spare Russia at the expense of others; failing that, he had allied himself with the West to defeat their common military foe. But beyond Stalin's military objective was a political one, and no common ground was to be found there between Western democracy and Communist totalitarianism.

Truman was in a tight spot. Roosevelt had proclaimed a lofty ideal: after the war, the nations of the world were to create in concert the world machinery for international peace-keeping that would "outlaw" war. Truman's first decision upon Roosevelt's death had been to direct that the San Francisco Conference convene as scheduled to draft the United Nations charter. An open break with Russia now would shatter not only the ideal that was dreamed of for the UN; it would dash the more modest hopes for it, as a useful world forum, which were realistic and attainable. Yet Russia was riding roughshod in Europe over the very values for which the Western allies had fought. And there was more to Truman's dilemma. On the one hand, Ambassador Harriman on the scene in Moscow and some Soviet specialists at the State Department believed the new President should denounce the Russians in no uncertain terms. On the other hand, there were the military chiefs of staff, fearful of Russia's staying power as an ally and eager to have it enter the war against Japan; they warned against doing or saying anything that might further test the fragile alliance. Still others, led by Secretary of Commerce Henry Wallace, argued that the only way to ensure that Russia would be a good partner in peace was to be indulgent and tolerant when it interpreted agreements any way it chose or ignored them at will.

Characteristically, Truman sought out a middle road. He was not going to saddle the U.S. with the onus of destroying hopes for the UN before the organization had been given a chance, but he was not going to let the Soviet Union suppose that the U.S. did not know what was going on in

Eastern Europe. He was not going to act as if nothing bad was happening there. And he made his point sharply in his first encounter with a Soviet official. Soviet Foreign Minister Molotov, no doubt with instructions from Stalin to obtain a firsthand impression of the new President, stopped in Washington en route to the San Francisco Conference. Harriman and Charles E. "Chip" Bohlen, one of the State Department's top Russian experts, escorted Molotov and Soviet Ambassador Gromyko to the White House on April 23, 1945.

Truman steered the conversation directly to the subject of the sanctity of agreements among nations. The U.S. and Britain, he said, were scrupulously observing every agreement made at Yalta and elsewhere, but this was not to be a one-way street. The West would uphold its end of every bargain honorably, Truman told Molotov, but it demanded the same of the Soviets. That had not been the case in Poland, the President said bluntly, where the free choice of the people had been thwarted. The U.S. wanted friendship with Russia, Truman said, but he was informing the foreign minister here and now that this could only be on the basis of mutual observance of agreements. He wanted it clearly understood that the U.S. did not go along with what was happening in Poland, and that he expected Molotov to convey precisely that message to Premier Stalin.

"I have never been talked to like that in my life!" Molotov sputtered indignantly.

"Carry out your agreements," Truman shot back, "and you won't get talked to like that!"

The point was driven home with only partial success. The Soviets made a pretense of consulting Poland's exile government in London, inviting 20 of the exile leaders to Moscow in May. Sixteen were promptly imprisoned for plotting against the Soviet occupation regime, but four were given positions in the Polish government. It was less than half a loaf to settle for, but accepting the Soviet gesture of compromise seemed to be the only way to keep the Polish controversy from wrecking the UN. The U.S. and Britain abandoned their refusal to agree to seat Poland's puppet government, in the hope that now that a democratic element at least had a foot in the door it could, in time, open it wider. That hope was not to be realized, but the concession enabled the San Francisco Conference, after 63 days of hard negotiations, to complete the document that established the UN.

A New Style and Image

In the meantime, Truman's early conduct in office was dispelling the shock that engulfed the country at Roosevelt's death. The dimension of that event, and its impact on people, is difficult to imagine. The multitude of measures he introduced to deal with the national trauma of the great depression made his influence on the daily life of all the citizens of the country the most direct and pervasive of any President in history. He had been the dominant figure of American life for more than a dozen years. He was an institution, bigger than life. Then with wrenching sudden-ness he was gone.

For the rest of their lives, all the Americans within earshot would remember where they were and what they were doing on the day they heard the news that Roosevelt was dead. But now the improbable Harry Truman was easing tensions in the nation's capital. Within weeks he was lifting the spirits of his countrymen and inspiring their confidence with the firmness and vigor he was displaying in office. He met the press, and the reporters liked his frank-ness. He answered their questions with candor when he thought answers were required and refused to answer others, but without a trace of evasion. The words he used were plain, and left no implication that something must be read into them. The new President showed that he intended to use the White House press conference as a channel of public information and to clarify official acts and policies, rather than as an instrument for propaganda and pressure. He met and talked reassuringly with the chief assistants of his predecessor and with congressional leaders from both parties. His quickness in making decisions was impressive, as was the confidence he showed in tackling difficult problems that were new to him.

It was becoming clear, too, to the people and to the new President as well, that he could not simply carry on for Roosevelt. There was too much change coming about, and things were happening too fast, even if there had been a clear chart left for Truman to follow. The fact was that, short of 82 days, the new President would occupy the White House for a full term. The great postwar problems at home and abroad would be for Truman to face with policies of his own. He would have to develop a Truman administration and a Truman program. And it was obvious from the outset that the Truman presidency would have its own distinctive style and character.

The new President immediately set in motion his own routine of White House business, and the most conspicuous change was in the speeded tempo of activity. He was up early, moving briskly through the day, and working intensely. Whereas Roosevelt's calling lists were meager, Truman's were jammed from early morning to noon. The list often extended well into the afternoon, as Truman departed from the practice of past Presidents of keeping their afternoons free of official callers. If he didn't get to the paper work in the afternoon, he would work on it into the evening, taking documents to sign and reports to study in the private quarters of the executive mansion. The Trumans did not care for the social whirl, and indicated that even after the war it would be held to the minimum demanded by protocol, a sharp contrast to the life of the society-loving Roosevelts before the war.

The new President was showing himself to be a capable administrator. His cabinet meetings were direct and businesslike, lasting about three-quarters of an hour, or half the time given to them before he entered the White House. He placed a maximum of responsibility upon his subordinates. He would call several into his office and assign them enough work in 10 minutes to take up days of their time. He did not harass them by calling for the results prematurely. When reports were submitted he went over them carefully and expressed satisfaction or asked for more details on certain points. If he regarded the report as unsatisfactory he simply assigned it to someone else.

The new chief executive's workday routine was noted with interest and reported to an unprecedented degree. Stationing an army of news media representatives at the White House to provide blanket coverage of presidential activity in minute detail was a comparatively new practice that had taken hold during Roosevelt's tenure. For one thing, the federal government to an unprecedented degree had become the place where the action was. The occupant of the White House had become the chief actor to an extent that eclipsed even the days of Teddy Roosevelt. Another reason the White House became the fountainhead of news reporting was, of course, the war. Reporters were always there for battle news, word on allied and enemy strategy, and wartime appeals to the home front. And after all, it had been a dozen years since there had been a new President. So with Truman the presidential office and residence became a goldfish bowl as never before.

The public was told when the President got up in the morning and when he had breakfast. Almost every move he made was faithfully recorded until it was time to report what time he went to bed. It was reported with interest that after arising at 6:30 in the morning and exercising, he shaved himself with a safety razor. This was notable because Truman had dispensed with the services of a veteran black doorman and barber who had shaved Presidents through many administrations. It was noted that Truman used the telephone frequently — a custom begun by Herbert Hoover, who was the first President to have a phone installed at his desk; before that, Presidents went into a side room for phone calls. Truman averaged around 30 calls a day, and liked to place calls himself in order to talk directly with members of Congress, cabinet officers, other officials, or private citizens. Truman liked to take a break in the late afternoon to seek relaxation by having a swim and a rubdown. He then would return to his office for a final spurt of work before going to the living quarters of the mansion around 6 p.m. and retiring before midnight.

In the days since fate had thrust Truman into the highest office in the land, so much had been printed in the newspapers about his humility that the personality and self-assurance he revealed in his personal contacts with the press came as a surprise. His tolerance of other views would quickly give way to firmness when he thought the time for that had come. His sense of being in command, the unmistakable air of confidence and even of testiness he displayed in the give-and-take of highly informal press conferences was not the humble manner that many news accounts had depicted. Descriptions of Truman during the first shock of the succession had highlighted his hope that his relationship with old friends would remain unchanged, his saying "Call me Harry," and his asking in all sincerity for prayers to aid him. The accounts gave an impression of a President who was preoccupied with his inadequacies.

The nature of the times, the suddenness of the succession, and the towering stature of his predecessor were compelling reasons to let the American public and the world know at once that the new President was not introspectively examining his shortcomings, real or imagined, but that he was in fact fully prepared for whatever challenges came along. Whether Truman sensed this or was advised accordingly, he quickly took the accent off humility. He conducted himself as one who does not shrink from responsibilities and has assumed them firmly, and the effect was electric. His performance with the press testified that he was not timid about his job and not the least bit reluctant to take extemporaneous questions from correspondents. In short, he began showing early on that he intended everyone to know that the President of the United States was just that, and that no apologies or pleas for acceptance were necessary.

Some of the show of self-assurance that surprised people who did not know Truman can be attributed to his expectation that others respect the presidency, as he did, wholly apart from the person occupying it. Some of the confidence reflected Truman's stubborn conviction that he was doing his level best and that no one could ask for more than that. And some of it must be attributed, of course, to his realization that tremendous power had come to him. As a senator he had an exceptional record, but he was one of many senators and his word was not final. As vice-president he was constitutionally relegated to the sidelines, and matters of great moment during his brief tenure were weighed and settled without his knowledge or counsel. But suddenly the paramount concerns of the nation and the world came to him for review and decision. The power of the nation behind him was such that no decision by any inhabitant of the planet was more effective than his own. President Truman was making that felt. He did not overestimate it or minimize it, but his awareness of it was clear.

At the same time, Truman reaped some advantage in good will as he began his presidency. He benefitted both from the natural impulse of most people to rally around as he shouldered the burden in an atmosphere of crisis, and from the refreshing change from the urban East to the homespun Midwest represented by the Trumans and their close friends and personal interests. The President's hometown of Independence, Missouri, seemed ideally named and situated. It had a powerful appeal in a country locked in a war that had millions of American boys in strange, faraway lands, longing to be back in such towns as Independence. Despite his long association with a big-city political machine in Kansas City that had all the blemishes associated with New York or Chicago, Truman's image was that of a small-town man.

There were plenty of political troubles in store for Truman. The war raged on and the cold war lurked in its shadows. The economy hurtled like a runaway locomotive toward the inevitable cliff of reconversion from war to peace. The opposition in Congress would take form soon enough, and the factional strife would resurface in the Democratic Party. But for a time there was a big plus for the new President in what were widely regarded as typically American roots in the folksy atmosphere of the midlands. When he and his family would occasionally leave Washington for a weekend excursion, it was quite naturally to the old home town. They stayed in the family's old house in Independence. The President would spend a few hours talking with his country and small-town friends; he would visit his mother, 92 years old, at the Grandview farm. It all struck a responsive chord in the American ideal of the majority of the people. The President's plain, down-home qualities, the homey atmosphere of Independence and all that went with it, went over well with the American people.

New Faces from New Areas

The nation's grief was giving way to Truman's good cheer, and was further cast aside by his announcement to the nation on May 7, 1945, that Nazi Germany had surrendered and the fighting in Europe was over. The business of getting on with the war against Japan was accompanied by clearer signs as the summer began that the Truman administration was taking shape. There also were signs that Truman's "honeymoon" from political problems was waning. Before that period of grace ended it would help him win approval on Capitol Hill of key legislation to reduce tariffs, to adhere by treaty to the UN Charter, and to authorize a U.S. delegate to the UN Security Council.

The new chief executive devoted himself constantly to the task of becoming educated to the office, but not to his predecessor's way of doing things. Part of Truman's own approach to the conduct of the presidency was a departure from Roosevelt's practice of bypassing heads of departments and agencies or creating new ones to do their work. Truman's political action plan was far more orthodox. He wanted orderly processes to be followed in administration. He preferred to place a full measure of responsibility on the ranking officials of the executive branch. He would then deal directly with these officials on the matters entrusted to them. He wanted organization to be tightened, and promptly asked Congress for authority to reorganize the executive branch to make it operate more efficiently and economically. Truman expected his officials and their departments or agencies to know their fields and where the lines were drawn around them. He did not want one department intruding on another. And while he emphasized that directing officials should exercise responsibility, he also insisted that he know what was going on.

His boyhood friend and high school classmate, Charlie Ross, quickly became the President's closest adviser in the White House. Truman selected Ross, who had become managing editor of the *St. Louis Post-Dispatch,* as his press secretary. Soon Truman changed the make-up of the cabinet considerably. Within six weeks as President, he had replaced four of the ten cabinet officers, and his appointments showed a dramatic geographic shift away from the eastern seaboard. To be attorney general, Truman named Tom Clark of Dallas; for secretary of labor, he picked Judge Lewis Schwellenbach of Spokane, Washington. He named Bob Hannegan of St. Louis as postmaster general. Representative Clinton Anderson of New Mexico, who was chairman of a special House committee investigating food problems, was urging that they be concentrated under a single head. He was put in just that position; Truman made him secretary of agriculture. With Secretary of Commerce Wallace, who was from Iowa, Truman's reconstituted cabinet was without precedent in that half of its members were from west of the Mississippi.

The next two Truman cabinet appointments in the summer of 1945 carried extra significance. They were among the most important cabinet posts, the appointees were from the deep south, and the appointments reflected Truman's fundamental faith in the democratic process and his devotion to the profession of politics.

Truman decided on his first day in office that he wanted James F. Byrnes, from South Carolina, to be his secretary of state. He conferred the day after Roosevelt's death with Byrnes, who had made shorthand notes of all the secret meetings he attended with Roosevelt at Yalta and transcribed them for the new President. Truman's primary reason for turning to Byrnes for this most important cabinet post was the question of succession to the presidency.

Under existing law, dating from 1886, if a President died, the line of succession after the vice-president would pass to the cabinet offices in the order of their creation, beginning with the secretary of state. This meant that Secretary of State Stettinius was the next in line to be President. But Stettinius had never been a candidate for any elective office, and Truman believed any man who stepped into the presidency should have held at least some office to which he had been elected by a vote of the people.

Seeking a change in the succession law would be a top priority for Truman, but he knew it would take time to obtain the legislation. Pending a change in the law, he felt obliged to choose a secretary of state qualified to succeed, if necessary, to the presidency. He regarded Byrnes as such a man, in light of the South Carolinian's many terms in the House and Senate, where he had chaired important committees. His record was so impressive that Roosevelt had named him to the Supreme Court. And Byrnes later gave up that lifetime position of great prestige and resigned from the Court when Roosevelt asked him to move into the White House as his assistant in charge of war mobilization. Truman believed Byrnes' background and ability would make him an excellent secretary of state, but he had still another, more personal, reason for asking him. Byrnes had felt that his record of service made him the logical choice to be Roosevelt's running mate in 1944, and Truman had agreed to back him before the convention began. Truman could imagine how it must have hurt his old friend when the convention and Roosevelt willed otherwise, and he thought that summoning him to be secretary of state might help balance things up.[1]

Out of consideration for Stettinius, who headed the U.S. delegation negotiating the UN charter at San Francisco, the appointment of Byrnes was delayed until the work of the conference was done. Truman then named Stettinius to be the first to fill the U.S. seat on the new UN Security Council. The President's next move was to appoint a new secretary of the treasury, who would be next in line of succession to the presidency. The incumbent, Henry Morgenthau, was largely a figurehead in the post. Morgenthau had become an active proponent of a plan he had drawn up to strip postwar Germany of all its industrial potential and force its people to remain nothing more than a pastoral, purely agrarian society.

Truman did not like the plan, but Morgenthau kept pushing it. When he learned Truman would soon go to Potsdam for postwar planning with Churchill and Stalin, Morgenthau appealed to the President to take him along. Truman said he thought the secretary of the treasury was needed more in the U.S. than in Potsdam. Morgenthau persisted to the point of arguing that if he could not go he would feel compelled to quit, whereupon Truman asked for his resignation.[2] To replace him, the President chose Fred M. Vinson of Georgia, director of the Office of War Mobilization and Reconversion, and formerly chairman of the tax subcommittee of the House Ways and Means Committee. Truman appointed an old army friend, John Snyder — who had become executive vice-president of the First National Bank of St. Louis, and who had been in Washington administrative posts including that of Federal Loan Administrator — to succeed Vinson.

By mid-July, three months after he became President, Truman's cabinet had only four Roosevelt appointees left in it. It was made up of men with government experience, and most of them had political experience as well — something Truman put great stock in. He believed a person who understands politics understands free government. His preference was for those who knew what it was like to go to the people, those who had met the test of convincing a majority that what you are doing deserves their support.

Truman's Political Philosophy

The new President's call for Congress to give an elective character to the presidential succession embodied his belief in this precept — that a person is better suited to hold a position of public trust by having had, at some time, the intense political experience of having to win an election. In his request for a change in the existing legislation, Truman pointed out that because of the circumstances under which he became President, there would be no elected vice-president for almost four years. The existing statute governing succession gave Truman the power to name the person who would be his immediate successor in the event of his own death or inability to act. He told Congress he did not believe that in a democracy that power should rest with the chief executive. He asked Congress to change the law so that if a President and the vice-president succeeding him were to die in office, the next to assume the office would be not a presidential appointee but the speaker of the House of Representatives. That way the successor would be an elected representative of the people in a congressional district as well as the leader chosen by the majority of the elected representatives of the people.

Just as Truman was a thoroughly practical and pragmatic person, so was his political philosophy. He was a politician by profession and was proud of it. Although he saw trends in political action away from encouraging the old-fashioned virtues of thrift, truth-telling, and equitable government, he believed those virtues to be so fundamental in the American make-up that politics was obliged to reverse the trend.

Truman was not a worrier. He thought of himself as an instrument for the public welfare; worry would blunt the instrument, so he simply would not permit it. Reviewing history's exhibit of such instruments, he believed Thomas

Jefferson was the best. Truman was undaunted by the fact
that others regarded the Democrats of his day as dubious
descendants of Jefferson's principles; the new President
believed he was a real and legitimate heir.

Like Jefferson, Truman abhorred bigness. He would
rather see a hundred small insurance companies than four
big ones, a hundred industrial corporations and labor unions
where a few dominated the scene. Bigness, in his view,
gave too much power to groups and to individuals and
tended to thwart true democracy. Truman wanted the federal establishment whittled down to more manageable
proportions, both in respect to sheer bulk and in efficiency
of operation.

As a party man, Truman was a firm believer in the
two-party system. However much the parties were broken
down by coalitions and made up of unrelated and warring
elements, he believed they represented the best system ever
devised for establishing responsible government. Within
the party, Truman believed a man should fight for his ideas
as hard as he knows how — in the caucus, the convention,
or whatever the party forum. But losing, he should follow
the majority. Truman would not be disloyal to his party's
platform, and felt committed to the broad social and
economic objectives for which its departed chief had stood.

Although his background and traditions were of a conservative tendency, Truman's political experience was
nearly all on the side of liberalism. The new President
defied stereotyping, however, and it became evident even
in the early months of his administration that Truman was
destined to play his own role in his own way. He would not
speak the lines of his predecessor. He would be his own
man in his own mold. His inclination was to digest the
innovations already made rather than to experiment with
others. He would work to lessen the wartime controls over

business, for Truman was a devout disciple of the theory of free business enterprise within the firm restraint of antitrust laws.

In the sphere of social legislation, Truman showed his hand early by unqualified endorsement of a bill to abolish the poll tax — often abused as a device to keep blacks from voting — and by his support of a permanent Fair Employment Practices Committee. Both were issues on which he would lose. The two actions were not conclusive, but they were significant in that had he chosen to do so he could have ducked the issues.

These various signs of Truman's political philosophy were straws in the wind. They did not point in the direction of a particular doctrine. Truman did not embrace a dogmatic approach to government and society. He was not given to theorizing of a visionary nature. The signs of his fundamental attitudes and beliefs did not form a portrait of an ideologist. What they did do was point to a tenure to be marked by progressivism and pragmatism, and they pointed more toward the middle of the ideological road.

Off to Confer at Potsdam

Harry Truman scarcely had time to get his feet wet in international politics before the Potsdam Conference totally immersed him in it. Even as he became President, the ideal of postwar cooperation between Soviet Russia and the West was unraveling as rapidly as the Red Army's advance into central Europe. The Russians summarily ignored Allied agreement to cooperate in the administration of liberated areas. They imposed Communist regimes in country after country and rudely refused access to the areas by their

Western allies. As they did so, Churchill wrote an eloquent
appeal to Stalin:

> There is not much comfort in looking into a future where you and the
> countries you dominate . . . are all drawn up on one side, and those
> who rally to the English-speaking nations and their associates are on
> the other. It is quite obvious that their quarrel would tear the whole
> world to pieces and that all of us leading men on either side who had
> anything to do with that would be shamed before history. Even
> embarking on a long period of suspicions, of abuse and counter-
> abuse, and of opposing policies would be a disaster hampering the
> great developments of world prosperity for the masses which are
> attainable only by our trinity. I hope there is no word or phrase in
> this outpouring of my heart to you which unwittingly gives offense.
> If so, let me know. But do not, I beg you, my friend Stalin,
> underrate the divergencies which are opening about matters which
> you may think are small to us but which are symbolic of the way the
> English-speaking democracies look at life."[3]

Truman, reading the letter in his first weeks in office,
was deeply troubled that Stalin was turning a deaf ear to
such reasonable, conciliatory appeals. While there might
still be time to prevent a total collapse of prospects for
East-West cooperation in postwar Europe, Truman determined that he must deal with the Soviet dictator face to face.
He must meet Churchill and Stalin in person and sit down at
the conference table with them. So he took steps to set up a
conference, making the overture to Churchill through the
U.S. Ambassador in London, and dispatching on a mission
to Moscow, Harry Hopkins, Roosevelt's most trusted confidential emissary who had won Stalin's affection and respect as the former President's personal deputy. The choice
of Hopkins was designed to convey to the suspicious Stalin
that, although Roosevelt was gone, American policy objectives were unchanged and the new President was willing to
work with the Russians as his predecessor had done. Stalin

agreed to meet with Truman and Churchill, suggesting as
the site for their meeting the town of Potsdam, a suburb of
the German capital city of Berlin, inside Russian-held territory.

The conference the three leaders conducted there lasted
seventeen days. Its sessions and all that they dealt with
make up a thicket of diplomatic stickers that do not need to
be analyzed thorn to thorn. But the conference deserves to
be recounted in its essence, not so much for what it accomplished as for what it signified and what it meant as an
educational experience. For Truman and Churchill, Potsdam would prove what the prime minister had warned about
and the President feared — that Stalin was bent on building
a European empire. He was busy subjugating it by military
force. He had no intention of living up to previous agreements that might hamper that objective, or of examining the
prospect of new ones in good faith and a spirit of compromise.

Churchill came to Potsdam widely regarded as the premier statesman of the world, and left there no longer holding office in his own country. Before the conference was
over, the British electoral process, reflecting the unrest and
impatience that swept the world as war tensions relaxed —
unrest and impatience of a kind that would soon enough
beset Truman — unseated Churchill and introduced the
unfamiliar name of a scholarly Socialist, Clement Attlee.
By the end of the conference, Churchill had learned that his
initial misgivings about Truman were misplaced; that however the new President's image contrasted with that of his
predecessor, the reins of leadership in the West were in
good hands and would be held firmly. Truman's firmness
must have been educational for Stalin as well. Unlike
Roosevelt, Truman showed that he was not inclined to
make concessions now in return for some vague promise
about the future.

President Truman and a party that included Secretary of State Byrnes, Press Secretary Ross, and a group of military and State Department specialists arrived at Potsdam after crossing the Atlantic in nine days aboard the cruiser *Augusta,* accompanied only by another cruiser, the *Philadelphia.* The voyage mixed relaxation and hard work. The President ate in the ship's mess, pushing an aluminum tray through the chow line along with his shipmates. He stayed in touch with Washington and the other, ongoing business of the presidency, and studied papers and documents that were his homework for the conference ahead. In the evenings he'd see a movie and play poker. He and his aides saw Potsdam as a last chance to implement the plans made at Yalta. That earlier conference had been the high-water mark of optimism and idealism. This one was being approached hopefully but with no illusions.

Confronting the Cold War

The Potsdam Conference began amid acrimony and distrust about Poland, and never really got out from under the cloud that situation had created. Stalin held the trump cards, with his red Army controlling all of Poland and with a handful of obedient Polish Communists posing as the government. At Yalta it had been decided that Poland would have a new eastern border, and would get some new territory on the west from Germany in a final peace settlement. The Soviets carved far more territory out of Germany than the Yalta agreement — albeit vague — had envisaged. The area they laid claim to would drive millions of Germans from their traditional homes. It would cede almost one-quarter of Germany's most productive agricultural region to Poland and rob the rest of Germany, already facing famine, of an important source of food.

It nevertheless became clear after days of wrangling that drained the patience of the participants that the Poles, with Soviet backing, had established squatter's rights that could be stripped away only by force of arms. Stalin sat tight, snug in the knowledge of having presented a *fait accompli* in Poland that the U.S. and Britain would not go to war to undo. Secretary Byrnes finally devised a rather feeble formula for getting off the hook and on to other business. It was decided that the conference would accept the Polish situation as a temporary one pending final solution of the main issue, Poland's western boundary, when a German peace treaty could be drafted. More than a generation later, such a treaty has yet to be drafted.

Having gone to Potsdam in the belief that the conference would establish the terms and the machinery for producing peace treaties with Germany and its former satellites, Truman was frustrated further as Stalin flatly refused to do anything but paper over with ambiguity the futures of Hungary, Romania, and Bulgaria. Again, all three had been taken over already by the Red Army. In each, the Soviets had installed only Communists in positions of control. They made a travesty of earlier agreement on joint Allied administration to help provide stability during a period of transition to democratic governments that were to be chosen through free elections.

The three leaders at Postdam took up the subject of Germany with little likelihood that, on this central issue, there would be a meeting of minds that already had different conceptions of the direction Germany's future should take. Stalin's country had suffered most at the hands of German invaders — twice within a generation — and he wanted Germany to be rendered permanently unable to be a military threat to Russia again. He wanted to erect on German soil a forward bastion of Communism in the heart of Europe.

Churchill wanted to curb Germany's military potential, but he took a longer political view. He wanted a successor state in Germany to be viable enough to play again its historic role of countering Russian designs on expanding to the West. Truman wanted to see Germany reconstituted along democratic lines, and not in a state of indefinite dependence on American charity. But Truman had been briefed to pursue as the primary negotiating objective at Potsdam the adherence of Russia to its promise at Yalta to launch a second front against Japan three months after the defeat of Germany. The U.S. and Britain thus had no agreed strategy on Germany, and Truman was conditioned to put uppermost emphasis on Russia as an ally against Japan.

The fact that Stalin again held the best cards when the future shape of Germany was on the table is, in retrospect, clearly related to the U.S. decision in the closing weeks of the war to halt the rapid advance of American forces across Germany. Once again, Churchill had warned in prophetic words — this time in a communication to his foreign secretary in May of 1945 — of the peril he saw unfolding in the Red Army's advance.

> I fear terrible things have happened during the Russian advance through Germany to the Elbe. The proposed withdrawal of the United States Army to the occupation lines which were arranged with the Russians and the Americans in Quebec . . . would mean the tide of Russian domination sweeping forward 120 miles on a front of 300 or 400 miles. This would be an event which, if it occurred, would be one of the most melancholy in history. After it was over and the territory occupied by the Russians, Poland would be completely engulfed. . . . The Russian frontier would run from the North Cape in Norway . . . along the frontier between Bavaria and Czechoslovakia . . . across Austria to the Isonzo River, behind which Tito the Communist partisan leader in Yugoslavia and Russia will claim everything to the east. Thus, the territories under Russian control would include the Baltic provinces, all of Germany to the

occupational line, all of Czechoslovakia, a large part of Austria, the whole of Yugoslavia, Hungary, Rumania, Bulgaria until Greece in her present tottering condition is reached. . . .

This constitutes an event in the history of Europe to which there has been no parallel, and which has not been faced by the Allies in their long and hazardous struggle. . . .[4]

The "occupational line" Churchill referred to had to do with a rough agreement dividing Germany into three zones which the British, American, and Russian armies were to occupy at the end of the war. This was accepted rather hastily and in a general way at a meeting of Roosevelt and Churchill in Quebec in September of 1944. There were no definite arrangements made because the Russians were not present, but later at Yalta all three powers had accepted the zones drawn up in this draft agreement and had made provision for a fourth zone for France.[5] Increasingly alarmed about Russian intentions, Churchill favored having the Anglo-American forces take as much territory as they could get for bargaining purposes after the war. This was especially true when the Western forces surged forward with a speed that could not have been foreseen even at Yalta. They passed their planned, postwar occupation line and found themselves in a position to beat the Red Army to Berlin. Churchill argued that when the fighting ceased, U.S. and British forces should not withdraw to their occupational line until the Western allies were satisfied about Poland, about the nature and duration of the Russian occupation of Germany, and about conditions in the Russian-controlled countries of the Danube Valley. He believed these matters could be settled only while U.S. forces were there in full strength.[6]

General Dwight Eisenhower, the supreme commander in Europe, objected to taking Berlin on grounds that doing so would inject political considerations into military operations. Berlin, he contended, might be a matter of prestige, but Berlin itself was no longer a particularly important objective.[7] It is hard to imagine this failure to grasp the political, psychological, and military advantage of capturing the city that represented the very heart and soul of Germany. Berlin was the nerve center of the Nazi regime and the political, economic, and cultural capital of the German nation. Berlin was to Germany what Paris has always been to France and London has always been to England. But Berlin at any rate had been relegated to the Russian zone by the occupation lines accepted at Yalta. Whatever other considerations might seem wiser in retrospect, Truman regarded the U.S. commitment on the occupation zones as an established fact. He had no intention of breaking the very kind of agreement he expected the Russians to honor.

The result, however, was that U.S. and British forces had been pulled back to within their prescribed occupational line to allow the Red Army to come forward to meet them. And Stalin again on this issue could sit tight at Potsdam; the mold for a divided postwar Germany was irrevocably cast. The U.S. and Britain had no leverage they could apply in negotiating with the uncooperative Russians on the complex problems of Germany's political control, economic reconstruction, and reparations payment.

Rather than dispute every detail, the negotiators disposed of the question of political control over occupied Germany by avoiding details and agreeing to nothing more than a broadbrush outline. It allowed each occupying power to carry out, in its own zone of occupation, the policies of an Allied Control Council. The policies were to provide, among other general objectives, for a gradual resumption of local self-government based on democratic principles. The wording, however, was so general that before the summer ended, the Soviets — without appearing to break openly the letter of the agreement — had set up a Communist regime in their zone and suppressed all other political activity.

The questions of rehabilitating the economy of Germany and of exacting war reparations from it became enmeshed, and they were embroiled in East-West argument from the outset. Truman recommended that, to get the German economy moving again, the occupying powers should treat the whole country as a single economic unit. He proposed setting production priorities to assure a minimal living standard and adequate supplies for the occupation forces, and allowing an unhindered flow of commodities and manufactured goods across the occupation lines. Stalin rebuffed the idea, with an eye to the assets the Soviets held in the coal mines and rich farmlands of their zone.

In Stalin's view, reparations came first and the needs of the German people came somewhere down the line. At Yalta, he had said the Soviet Union's war claims against Germany would probably amount to $10 billion. At Potsdam, he said the bargaining should begin with that figure. Without waiting for the niceties of an agreement, the Soviets meanwhile had been stripping the territory they occupied — not only in Germany but that of its former East European satellites as well — of anything they could transport to Russia. They confiscated British-owned refineries in Romania, and brushed the action aside as a trifling matter when Churchill voiced disapproval. The Russians dismantled entire factories and shipped them away, carting off as war booty anything they laid hands on in the way of industrial stocks, supplies, equipment, food, and fuel resources.

Truman and Churchill would have no part of Stalin's most outlandish demands — that the conference grant Russia at least $10 billion in reparations from Germany and the right to use forced German labor. They had no choice, however, but to abandon the key concept of treating all of Germany as a single economy, occupation lines notwithstanding. By blocking this, Russia further assured the ultimate, lasting division of Germany into East and West. Stalin's refusal to cooperate left no alternative but an unhappy compromise by which each occupying power would satisfy its own reparations claims in its own zone.

The U.S. and Britain made no claims for reparations, but there was no way to keep the Russians from ripping away whatever they chose to extract from the territory they held. The upshot was that effective control of each occupation zone — economic, political, and military — would rest with each occupying power. Perhaps it was naive to have expected otherwise. At any rate, the Russians would repeatedly frustrate the efforts of the Allied Control Commission to work out unified approaches and policies for the occupation of Germany. Potsdam merely underscored the fact that the die had been cast for "the German problem," which would be at the center of the cold war for many years to come.

Japan and The Bomb

Oddly enough, even as the cold war battle lines were hardening at Potsdam over issues in Germany and Eastern Europe, the U.S. was thinking mostly of Japan, where the war was not yet won. Truman went to Potsdam convinced that his most urgent objective there was to get Stalin to reaffirm the commitment he had made at Yalta for Russia to enter the war against Japan. The new President, at this early stage in office and involved in a summit conference of this order, was inevitably dependent upon the judgments of the advisers he inherited along with the presidency. The man he had picked to be his secretary of state was a carry-over from

Roosevelt's inner circle of strategic planners and advisers. So were the military chiefs of staff who also accompanied Truman to Potsdam. And at Potsdam they remained preoccupied with the immediate task of winning the war, rather than with its consequences.

These advisers were not about to sit back and relax because Nazi Germany had fallen. They were uneasy that victory in Europe might be accompanied by a slackening — even though it might be a subconscious one — of the U.S. war effort. They were not unaware that enormous difficulties would be involved in administering occupied Germany and the newly liberated areas, rife with the problems of hunger, homeless refugees, and economic dislocation. But the fear of the moment was that this might detract, at a most critical time, from the overriding priority of pressing on to victory over Japan. As troubled as the U.S. was by Soviet behavior, many U.S. planners could not help but relate that, too, to the immediate effect it could have on the war against Japan. Several key advisers reasoned that if the Soviets were welshing on their agreements, they might well disregard their commitment to create a second front in the war in Asia.

In what is perhaps the most notorious of Roosevelt's secret agreements at Yalta, Russia was promised a redress of its losses in the Russo-Japanese War of 1904, including territorial gains in Japan's Kuril Islands and a free hand in Outer Mongolia, in return for Russia's pledge to wage war on Japan three months after the war was over in Europe. Although of vital significance for the future of China, the agreement was concealed from the Chinese until the trap was ready to be sprung on the Japanese. Meanwhile, tension was mounting between Russia and the West; Stalin's stunning disregard for Yalta agreements in Europe was causing considerable doubt in the summer of 1945 as to whether the Soviets could be counted on in regard to Japan.

As a result, Truman came to Potsdam harboring genuine fears that Russia might not keep the bargain.

It was not that the new President did not receive some contrary advice. Ambassador Harriman, for one, took the position that it would be harder at that point to keep the Soviets out of the Japanese war than to get them in. In his view, the Soviets had much to gain, at little risk, by getting in on the kill at the eleventh hour. But those taking this position were clearly in the minority. Truman's military chiefs of staff went promptly to work with their Soviet counterparts at Potsdam, concentrating their attention on plans for moving Russian forces against Japanese positions in Manchuria. Truman went along with the thinking of his military chiefs — that any political disadvantages of having the Soviets as allies against Japan were outweighed by the risk of excluding them. As his first order of business at Potsdam, Truman sought and succeeded in obtaining Stalin's reassurance that Russia would join the war against Japan.

The word of the Soviet dictator, however, was by this time hardly sufficient to put Truman's mind at ease when it came to the problem of defeating Japan. His own chiefs of staff, providing the best advice that the country's most able military and strategic planners could come up with, had told the President they estimated it would take another year and a half to subdue Japan, at a cost of at least a half million American casualties. U.S. war plans, drawn up on the eve of the test explosion of the atomic bomb, called for an amphibious landing on the southernmost of the Japanese home islands in the fall of 1945. This landing was to be followed approximately four months later by a second massive invasion, which then would be followed by another with troops transferred from Europe. Fierce fighting against fanatical, last-ditch resistance, with terribly heavy losses on both sides, was envisaged until late fall of 1946.[8] It was known that Japan's armed forces still had four million men to defend North China, Manchuria, Korea, and the Japanese home islands, and that it was organizing a national volunteer army at home for a final stand.[9] If their emperor told them to fight to the last man, the Japanese would fight to the last man.

The bloody saga of nearly four years of savage fighting in the South Pacific left no doubt that Japanese resistance would grow increasingly determined and that the toll in lives would soar higher as the war came closer to Japan itself. As the *New York Times*' correspondent covering the war in the Pacific cabled to his home office after the hard-won U.S. victory over the Japanese defenders of Okinawa, late in June of 1945:

> The war with Japan may well last for years instead of months as some optimists hope. However soon it is won the cost in life, blood and money will be high.
>
> Final victory over the Japanese can be achieved only by ground action. Large-scale bombing and fleet action unquestionably will reduce the enemy's power of resistance, but when his soldiers and sailors hole up in caves as they did on this island, they can be flushed out and killed only by foot soldiers supported by tank and flame throwers.
>
> There is virtually no evidence that the will to resist of the average Japanese soldier is weakening. The record number of prisoners taken in the final days of this campaign can be considered only a minor gain for our psychological warfare efforts when it is measured against the unabated fanaticism with which the enemy fought.[10]

It was in this context that Truman made the decision to use atomic bombs on Japan. Informed at Potsdam that the experimental bomb was ready, Truman saw the possibility that it, rather than the unreliable and intractable Russians, might be *the* decisive factor in speeding the end of the war. There was no assurance that atomic bombs would bring a sudden end to the conflict. But the only alternative to their use that was foreseen at that time was an indefinite continuation of butchery, whether or not the Soviets significantly helped turn the military tide against Japanese forces on the Asian mainland.

Once Truman and Churchill learned that the awesome new weapon was a reality, Truman told Stalin about it — blissfully unaware that the Russian premier probably knew more about America's atomic-bomb project than he did when he became President. Stalin displayed no particular interest other than to express hope that the U.S. would make "good use of it" against the Japanese. [11] From Potsdam, the allies at war with Japan issued an ultimatum that had been drafted in Washington and brought along by Truman for approval. It warned the rulers of Japan that utter destruction was in store for their homeland if the terms of unconditional surrender such as Germany accepted were not met immediately. The warning — later to be known as the Potsdam Declaration — was issued on July 26, and broadcast to Japan repeatedly for the next 24 hours. Two nights later, millions of leaflets were dropped on Japan by U.S. planes. The leaflets repeated the essence of the Potsdam Declaration with an ominous new note — they listed 11 cities and warned that at least four would soon be chosen for total destruction from the air.

Although it is now known that the inner circle of Japan's leadership was divided over whether to continue or abandon the war effort, the outside world then knew only the outright rejection of the Potsdam Declaration broadcast on July 29 by Japan's premier. He defiantly announced that his government would disregard the declaration and fight resolutely on. That rejection sealed the matter of using the atomic bomb.

The bomb had been in the works for years, and military considerations dictated its development from the beginning. It had been suggested to Roosevelt by the brilliant scientist Albert Einstein. The U.S. and Great Britain were pooling their scientific knowledge that could be useful to the war effort. There was no doubt that German scientists were trying to come up with an atomic bomb. Once the U.S. was in the war, thousands of Americans in science, industry, labor, and the military joined forces in a top-secret crash program costing $2.5 billion to win the race of the laboratories and produce the first atomic weapon.

When Truman became President and learned the full story of the atom bomb project, he set up a high-level civilian committee to study carefully the implications of the weapon's use. Secretary of War Stimson chaired the group, which included four cabinet and subcabinet-level officials in the foreign policy and national security field, plus three leaders in the scientific and educational community — the president of the Carnegie Institution of Washington, who headed the government's Office of Scientific Research and Development; the president of the Massachusetts Institute of Technology, and the president of Harvard University. This group was assisted by an advisory committee of several scientists, including the leading scientists involved in developing the bomb. On June 1, 1945, the conclusions reached by the study group and by the advisory group were given to Truman: use the bomb against the enemy as soon as possible. The groups concluded that they could propose no technical demonstration of the bomb's power — such as dropping it on a deserted island — that would be likely to end the war. They saw no alternative to using it against an enemy target. They recommended that this be done without specific warning and against a target that would clearly show the weapon's devastating strength.[12] This opinion was added to that of the President's top military advisers and of America's allies.

The last word rested with the President. Characteristically, Truman did not dodge the decision or the full responsibility for having made it. On August 6, 1945, as President Truman was sailing home from the Potsdam Conference, the first atomic bomb was dropped on Hiroshima, Japan. This was the first of four target cities finally selected because of their military importance. The bomb exploded in the air above Hiroshima, instantly killing about 70,000 people. The number of dead was actually less than the 84,000 killed in a single fire-bomb raid on Tokyo five months earlier, but the one atomic bomb destroyed nearly five square miles and demolished more than 80 percent of Hiroshima's dwellings. No factual report was made to the Japanese people, but a Japanese investigating team, headed by the country's leading nuclear physicist, knew exactly what kind of a bomb this was.[13]

"Let there be no mistake about it," Truman said afterward. "The final decision of where and when to use the atomic bomb was up to me." He said he "regarded the bomb as a military weapon and never had any doubt that it should be used."[14] A second one hit the city of Nagasaki two days after the first one was dropped. Before a third bomb could be made ready, the war with Japan was over.

Potsdam in Perspective

The Potsdam Conference was not the historic beginning or ending of anything. It was not the last chance for Soviet-American cooperation and it was not the beginning of the cold war. When the "hot war" of shooting and bombing ceased in Central Europe, it was succeeded by the hostile confrontation that came to be characterized as "cold war." Waging the hot war to its conclusion concealed the growth of the cold one, but it had already taken root and its roots were deep. The agreements worked out at Potsdam might have formed a sufficient basis for postwar cooperation had their spirit been observed. But the Russians had no such intention, as was clear before the conference adjourned.

It probably is impossible to determine precisely what started the cold war. Maybe it started when Russia seized additional German territory for Poland and took more of Poland for itself. Perhaps it began when Russia refused to abide by Allied agreements concerning the liberated areas of Eastern Europe. It may have started when Stalin decided to disregard Yalta agreements or twist them to his own advantage. All this transpired in the spring of 1945; it was happening before Harry Truman became President and before a Potsdam Conference was scheduled. Whether or not that conference had been held when it was, the ''iron curtain'' Winston Churchill would describe in March 1946 had already fallen in the summer of 1945.

The meetings at Potsdam were significant, of course, in several respects. In the eyes of the U.S. delegation, the top priority was to hold Russia to its promise of declaring war on Japan, and this was accomplished. Truman believed it was imperative for him to deal with Stalin face to face, and he did. Otherwise, the negotiations were not especially productive, but they were highly instructive for the new President.

Truman regarded this extensive encounter with the Russian premier as the most significant thing about Potsdam. It enabled Truman to see what had to be faced in the future. Potsdam was not the brief, formal diplomatic event that ''summit'' meetings have come to be — not one of those dramatic productions for news media at which leaders sign agreements already worked out by negotiators at lower levels. At Potsdam, Truman and Stalin sat down at the bargaining table together for 17 days. The two leaders, along with the British prime minister, dug into the issues directly for the duration of what was a long, working conference. Afterward Truman, committed to the rule of good faith, did not give up hoping for the best. But he was convinced that there was no doing business with Stalin except on Soviet terms. "Force," Truman concluded, "is the only thing the Russians understand."[15]

On the voyage home from Potsdam, Truman — President for less than four months — had time to reflect on what the encounter there portended about the nature of the postwar world. He had gone to Potsdam in good faith. He could easily have put off a meeting of heads of state in order to allow more time for preparation and to become more established in the presidency. He could have called for a foreign ministers' conference instead, and sent his secretary of state. By going ahead when he did, Truman made the boldest and most direct effort he could to prevent a total collapse of the dubious prospect of postwar cooperation with Stalin. But two worlds had clashed at the conference table in Potsdam. The profound division between two utterly, fundamentally conflicting ways of life had penetrated all the rhetoric, argumentation, and nit-picking of the negotiations. Truman's eyes had been opened to the emerging pattern of the cold war. He saw the iron curtain in the making, and he saw it firsthand, not merely through the eyes of others.

The conference kept Truman away from the U.S. for nearly a month, but it enabled him to perceive that the great test of his administration would be an international one. The guns at last went silent in the Pacific, but the war's end could not now bring the President peace of mind. He knew now that Stalin's mind was set on conquest rather than covenants for peace. Truman saw now that the supreme challenge facing his country and his presidency would be to

stand firm in distant places to defend the concepts of freedom for which so much human suffering had already been
sacrificed. The summer was a sobering one for the new
President, but it made him a wiser man with a world view.
Truman came through it with a new sense of direction and
purpose, and with a firm grasp of foreign policy.

Truman's Domestic Challenge

Japan's surrender, formally signed in Tokyo Bay aboard
the U.S. battleship *Missouri,* was an event of almost unparalleled drama. It is not hard to picture a President going
there to be at the center of this historic ceremony. In fact, it
is hard to imagine a President not capitalizing on the
worldwide attention it commanded. But Truman stayed
home, leaving the ceremonial distinction to the commander
of the Allied war effort in the Pacific, General Douglas
MacArthur. Away from the limelight, the President worked
on a domestic program of 21 legislative proposals he would
deliver to Congress four days after the Japanese surrender in
a comprehensive "State-of-the-Union" message.

The President's program was designed to deal with the
problems of "reconversion" — the staggering task of turning from war production at full tilt to the building of a stable
peacetime economy that could absorb millions of returning
servicemen. It was a wide-ranging program that put forward a number of objectives Roosevelt had been seeking. It
included proposals for national health insurance, federal aid
to education, slum clearance and housing construction, a
series of flood control and hydroelectric projects, and the
establishment of a permanent Fair Employment Practices
Commission. Truman advocated reductions in corporate
and personal income taxes, financial aid for small
businesses, stabilization of farm income, and the elimina-

tion of monopolies. Truman also asked for highway improvement and construction, a permanent law empowering the President to reorganize the executive branch, and $18 million in emergency housing aid for needy families of servicemen. The President's message was filled with praise for free enterprise and expressions of confidence in the ability of American industry to create full peacetime production and employment. Truman asked Congress to go slowly and be selective about repealing wartime economic controls. And to the applause of many, he included organized labor among those who should maintain their wartime agreements for a time.

A variety of meanings were read into Truman's domestic program. Some commentators saw in it a lengthening shadow of the New Deal, and others saw disturbing signs of reaction. The more objective observers regarded it as indicating a path avoiding either extreme — a path displaying unmistakable signs of New Deal idealism but modified by practical Missouri conservatism. Members of Congress seemed pleased above all by the tone of the President's message. There were no demands, no warnings of consequences that could follow if his blueprint was not followed. Throughout the message Truman recognized Congress as an equal partner in government, with the same right and duty to veto what he might propose as were his to veto what Congress might legislate.

Perhaps the President's emphasis during his early months in office on a partnership with Congress encouraged the legislators to be more assertive. Truman took pains to show deference to Congress as soon as he became President. Roosevelt had often shown disdain for Capitol Hill, and Truman wanted to show a dramatic contrast in his own approach. Congress was where his heart was, and he genuinely believed it should be strong and active. This was also good politics at a time of transition to a new administration. Truman wanted the cooperation of Congress, wished to create good will there, and was well acquainted with congressional resentment of high-handed treatment by Roosevelt. But opposition to Truman was inevitable, no matter what kind of legislative proposals he made. And one reason was Roosevelt's departure. Before long, the absence of that dominant, sometimes domineering figure was bound to embolden the branch of government that for many years he had intimidated.

It is not abnormal when a presidential "honeymoon" with Congress and contentious components of his own party comes to an end. It is the honeymoon that is abnormal. Truman's began to wane before the war ended, and would have played itself out in any event regardless of feelings about his predecessor. But the end of the war gave an extra impetus to political partisanship. It had been suppressed as the country rallied around the flag for a united war effort. With the war won, that restraint was lifted, and Republicans and factions within the Democratic Party as well were ready to remove the kid gloves and go at it in earnest. Inevitably, partisan and intraparty opposition centered on the new man in the White House when Truman called for action on his domestic program.

In the postwar period, Truman faced an impossible situation. For the duration of the war, many groups had put aside the pursuit of selfish interests. The instant the war was won, they expected their demands to be satisfied. Labor wanted government price controls retained, but wage controls ended. Industry wanted to keep wage controls, but thought free enterprise demanded an end to price controls. Consumers wanted an end to wartime rationing so they could use the savings built up by good pay from plentiful jobs to buy the things they had done without. At the same time, there was much anxiety about the economic outlook. The sudden termination of most war contracts would close down war production plants and cause severe unemployment just as servicemen were returning home in need of jobs. Because the full employment of World War II had ended the great depression, most Americans — including economists — expected the coming of peace to bring back a depression.

The experience of previous Presidents in postwar periods had demonstrated that no amount of genius would have been able to prevent a surge of discontent during this turbulent transition. There was no way of avoiding inflation and dislocation. Five wartime years had made the American economy a monster of production. More than $300 billion — a sum inconceivable to the human imagination — had gone into equipping and paying the armed services, which, when the war ended, numbered more than twelve million even as the civilian labor force was at an all-time high. The country's gross national product (the sum of all the goods and services produced in the economy) had doubled, as had the average earnings. Price controls and the scarcity of consumer goods held down living costs, with the result that at war's end there was an incredible nest egg of $136.4 billion of personal savings in banks and bonds itching to be spent. Dollars were abundant and commodities were scarce — the classic conditions for inflation.

The Republican Party, which had not won a national victory since 1928, was understandably eager to use the tidal wave of postwar discontent as a means of toppling the Democrats from their monopoly of political power. The Republicans kicked off their campaign for the 1946 congressional elections the moment Truman presented his program to Congress. They found plenty of ammunition with which to take the political offensive in the public clamor for wartime decontrols, ends to shortages, wage hikes, etc. This was even more the case when inflation rather than deflation turned out to be the primary problem of the economy. The politics of depression enable a President to dispense favors to major economic blocs with massive spending programs to boost economic recovery. The poli-

tics of inflation call for holding the line against the demands
of major pressure groups.

In these circumstances, it was Harry Truman's political
misfortune to be a man committed to the middle of the road.
He was a politician determined to find a common meeting
ground at the center of all issues, where there could be
compromise and conciliation of conflicting interests. But
there was no mood for compromise on these issues, and
Truman's efforts to conciliate the competing interest groups
ended up alienating them. The President defended continued government price controls as necessary to stem inflation, but allowed some controls to be weakened or ineffec-
tively administered. The defense of price controls angered
those — businessmen, for example — who wanted them
abolished, while their discontinuance angered consumers.

With price controls becoming ineffective, organized
labor was more determined than ever to win wage increases, and in late 1945 and early 1946 a wave of strikes
rocked the country. Truman supported compromises that
granted wage boosts to labor and price increases to employers, a course of action not likely to stop inflation. Then
Truman's anger was aroused when the railway unions
brought the country to the verge of paralysis with a strike in
May of 1946. Truman regarded it as a flouting of the
national interest, and pulled out all the stops. In a special
message to Congress, he asked for the power to draft
strikers into the army so the government could operate the
railroads. The strike was settled before the message could
be acted on, but labor was alienated.

Costly Errors, Firm Command

In the months that followed, Truman made two colossal
mistakes, both of them rare instances in which he retreated

under political pressure. The first was on the question of continuing meat-rationing that had been imposed during the war. Public opinion was overwhelmingly against it, and the Republicans made a major issue of it. But the President firmly stood his ground, despite a strike by cattlemen and a deafening public and political clamor. Finally, after Democratic candidates for Congress thoroughly bombarded him with the estimate that if meat-rationing continued, the Republicans would surely regain control of Congress, Truman ordered all price controls on beef dropped — one week before the election. He did so in the belief that he could not keep the Republicans from making decontrol of beef the first order of business in the new Congress anyway — this was their campaign promise — so he decided to beat them to the punch. But the move came too late to save the Democratic majority in Congress. The Republicans won control of both houses, and were absolutely convinced that a Republican President in 1948 would be the inevitable result of their return to power. One can only speculate on how different the legislative record of the Truman administration might have been if the Democrats had not lost control of the first Congress to be elected when Truman was President. Instead, Truman was confronted by the steadfast opposition of a party jubilantly feeling its oats and eager to roll back the Roosevelt New Deal.

The second costly error Truman made was in bowing again to public pressure and demobilizing American military forces too soon. Three days after announcing Japan's surrender, the President said he would ask Congress to enact a program of universal military training for all healthy young Americans. But it was not the right time, politically, for such an appeal to maintain the nation's military strength. The war was over, and there was a stampede to be done with every reminder of it. In the elation of military victory, men who had been the most willing of soldiers could not get out of the service fast enough. Those who had once volunteered for extra duty now demanded early discharge. Congressmen were besieged with mail from millions of wives and parents. Congress got the message, and resoundingly defeated the President's call for universal military training.

A military demobilization was set in motion in deference to the political pressure that the public mood generated. Truman believed it to be an unwise course, but gave in and compromised on it anyway. How disastrous this mistake was will always be open to debate. Its consequences cannot be accurately measured, of course, against what might have happened or not happened otherwise. It seems reasonable to assume that, at the very least, the hasty dismantling of the world's mightiest military machine and the rapid reduction in the size of the U.S. fighting force created power vacuums in crucial areas, especially Central Europe, at a crucial time. This almost certainly emboldened Stalin; encouraged internal subversion and Soviet challenges; and helped foster a period of tension, threat, and crisis that the U.S. was then called upon to react to and cope with in the years to come.

The demobilization was in fact a product of a public opinion that had been misled by Roosevelt's misjudgment that a cooperative U.S.S.R. could be counted on after the war. Truman's action in going along with it suggests that he still had not given up hope entirely that this kind of Soviet attitude might be brought about. Perhaps on the dilemma of demobilization as on his delayed ending of meat-rationing there was no realistic way Truman could have acted otherwise. But these were nevertheless political retreats for which his administration paid a heavy price in domestic and foreign policy. They were bitter lessons for the new President, and they explain the bold, uncompromising quality that later characterized his own campaign for the presidency.

His mistakes did not obscure the clear fact that Harry Truman had fully taken command of the presidency. Although probably no President since Andrew Johnson — another of the several postwar Presidents who all were burdened by trouble with Congress — entered the White House under such trying conditions, Truman established convincingly from the beginning that he was in charge there. He showed himself to be a man with definite ideas of his own. The portrait of the Truman presidency emerging from his first year or two in office was not without blemishes, but there was much in it to admire both in style and substance. It was not thrilling, but there was much of comfort and reassurance in it. There was little to be seen of what could be called flaming leadership or sweeping domestic innovations, but much that was good and human and courageous. Shining out was political experience, conviction, and common sense.

IV Rescuing Western Europe

The winter of 1945-1946 drained away whatever was left of Harry Truman's patience with the Russians. Hunger and misery engulfed Europe, where millions of displaced persons were homeless and where military operations in the waning months of the war had disrupted plantings and harvests and destroyed livestock and crops. The processes of distribution had been broken down. Western Europe, always a deficit area in food production, had been cut off from its usual sources of food in Eastern Europe. The hands on the clock of starvation, it was said, were pointed at 11:59. On Truman's orders, the U.S. rushed in hundreds of millions of dollars worth of food supplies and other necessities. At the same time, the U.S. continued through negotiation and compromise to seek cooperation with Russia.

In the face of all this, Russia's response became like a broken record of more demands for more concessions from the U.S. All the while, Moscow's Communists consolidated and extended their control over the areas of Europe the Red Army held captive. Soviet behavior gave signs at every turn of a quest for expansion and conquest threatening the very survival of America's allies.

In December of 1945, President Truman had sent Secretary of State Byrnes to Moscow for another try at dealing with the Soviets. After his return, Truman called Byrnes into his office on January 5, 1946, and read him a memo he had written out in longhand. The President was irked at not having been informed of what was taking place at the Moscow meeting and with Byrnes for taking upon himself too much authority for the conduct of foreign affaiirs. Truman took Byrnes to task, and in the memo revealed his impatience with Soviet actions. He told Byrnes angrily that "unless Russia is faced with an iron fist and strong language another war is in the making." The President said he thought it was time to stop trying to compromise — that he was tired of "babying" the Soviets.[1] The words were not, however, a declaration of U.S. foreign policy. The President was upset with the Russians and fed up with trying to deal with them. He was determined that the U.S. be tougher in taking a stand and in letting the Soviets know where it stood. But Washington did not have a consistent plan of action to match Moscow's. There were complaints, in fact, by columnists and commentators that the U.S. seemed to have no Russian policy at all.

It was at this extremely tense time in Soviet-American relations that a rapid series of alarming developments produced the conviction that Russia was not an estranged ally but an enemy. On February 9, 1946, Soviet Premier Stalin made a rare public speech in which he stressed the incompatibility of communism and capitalism, and clearly implied that future wars were inevitable until communism took capitalism's place. Most American observers agreed with the reaction of *Time* magazine, which viewed the speech as the most warlike pronouncement uttered by any top-ranking statesman since World War II had ended. Even liberals like commentator Eric Sevareid and Supreme Court Justice William O. Douglas got the message that the primary objective of Soviet foreign policy was now to extend communist ideology to the other parts of the world. Sevareid said the line the American Communist Party was taking, coupled with that espoused by Communists in Western Europe and elsewhere, made clear as daylight that international communism was organized and operating effectively. "If you can brush aside Stalin's speech of February 9," Sevareid said, "You are a braver man than I am." Douglas put it more bluntly; he said Stalin's speech constituted the "declaration of World War III."

Stalin's address came at a time when the Soviets had just used their veto in the United Nations Security Council for the first time. It was not on a matter vital to their national security, but a relatively minor issue connected with the presence of Anglo-French forces in Syria and Lebanon. The week following Stalin's speech brought news of a Canadian spy case in which 22 persons were arrested for having obtained secret data on the atomic bomb for the Soviet Union. The Canadian spy case frightened Americans not only because it involved the atomic bomb but because of the connection it indicated between Soviet espionage and the world communist movement.

Among Washington policy-makers, another bombshell arrived the next week in the form of a long cable from the U.S. Embassy in Moscow. Averell Harriman was on his way home then, having completed his assignment as ambassador and having left his second in command, George F. Kennan, in charge of the Moscow embassy. Kennan was an experienced foreign service officer and Soviet expert who for years had been a serious student of Russian history and communist ideology. He was surprised soon after taking charge of the embassy to receive a cable from the State Department seeking in exasperation an explanation of why the Russians behaved the way they did. Kennan, long having yearned to have the ear of the people at the top of the State Department on this very subject, really let them have it. Eagerly seizing the opportunity, Kennan composed an 8000 word telegram. It was a highly persuasive essay analyzing the background, motivations, and methods of Soviet policy, its relationship with communist ideology, and its probable future course.

According to Kennan, Russia would exert constant pressure to infiltrate, disrupt, and paralyze the West. Moscow would exploit to the fullest its international communist organization and every concession it could extract at the official level through diplomacy. Kennan described the Soviet government as a political force committed fanatically to the belief that there could be no permanent compromise with the U.S. Russia, he wrote, believes it desirable and necessary for the internal harmony of American society to be disrupted, its traditional way of life destroyed, and the international authority of the U.S. to be broken to secure Soviet power. Kennan said the Soviet government possesses complete power to direct the energies of one of the world's strongest peoples and the resources of the world's richest national territory. He pointed out that Moscow had an elaborate and far-flung apparatus for exerting its influence in other countries, and that it was seemingly closed off to considerations of reality in its basic reactions. Kennan called the problem of coping with this force the greatest task U.S. diplomacy would ever face. Placing limits on Soviet ambitions, he said, would depend on the degree of cohesion, firmness, and vigor the Western world could muster.[2]

The impact of Kennan's cable exceeded the career diplomat's wildest dreams. According to Joseph M. Jones, a State Department official, Kennan acquired great prestige in the department and in the upper echelons of the government as a result of the "realism and incisiveness" of the February dispatch, which "so impressively analyzed Soviet motivations and designs as to contribute markedly to the stiffening of U.S. policy toward Soviet expansionism."[3] It was, in short, one of those cases of being in the right place at the right time. Kennan's analysis could not have been better timed to have greater effect, and it was widely circulated among American policy-makers. They

found in it an articulate intellectual rationale for the shift of
mood that was already taking place toward a stronger stand
against the Soviets. President Truman read it, the State
Department sent Kennan a message of commendation, and
Secretary of the Navy Forrestal — who before long would
become the country's first secretary of defense — had it
reproduced and made required reading for hundreds if not
thousands of higher officers in the armed services.

The ominous message of Kennan's analysis was this:
internal factors alone determined Soviet Russia's foreign
policy, so there was nothing the U.S. could do, no matter
how well-intentioned, that could diminish this hostility
toward the West. The only course left to the U.S. was to
resist as effectively as possible communist attempts, exter-
nal and internal, to overthrow Western institutions, in the
hope that eventually internal changes within the Soviet
Union would produce some change in Soviet policy. This
conviction was taking hold in the Truman administration.
The Kennan cable helped it do so, as did stinging Republican attacks on the administration for pursuing policies of
"appeasement." The administration's policy was in the
process of hardening, in the direction Truman had indicated
when he called Secretary of State Byrnes on the carpet early
in January.

The first public expression of the administration's
tougher stance came in a speech Byrnes gave on the last day
of February. Byrnes took note that the U.S. had approved
many adjustments in favor of the Soviets and had resolved
many serious doubts in their favor. In the interest of world
peace, however, it should be made plain that the U.S.
intended to defend the United Nations charter, through
which the major nations had pledged themselves to re-
nounce aggression. "We will not and we cannot stand
aloof," Byrnes said, "if force or the threat of force is used
contrary to the purposes and principles of the Charter." No

nation, he continued, had the right to station troops on the territory of another sovereign state without its consent. No nation had the right to prolong unnecessarily the making of peace. No nation had the right to seize enemy property before reparations agreements had been made. The U.S. did not regard the status quo as sacrosanct, but it could not overlook "a unilateral gnawing away at the status quo." In a manner reminiscent of Theodore Roosevelt, Byrnes' speech concluded with the declaration that "if we are to be a great power we must act as a great power, not only in order to ensure our own security but in order to preserve the peace of the world."[4]

As if in response, Stalin immediately displayed once again the way he liked to use the Red Army. It had been agreed at Potsdam that the allies would withdraw their forces from Iran by March 2, 1946. Britain announced it would do so. Russia, however, did not intend to go until it had extracted an oil concession from the Iranians. Even at that, the Russians had in mind withdrawing only from central Iran and keeping their troops in the northern part of the country. On March 1, Moscow announced that Soviet forces would remain in Iran past the Potsdam deadline, "pending clarification of the situation." Although Stalin's bid for Iranian oil fields ultimately was unsuccessful and the Red Army was pulled out, here was another example of Russia breaking an agreement and ready to use armed force to back up aggressive demands. It had its effect on an American public that was becoming increasingly alarmed about Russian intentions.

American opinion was further aroused by the eloquent, forceful address Sir Winston Churchill delivered at Westminster College in Fulton, Missouri, on March 5. Truman had been asked to speak, but instead passed the invitation along to the former British prime minister, who was vacationing in Florida as a private citizen. The distinguished

Briton, greatly admired in America for his inspirational statesmanship throughout World War II, introduced "iron curtain" to the Western world's vocabulary in the Fulton speech. "From Stettin in the Baltic to Trieste in the Adriatic," Churchill said,

> an iron curtain has descended across the Continent. Behind that line lie all the capitals of the ancient states of central and eastern Europe. Warsaw, Berlin, Prague, Vienna, Budapest, Belgrade, Bucharest and Sofia, all these famous cities and the populations around them lie in the Soviet sphere and all are subject in one form or another, not only to Soviet influence but to a very high and increasing measure of control from Moscow.[5]

In somber, ringing phrases Churchill warned that the Russians want "the fruits of war and the indefinite expansion of their power and doctrines." He said the Western powers could not hope to preserve peace by allowing the Russians free rein. Churchill expressed the conviction that there is nothing for which they have less respect than for military weakness.

An opinion poll taken in mid-March of 1946 showed emphatically that the American public favored the strong stand Truman was determined to take against the Soviets. When asked about their attitude toward Soviet policy in international affairs, only seven percent of those polled expressed approval of Soviet policy; 71 percent disapproved. Only three percent felt the U.S. was being "too tough" with Russia; 60 thought the U.S. was being "too soft."[6] The time had come in Truman's policy of patience with firmness to put the emphasis on firmness. The American people plainly agreed. The communist side, for its part, acted as if it were issuing invitations for Truman to do just that. It was as if the Communists — not just Russia but the satellite states it had set up — were doing their utmost to test the West's will to resist belligerent behavior. And when

Truman at last would react with a show of force, the Communists responded as if to demonstrate that force was indeed the only language they could understand.

Tension and Danger Increase

An explosive situation had developed in the strategic area of Trieste, with the communist leader of neighboring Yugoslavia, Marshal Tito, demanding control of the territory. It was to be occupied by Britain and the U.S. while a territorial settlement was negotiated, but Tito's obstinate actions and demands, backed by Stalin and coupled with the threat of partisan violence, were so grave as to bring fears that they might force a war with Yugoslavia. Tito's demands were accompanied during the summer of 1946 by armed provocations alongside Trieste and threats to take the territory by force. The West feared a sudden attempt by Yugoslavia to seize Trieste, and while the Big Four foreign ministers — representing the U.S., Russia, Britain, and France — were meeting in Paris in search of a peaceful diplomatic solution, Tito's air force shot down two U.S. transport planes. It was an act widely regarded as a test of American reaction to force.

The passengers in the first U.S. plane were miraculously spared death but the Yugoslavs held them incommunicado. The passengers of the second plane were killed, although this was not known at first since American authorities were refused permission to investigate. Truman's restraint gave way to indignation. He dispatched an ultimatum as blunt and furious as any in U.S. history, warning Tito to free the fliers in 48 hours or face action before the UN Security Council. Truman alerted five U.S. armored divisions to move to the Brenner pass, ordered units of the Mediterranean fleet to steam into the Adriatic, and notified several air force squadrons to be ready for take-off. Only then did the turmoil subside. The Communists backed down quickly, with Tito permitting an investigation and giving strict orders to the Yugoslav military forces not to fire on foreign planes in the area. Tension over Trieste abated rapidly and the four foreign ministers reached a compromise territorial solution.

The summer of 1946 continued to be tense and dangerous, however, as the Soviets appeared to be climaxing a campaign to bring Turkey under Russian control. In August, Russia massed 25 divisions at the Turkish border. Moscow then proposed a new administration of the Black Sea Straits which would mean Soviet control of that long-coveted waterway, setting up Soviet naval and air bases in Turkey, and the virtual end of Turkey's independence. Upon receiving the Soviet proposal, Truman had the acting secretary of state, Dean Acheson, work out a coordinated government position on standing resolutely with the Turks to meet the Soviet threat. In the meantime, Truman sent a naval task force to the Mediterranean to underscore American concern. The President believed that giving in to Soviet demands to control and dominate Turkey would in all probability also lead to communist domination of Greece. The consequences would be disastrous. Truman's position was that the U.S. might as well learn then as in five or ten years whether the Russians were bent on world conquest.

The U.S. issued a diplomatic note telling the Soviets firmly that the straits were a matter of international concern and that the U.S. could not accept Moscow's proposals. The diplomatic message was not an earth-shaking document, and it did not lay the matter to rest once and for all. But the decision-making that lay behind the U.S. note was highly significant. It meant organizing military and foreign policy officials promptly to work up essential background and position papers. It meant adopting a stand countering

Russia that could lead to armed conflict. Truman quickly and carefully weighed the consequences and chose to take the risk. He was making clear that the U.S. would not back down in the face of Soviet sabre-rattling over Iran, Trieste, and Turkey. He was conveying the message that Washington was willing and able to call Moscow's hand. But it seemed that no sooner was Truman's point made in one case than the Communists would probe another. During the rest of 1946, tensions remained high and the international scene left little ground for optimism. The Soviets were ever more assertive and uncooperative. They swiftly consolidated areas into their orbit, drove hard bargains at the conference table, and aimed diplomatic and propaganda offensives at the U.S.

In the fall of 1946, President Truman asked for a comprehensive study of Soviet-American relations, which he knew would be the central problem of American foreign policy. The result was an important state paper prepared through the secretary of state, the secretary of war, the attorney general, the secretary of the navy, Fleet Admiral Leahy (who had been Roosevelt's chief military adviser), the joint chiefs of staff, Ambassador Edwin W. Pauley (in charge of negotiating postwar reparations), the director of central intelligence, and other persons with special knowledge of foreign affairs.[7] The document was imposing in its scope and depth, comprising nearly a hundred thousand words and divided into an introduction and six sections. It dealt with Soviet foreign policy, Soviet-American agreements, Soviet violations of its agreements with the U.S., conflicting views on reparations, Soviet activities affecting American security, and U.S. policy toward the Soviet Union.

This study Truman asked for was drafted on the premise that only through an accurate understanding of the Soviet Union would the U.S. be able to make and carry out policies

that would reestablish international order and protect the
U.S. at all times. The key, according to the study, was to
realize that Moscow's leaders adhered to the Marxian
theory of ultimate destruction of capitalist states by communist states, but that they sought to postpone the inevitable conflict while they strengthened and prepared the
Soviet Union for its clash with the Western democracies.
The study said Moscow's main concern regarding the other
nations of Western Europe was to prevent the formation of a
Western bloc. It noted, too, that Red Army troops and
Russian planes in combat readiness outnumbered American
units opposite them in Germany, Austria, and Korea in
overwhelming strength, placing U.S. forces literally at the
mercy of the Soviet government.

The study — then, of course, a top-secret document —
told the President that the Soviet government would never
be easy to get along with. The American people would have
to accustom themselves to this, not as a cause for despair
but as a fact to be faced objectively and courageously. If
Soviet cooperation could not be enlisted in solving world
problems, the U.S. should be prepared to join the British
and other Western countries in an attempt to build up "a
world of our own" which would pursue its own objectives.
It would recognize the Soviet orbit as a distinct entity with
which conflict was not predestined but with which common
aims could not be pursued. Unless America was willing to
sacrifice its future security for the sake of "accord" with
the Soviet Union, the U.S. must, as a first step toward
stabilizing the world situation, try to stop additional Soviet
aggression. The larger the area the Soviets controlled, the
larger the military requirements of the U.S. In short, the
U.S., while scrupulously avoiding any act that would be an
excuse for the Soviets to begin a war, should be ready to
resist vigorously any Soviet efforts to expand into areas
vital to American security.

The top secret report reiterated to Truman that the language of military power was the only language the disciples of power politics understood. It noted that compromise and concessions were looked upon by the Soviets as signs of weakness — as retreats that only encouraged them to make new and larger demands. The U.S., it maintained, must use the language of military power if Moscow's leaders were to realize that America was determined to uphold the interests of its citizens and the rights of small nations. The report concluded that, in addition to maintaining its own strength, the U.S. should support and assist all democratic countries that were in any way menaced or endangered by the Soviet Union. Such action was deemed necessary if there was ever to be any realistic prospect of achieving understanding and accord with Moscow on any terms other than its own. This need to contain the expanding empire of totalitarian communism was being clearly perceived in the fall of 1946. The evidence was overwhelming and was continuing to accumulate. But it was not until the beginning of 1947 that the catalyst came that led Truman to transform this containment concept into policy.

By agreement stemming from the late stages of the war in Europe, Britain and the U.S. shared a responsibility for preserving the political integrity of Greece and Turkey. Britain's part of the bargain, by far the biggest part, was chiefly military, and the role of the U.S. was almost wholly economic. But constant and massive communist pressure threatened both Greece and Turkey with collapse. A crisis appeared imminent in the tottering Greek government. A well-organized effort was obviously under way to bring Greece into the Soviet orbit. If Greece fell, Turkey would be drawn under with it. Once communist power broke through these political barricades, the entire Mediterranean area, notably Italy but including the rest of Europe's southern flank, would be in jeopardy — and so, too, would be the concept of a free-world counterforce to communist aggression.

The situation in Greece grew worse during the fall and winter. In December of 1946 the UN Security Council set up a commission to investigate outside aid to Greek communist guerrillas. Several times during the year the Greek government had called upon the U.S. for more financial aid. Truman responded with what aid he could authorize under the limited appropriations and authority that existed. In January of 1947 he sent an economic mission to Greece to make a thorough survey of the situation. It brought back a report that unless Greece got immediate assurance of large-scale military and financial aid, the last vestiges of Greek governmental authority would disintegrate in a matter of weeks. Resulting inflation, strikes, and public panic would provide a clear field for the communist guerrillas to take over the government.

Early in January of 1947, Britain told the U.S. that it was in dire economic straits. It had sold half its overseas assets and piled up huge debts during the war. With postwar production and exports hampered by manpower shortages and low productivity, and with more goods being imported, Britain was going still further into debt. The British cabinet viewed with alarm the budget outlook for the fiscal year to begin on April 1. Loans and grants to foreign countries in support of political commitments were a heavy drain on the budget, and cutting back British troops stationed overseas seemed the only way to ease some of the financial strain and reduce the critical domestic manpower shortage.

The extent of Britain's problems, however, and of the desperate situation in Western Europe generally were not, at this point, fully or widely appreciated in the U.S. What was perhaps most remarkable about the transformation of American foreign policy during the next few months was that it took place in a political setting that was not a favorable one. Washington had been concerned throughout most of the critical year of 1946 with the congressional elections that November. After the Republicans captured Congress, the question of the day was not whether the President would now lead the country to accept new worldwide responsibilities. The question seemed to be how far, after this repudiation of the Democrats at the polls, the new Congress would cut back New Deal legislation, reduce appropriations for armed forces and foreign relief, and carry the country back to isolation. Wreckage, misery, national weakness, and vulnerability to communist takeover characterized much of the free world bordering the totalitarian states Stalin was setting up. These facts were present, but the American people, after years of war's sacrifices and disruption, were primarily intent on pursuing prosperity and bringing their lives back to normal.

Britain Bows Out

There was nothing in the cables or memoranda circulating in Washington on the gray afternoon of Friday, February 21, 1947 to suggest that the most revolutionary advance in American foreign policy since 1823 would occur in the weeks ahead. George C. Marshall, whom Truman had just made the new secretary of state, had just left for Princeton, New Jersey, where the next day he would make his first speech since assuming office. The British ambassador in Washington telephoned for an immediate appointment. Undersecretary of State Dean Acheson was consulted on what to do about the urgent call. The ambassador wanted to deliver two notes concerning a decision by the British government to end aid to Greece and Turkey. Acheson arranged for the first secretary of the British Embassy to come to the State Department in order to put the substance of this communication into working channels with the least possible delay.

The message from the British was a bombshell. It recalled the military and strategic importance of Greece and Turkey, recounted their urgent needs, and pointed to the imminent danger of Soviet control. It then informed the U.S. that, in order to cope with the danger of their own economic collapse, the British could no longer furnish assistance. British aid would cease within six weeks — by March 31 — after which, if Greek and Turkish independence was to be preserved, the U.S. alone would have to do it. The brief discussion that took place between two minor diplomats that bleak Friday afternoon was the decisive first step by which Britain handed over virtually the last of its responsibility for preserving the world balance of power to the U.S. It set momentous developments in motion. It was the catalyst for an American policy that did nothing less than shape the history of the world.

Up to this time, American foreign policy had historically been based on *Pax Britannica* — the power of Britain's navy to rule the waves, and the economic power of the British empire to impose a relative degree of stability on the turbulent political life of Europe, Asia, and Africa. The seemingly indestructible imprint of the British Crown marked the century from 1815 to 1914, during which the world was free from large-scale international warfare at the same time the industrial revolution opened new vistas of material abundance. Thus sheltered, the U.S. — enjoying the additional advantage of wide ocean barriers — grew and prospered in untroubled isolation. The simple American foreign policy principle of no "entangling alliances," such as George Washington advised against, was breached in World War I, which also undermined the long-standing primacy of Britain in Europe's power structure. The initial blows of World War II made shockingly apparent the extent of Britain's weakening. Suddenly the initiative in world politics, and the military muscle behind it, belonged to the rampaging dictatorships of Germany, Japan, and Russia. America's intervention in World War II averted Britain's imminent collapse. By the end of the war, however, only the facade of its former power remained. The sea power on which British diplomacy was based was now but a feeble anachronism in a new age of air power. Britain was on the verge of economic ruin, and its overseas empire was crumbling away. The Western European nations on the continent were similarly crushed and impotent.

In this enormous political void of Europe, only Russia was left with the strength and will of a conqueror. And conquer is what the Soviets evidently meant to do — to establish out of the rubble of war the dictatorial world order prophesied by Marx and Lenin. America was the only power with the potential to thwart the Soviet ambitions for empire.

Postwar U.S. policy toward Soviet imperialism had been purely pragmatic. The American government had reacted with alarm, meeting the increasingly frequent challenges as each arose. Problems of communist expansion were dealt with as each one came up, one instance after another. Truman told this author in an interview after his presidency that there was nothing written out or outlined to follow during 22 trying months following the end of the war in Europe. "There was nothing planned," he said. "We simply acted when it was necessary to do so."[8] But the implications of filling Britain's shoes extended far beyond the two tactical challenges immediately at hand in Greece and Turkey.

James Byrnes had spent most of his 18 months as secretary of state across the conference table from Soviet Foreign Minister Molotov. Byrnes' perseverance had resulted in agreement on peace treaties with Italy and the former German satellites in Eastern Europe. The treaties generally confirmed the existing division of power in Europe, but the U.S. hoped they would result in reduced tensions through the withdrawal of occupation forces and the restoration of more normal relations. It was also hoped that they would prepare the way for settlement of the German problem through patient, realistic bargaining.

The hopes were not to be realized. After the treaties were signed in Paris in February of 1947, Russia intensified its policy of consolidating its East European bloc and exerting pressure at its edges. Russia was revealing, as it had consistently since the summer of 1945, its determination to push outward at one point or another along its perimeter until it was blocked by the application of counter force. There was now no question but that America alone could apply such counter force. The time had come for the U.S. to adopt a foreign policy broadly and systematically aimed at restraining the Soviets.

When the British ambassador met with Secretary of State Marshall on Monday, February 24, to communicate the British notes officially, the call was something of an anticlimax. Undersecretary Acheson had directed a task force that worked all weekend and had a comprehensive memorandum ready for the secretary of state on Monday morning. Before noon, Marshall conferred with Truman at the White House. Both shared the immediate recognition, which was virtually unanimous throughout the executive branch, that if Soviet expansion was to be checked, the U.S. must move into Britain's defaulted position.

There was full agreement on what had to be done, but the problem was to get authorizing legislation from a Congress no longer controlled by the Democratic party. Truman was concerned about his chances for getting a massive appropriation in a hurry, and time was of the essence. Greece and Turkey were in a precarious position, Marshall would soon be leaving for a conference in Moscow, and Truman would be away from Washington for several days on a state visit to Mexico — the first one ever made by an American President. Truman decided to invite congressional leaders to the White House the next day to brief them on the proposed course of action and get their reaction to it. He expected help from such bipartisan foreign affairs advocates as Senator Arthur H. Vandenberg and Congressman Charles A. Eaton, the Republicans who now headed, respectively, the Senate Foreign Relations and House Foreign Affairs committees. But Truman wanted to advise the congressional leadership as soon as possible of the gravity of the situation he was dealing with and the nature of his decision.

Truman explained to the legislative leaders the position the U.S. was placed in by the British notes. The British cabinet's decision to withdraw aid from Greece and Turkey had not yet been made public, so none of the congressmen knew how serious a crisis the U.S. suddenly faced. Marshall spoke to the group, too, and so did Acheson. Truman told the legislators he had decided to extend aid and hoped Congress wouuld provide the means to make the aid timely and sufficient.

The congressmen were deeply impressed. Senator Vandenberg said so and, speaking for the group, said it was clear that the country faced an extremely dangerous situation of which Greece and Turkey, although of great importance, were only a part. He recommended that the aid request be made in a message to Congress accompanied by an explanation to the American people in which the grim facts of the larger situation should be laid on the line publicly as they had been at the meeting.[9] Having alerted the congressional leadership to what was in the offing, Truman had the same thing done for the press. That night, Acheson held an off-the-record background conference with about 20 newspaper correspondents who regularly

covered the State Department and foreign policy developments. The newsmen had got wind of the White House
meeting, and now were told of the British notes and
Truman's decision to ask Congress for the aid. Even though
at this early stage it was unwise to release particulars,
Truman thought it important to provide an accurate press
briefing on the broad context of the situation.

During the days that followed, the necessary staff work
continued behind the scenes to work out all aspects of the
program. All barriers to bold action were down. Economic
experts busied themselves with estimates of how much aid
would be needed and could be effectively used. Political
officers were engaged in consultations with British, Greek,
and Turkish representatives. Legal officers were at work
drafting the enabling legislation, and other departments and
agencies focused on other planning that had to be done.
Truman was filled in on all this when he returned to
Washington on the night of March 6 after his visit to
Mexico. Truman cancelled plans to spend a few days resting in Key West, Florida, and called a cabinet meeting for
the next day.

The Truman Doctrine

The President reported fully to his cabinet on the facts of
what he considered to be the most serious situation a President had ever confronted. The cabinet endorsed his decision
to act, and there was considerable discussion about the best
way of advising the public of the issues involved. On this
point, Truman appointed a committee, headed by Secretary
of the Treasury Snyder, to make recommendations. The
committee met the next day and recommended to the President that, to emphasize the gravity of the situation, he
appear in person before a joint session of Congress. After

the cabinet meeting, Truman announced that he was post-poning indefinitely the vacation he had planned to begin the next day. He said he would meet with congressional leaders of both parties on Monday, March 10, to discuss the Greek crisis.

The Monday meeting was with a larger group of legis-lators than the one Truman briefed on February 27. There was much discussion. Truman answered questions, and encountered no opposition to the action he was determined to take. To stress the bipartisan nature of the issue at hand, Truman and Vandenberg together announced after the meeting that the President would appear in person on March 12 before a joint session to deliver a special message. A good indication of Truman's success in imparting a biparti-san character to this fundamental and far-reaching foreign policy move came that night. Vandenberg called a confer-ence of Republican legislators and gave them an hour-long talk on what was behind the forthcoming message to Con-gress. He told them Truman's statement would transcend politics, that it was national policy at the highest degree, with nothing partisan about it.

The next day Truman turned to the wording of the mes-sage he would deliver. The drafting of his speech had been started earlier, and the President did not like the first draft at all. It was filled with statistics, and Truman complained that it sounded like an investment prospectus. He sent the draft to Acheson with a note asking that the address be made into a general statement of policy. The speech was rewritten, but it still did not satisfy Truman. It struck him as half-hearted, and he picked up a pencil and began making changes. "I wanted no hedging," he said. "This was America's answer to the surge of expansion of Communist tyranny. It had to be clear and free of hesitation or double talk."[10]

At one o'clock in the afternoon on Wednesday, March 12, 1947 — less than three weeks after word came of

Britain's impending withdrawal — President Truman stepped to the rostrum and addressed the joint session crowded into the House chamber. The words he uttered would shape the history of the world. They announced a policy based on a conviction that wherever aggression, direct or indirect, threatened the peace, American security was involved.

Truman talked of the crises threatening Greece and Turkey as one aspect of the situation. UN assistance had been considered, he said, but these crises required immediate action and a kind of assistance that the UN and its related organizations were not in a position to extend. The UN's objectives would not be realized, Truman said, unless its members were willing to help free peoples maintain their free institutions and national integrity against aggressive movements that seek to impose totalitarian regimes upon them. Nations throughout the world must choose between alternative ways of life, the President said, and in that moment in world history the choice was too often not a free one. Truman drew the line sharply:

> One way of life is based upon the will of the majority, and is distinguished by free institutions, representative government, free elections, guarantees of individual liberty, freedom of speech and religion, and freedom from political oppression. The second way of life is based upon the will of a minority forcibly imposed upon the majority. It relies upon terror and oppression, a controlled press and radio, fixed elections, and suppression of personal freedoms.

Then came the dramatic sentence that set forth what was to become known as the "Truman Doctrine." The President said, "I believe that it must be the policy of the United States to support free peoples who are resisting subjugation by armed minorities or by outside pressures."[11]

The world was not static and the status quo was not sacred, Truman said, but the U.S. could not allow changes

in the status quo in violation of the UN charter by such
subterfuges as political infiltration. The U.S., by helping
free and independent nations maintain their freedom, would
be giving effect to the principles of the UN charter. The
President asked Congress to appropriate $400 million for
aid to greece and Turkey through June 30, 1948. He asked
for authority to train Greek and Turkish personnel in the
U.S. and to send American civilian and military personnel,
at the request of each country, to assist in and to oversee the
use of American aid. Truman clearly indicated the broader
implications of this action. He emphasized that immediate
and resolute action was needed in the cases of Greece and
Turkey in order to meet "a much wider situation." Truman
acknowledged that "this is a serious course upon which we
embark," but warned that "the alternative is much more
serious."

Congress agreed. Even though the Republicans were
eager to assert their newly won control of Congress against
the will of the White House, well over 70 percent of the
votes in each house solidly endorsed the Truman Doctrine.
A vote of 67 to 23 in the Senate and 287 to 107 in the House
approved the aid program for Greece and Turkey and the
foreign policy concept of erecting barriers to contain further
Soviet expansion. In so doing, the U.S. served notice that to
deny further strategic advantages to Russia, it would bolster
up nations and governments resisting Soviet pressure and
penetration. This policy acknowledged officially the cold
war between communist and non-communist worlds.
Henceforth America's energy in foreign affairs would be
chiefly expended in the building of economic and military
defenses for the free world.

Truman's foreign policy evolved from the realities of
nearly two years of bitter, disillusioning experience with
Soviet deceit and aggression. There was not really a reversal of U.S. policy toward the Soviet Union. Soviet-

American relations had never been good before World War II; there had never been the kind of Soviet-American cooperation Roosevelt apparently envisioned and Truman repeatedly offered after the war. Truman's stance was one of patience with firmness. It toughened as Russia proceeded month after month to conduct its diplomacy by deceit and delay, while in one instance after another persistently destroying democratic governments, seizing territory by force, and threatening a growing number of free and independent countries with military force and political sabotage.

The toughness Truman and the American people adopted was in reaction to Soviet actions. The actions are a matter of record. Russia became an aggressor, preying on those that were weaker. Truman's offers to Stalin to work together for peace were rudely rejected.

The U.S. had indulged the Soviets during the war, and Truman finally decided it was time to stop indulging them. The simple fact is that in the wake of World War II there was an immense power vacuum. The Soviet dictatorship moved aggressively to fill it by any possible means, including military action. Russia was, in its behavior, nothing less than an international bully, grabbing for more power and territory. Britain was no longer able to preserve the world balance of power, and Truman determined that the U.S., the only country that could do so, should do so.

Threatened countries were looking to the U.S. for help, and the U.S. would provide it. Those who would fault the U.S. for a "reversal" of policy toward the Soviet Union are rewriting history and misusing words. The Truman Doctrine was not arrived at in haste. Truman chose the course when at last it was clear there was no other way to hold the bully at bay.

The reason the Truman Doctrine represented a truly revolutionary advance in U.S. foreign policy was because with it America for the first time formally recognized and accepted the role and responsibilities of world power. The role came to America by default, but it could have been rejected. It had been before. America could have put its head in the sand, ostrich-like, as it did after World War I. It could have tried to remain aloof, attempting a separate existence as an island of prosperity and democracy, ignoring the problems for which smaller, weaker nations sought help. But Truman was determined that the U.S. this time would step into, rather than shrink from, the leadership role that other free world nations looked to it to fill. America had not sought this role, and could not relish the many hazards it held. The transition from war had not been to peace but to new kinds of invisible aggression and new dimensions of problems, dangers, and uncertainties. Truman was nonetheless convinced that America must shoulder the burden. And a burden it would be.

To Rebuild from the Rubble

World War II was the most destructive of wars. In much of Europe, rivilian populations had been military targets almost as much as the armed forces had been because they were part of the economic and industrial centers involved in a total war. Attacks on industrial areas, utilities, and transportation had brought war-ravaged economies to the breaking point. Europe desperately needed food, fuel, raw materials, machinery, and investment capital to bring about an economic recovery that would raise nations from the rubble of war. Peace could not be established unless the economic life of these nations could be restored.

In the spring of 1947, after two years during which the U.S. had given some $15 billion dollars worth of emergency assistance to alleviate suffering and prevent starvation and disease, it was apparent that an even larger and more comprehensive program was needed to rebuild the economies of Europe. At the same time, it was becoming evident in Greece that U.S. aid could be used by a government recipient to further partisan political aims of its own. Truman wanted American aid to Europe to take the form of some kind of joint endeavor, for two reasons. First, he believed that no amount of aid would lead to a lasting recovery unless the nations of Europe were willing to help themselves. He wanted some framework for U.S. aid that would encourage the Europeans to organize a common effort to work out solutions to their own economic problems with American help. Secondly, Truman wanted to encourage Europeans to develop the broadest possible view of a recovery program, rather than to think of it in narrowly nationalistic or partisan terms.

Late in April, Secretary of State Marshall returned in a pessimistic mood from the Moscow conference of foreign ministers. The Russians had turned a deaf ear to discussions of the helpless plight of Europe. Their conduct convinced Marshall that they were coldly determined to exploit the conditions there. The Soviets obviously were stalling for time while Europe disintegrated. In a radio address on April 28, Marshall told the nation that Europe's recovery was much slower than had been expected, and that new signs of disintegration were appearing as each day passed. The patient is sinking, he said, while the doctors deliberate. Whatever action was possible to meet these pressing problems would have to be taken without delay.

Before going to Moscow, Marshall had decided to establish a policy planning staff in the State Department to help develop long-range policy. He named George Kennan to head it. On April 29, he put Kennan and his small staff to work; they were to analyze the problem of European reconstruction and recommend action. They were to use the basic idea of a coordinated, multistate recovery program. The U.S. would prime it and help it solve the most pressing problems. But its aim over the long term was the creation of a strong, economically integrated Europe based on democratic political forces. This would be the next giant step in applying the Truman Doctrine.

The foreign policy the President had proposed on March 12 embodied the concept of containing Soviet expansion by strengthening nations that might be threatened — giving them the stability to maintain their independence. When it was first applied — to Greece and Turkey, which were of greater strategic than economic significance — U.S. aid was primarily military and in the nature of a holding action. The Truman Doctrine's next phase would be incomparably larger and more positive — to build a community of free and prosperous nations to forestall the communist advance on a weakened Europe.

Kennan must be credited with considerable influence in shaping some of the ideas that were incorporated in the plan Truman chose. Although Kennan's contribution was only part of a consensus that already was developing, it was he and his staff who gave it form and direction. The conception of the plan was so daring and its dimensions so staggering that Truman decided a trial balloon should be floated. His troubles with the Republican-controlled Congress were mounting. He wanted to make his thinking on this vast new program known publicly but indirectly so he could gauge the reaction.

The opportunity at hand was a long-standing speech invitation Truman had. He asked Undersecretary Acheson to substitute for him and discussed with him carefully the substance of his speech. Acheson, a striking figure with a magnificent mustache and an aristocratic bearing, delivered the little-noted speech in the town of Cleveland, Mississippi, with only about a half-dozen reporters on hand to

represent the regional press and wire services. But it was
not as unlikely a place as it might seem from which to call
the attention of the U.S. to the need to rebuild Europe. The
occasion for the speech was the annual meeting of the Delta
Council, an organization of farmers and small businessmen
who live in the Mississippi Valley between Vicksburg and
New Orleans. They are traditionally internationalist in outlook because worldwide markets are needed for cotton, the
main crop of the area.

Acheson told his audience that when Secretary of State
Marshall returned from the recent meeting of foreign ministers in Moscow, he did not talk with the President about the
front-page topics of communist challenges and the military
situation. They talked instead of food and fuel, and about
how short the distance is from food and fuel to either peace
or anarchy. The devastation of war, Acheson said, has
brought us back to the basics.

Perhaps few of the people present realized they had heard
a speech calculated to speed up a major policy development
in Washington. The words were heard only by those present
and those listening to the local radio broadcast. Acheson,
however, was speaking to a much wider audience: to the
staff of the Department of State, to the cabinet and the
whole government hierarchy, to the Congress, and to the
American people. He was also assuring the governments
and peoples of Europe that America recognized the problem
they had and the responsibility it had.

This was the first official statement of the importance of
the economic unity of Europe. The key point of that Delta
Council speech was that the reconstruction of Europe would
have to be treated as one problem. The address was also
remarkably frank about the motives for American aid. It
was "only in part suggested by humanitarianism,"
Acheson said, and "chiefly as a matter of national self-
interest." Acheson's speech went on to say that since world

demand exceeded America's ability to supply, America would have to concentrate its emergency assistance in areas where it would be most effective in building political and economic stability and in promoting human freedom and democratic institutions. This approach, Acheson explained, was merely common sense and sound practice:

> It is in keeping with the policy announced by President Truman in his special message to Congress on March 12 on aid to Greece and Turkey. Free peoples who are seeking to preserve their independence and democratic institutions and human freedoms against totalitarian pressures, either internal or external, will receive top priority for American reconstruction aid. This is no more than frank recognition, as President Truman said, 'that totalitarian regimes imposed on free peoples, by direct or indirect aggression, undermine the foundations of international peace and hence the security of the United States.'[12]

Even if the full implication of the Delta Council speech was not perceived immediately, or even widely noted by the American press, the ideas seemed to go over well. Upon Acheson's return to Washington, the pace of conferences around the President's desk quickened. Truman and his key advisers proceeded from the certain knowledge that a major crisis in the affairs of Europe was upon them. They understood that America alone had the capability, and the urgent obligation, to meet it. They agreed that doing so would require America to invest massive sums of money continuously over a number of years.

From this basic assumption, the plan took shape. Truman insisted on several points and gave it its form and direction. For one thing, Europe was to be the focus of the American aid effort. Economies were ailing all over the world. Europe's needs were as pressing as any, but its prospects were better. For maximum effect, the American effort should be concentrated where the chances of success were most promising, and that meant Europe. For another thing, the President wanted the enterprise to emphasize the positive; he wanted it to be in the nature of a fight *for* economic recovery and political freedom rather than a fight *against* communism. Truman also insisted that the program be devised not as a shot in the arm but as a sustained course of curative treatment. Finally, he was committed to the notion that the initiative in this effort and the responsibility for making it work must come from the nations that expected to benefit from it. This became the hallmark of the concept that emerged. It would end the openhanded dole but not impose an arbitrary plan. It would instead call forth a truly cooperative effort in which Europe would draw up its own scheme for its own economic salvation. European nations would do this together, and American goods and money would help make it work.

The Marshall Plan

With the form of the plan ready, the question became one of how best to propose it. It was novel in its approach and staggering in its scope. It could easily founder on an unpopular reception at home or abroad. To minimize the risk of having the idea shot down as soon as it was broached, it would have to be introduced with skill and finesse. The President would be the logical person to propose it, but Truman's popularity was in a period of eclipse. He was running into such trouble with the Republican-controlled Congress that he feared its disdain for him would be attached instantly to such a radical and far-reaching proposal. In short, a "Truman Plan" was not likely to be well received. Moreover, the President wished to give credit to his secretary of state's major role in developing the plan. So it was decided that the plan should be associated with Marshall, and that he should therefore be the one to propose it.

Marshall was not an electrifying orator, but he was a most impressive person. He was a man of dignity and selfless statesmanship, a rather colorless figure but a person of considerable stature at home and abroad. And he had an ideal forum available at just the right time — a commencement address at Harvard University. Marshall epitomized the responsible and compassionate international public servant embarked on a mission of lofty purpose as he described in a concise, 15-minute address from the sun-drenched rostrum at Harvard the European recovery program that would become known at once as the Marshall Plan.

Any government willing to assist in the task of recovery, Marshall pledged, would find full cooperation on the part of the American government; any government that maneuvered to block the recovery of other countries could not expect help from America. Truman and his foreign policy team must have had their fingers crossed as Marshall spoke. He was venturing in this carefully worded passage past the pitfall that worried them most: what if Russia came forward to accept aid under the plan? Other than qualifying eligibility to those European countries willing to cooperate, no mention was made of which ones would receive the aid. But it was recognized in Washington that a calculated risk was being taken. There was hope that the plan would appeal to some of the Soviet satellites, and to prospective satellites such as Czechoslovakia, and perhaps lead to a loosening of the communist grip on those countries. But it was known that if Russia took up the aid offer it could wreck the program, and that if Russia and all its satellites were to be among the recipients the necessary appropriations would be so colossal as to stand no chance of congressional approval, especially in view of the strong and growing sentiment against the Soviets.

Truman decided to take his chances with Russian acceptance or rejection and, in the event of the former, the reaction of Congress, rather than phrase the offer in a way

that would make the U.S. appear to be dividing Europe.
The offer was not made deviously. Nevertheless, it was the
desire not to put the U.S. in a position where it could be
blamed for dividing Europe that primarily accounted for
there being no direct reference to possible recipients of the
aid.

The Soviet Union, as if to provide dramatic contrast,
brought down the government of Hungary on the same day,
an event that shared front pages with the proposal of the
Marshall Plan. Three weeks later, the foreign ministers of
Britain, France, and the Soviet Union met in Paris to discuss making a joint assessment, on a continental basis, of
Europe's prospects for production and for mutual aid. Britain and France were proceeding with the basic idea of the
Marshall suggestion that Europe should produce a plan,
whereupon the U.S. would give such aid as might be
practical. The Soviet Union rejected participation. Label-
ling the U.S. proposal a threat to the sovereignty of small
nations and accusing Britain and France of splitting Europe,
the Russian delegation packed up and left for Moscow.

Britain and France went ahead and sent 22 European
states invitations to join in setting up a "committee of
cooperation" to draft a report on Europe's resources, prospects, and needs. Most of the Soviet satellite countries
awaited instructions from Moscow and then declined the
invitation. Favorable comments on the proposal had come
from Poland and Czechoslovakia before the break between
Russia and the West at Paris. Even after Moscow made its
position known, the two countries indicated an interest in
cooperation. The Czechoslovak cabinet decided in favor of
accepting "in principle" the Paris invitation. Then Poland
declined, charging that Germany was to be given priority
over its victims, that Britain and France were placed in
privileged positions, and that there were no guarantees of
the sovereignty and economic plans of small nations.

Czechoslovakia's premier and foreign minister flew to Moscow for consultations. Upon their return, the Czechoslovak government announced that it had ascertained that the Slavic states and other countries of Eastern Europe with which it maintained close relations would not take part. It then declined also, on the grounds that Czechoslovakia's participation would be interpreted as an act directed against the friendship of the Soviet Union and its other allies.

Sixteen Western European nations did join the drafting session. They established the Organization for European Economic Cooperation, which served to coordinate the American aid program. The program's aim was to combat the economic weakness that was vulnerable to exploitation "by any and all totalitarian movements," a condition Soviet communism was exploiting.[13] Congress enacted the Marshall Plan with the Foreign Assistance Act of 1948, allotting the European program $5.3 billion. It was a genuinely generous American initiative. In a very real sense it was humanitarian in its value and effect. But there is no doubt that its passage by Congress was aided by the widely held belief that economic instability was the breeding ground for communism and that this was the best way to combat it.

The Marshall Plan put the Soviets on the defensive. They were quick to realize that once it began to function, they could lose their chance to extend Soviet power by capitalizing on economic misery in Western Europe. Having failed to prevent allied cooperation for European recovery, Moscow struck back with countermeasures for its East European satellites. It hastened to bind them more tightly in a network of political and economic pacts, and made new efforts to tie their trade to Russia. The Soviets had already signed 20-year treaties of alliance with Czechoslovakia in 1943 and with Poland and Yugoslavia in 1945, providing for mutual military aid. Moscow began negotiating similar treaties with Bulgaria, Romania, Hungary, and Finland, completing them early in 1948 and giving the Soviet Union an unbroken chain of alliances from the Arctic to the Black Sea. The satellite states also concluded a network of military pacts among themselves, 11 of them by April of 1948. The Soviets encouraged close ties among the Balkan states, which tended to increase the pressure on Greece, and between Poland and Czechoslovakia, which tended to turn both states away from their interest in the West.

When the satellite countries "declined" participation in the Marshall Plan, there was talk of a "Molotov Plan" for the recovery of Eastern Europe. Actually such a "plan" had been in operation since 1945 in the sense that these countries, under communist direction, were pursuing roughly similar economic plans that allocated most of their foreign trade to the U.S.S.R. and to each other. Moscow now acted to sever whatever flow of trade and commerce had been resumed between East and West Europe and to block restoration of the normal and essential prewar flow of commerce between the two areas.

In the meantime, the Marshall Plan was having a notably favorable impact long before its initial aid shipment would arrive. It was bringing new hope to the cooperating nations of Western Europe. They attacked the task of recovery with renewed vigor despite Moscow's veiled threats and a barrage of Communist propaganda against the U.S. and the recovery program. The U.S. commitment instilled confidence where there had been doubt, despair, and uncertainty. At last there were grounds for optimism about the survival of free political and economic institutions. In Italy and France, where the prospect that communists could come to power was particularly strong, that prospect appeared to be arrested if not diminished. A real strengthening of West European economies was in the works.

The Blockade of Berlin

The course of economic recovery was to seal the split between East and West. Nothing could have made that split more stark and irreversible than did Moscow's stunning blockade of Berlin. It was a blatantly aggressive power play, cold-blooded and iron-fisted. It heated the cold war dangerously close to the kindling point, and dramatized as nothing else could the fact that Europe had been divided into two camps.

The city of Berlin, Germany's former capital, had become an isolated outpost of four-power administration surrounded by the eastern zone of Germany, where the Soviet army held sway. The city was 110 miles behind the "Iron Curtain" at the nearest point, connected with the Western occupation zones by rail, highway — the autobahn — and a river-and-canal network. On March 20, 1948, Russia's representative stalked out of the Allied Control Council in Berlin, formalizing the already obvious fact that four-power control of the city had become unworkable. On March 31, the Soviets declared that beginning the next day they would check the identification of all U.S. personnel passing through their zone, and would inspect all freight shipments. When American authorities objected, pointing out that agreements among the allies had assured free access to Berlin, the Russians claimed no such agreements had been made and that they had full right to control all traffic in their zone.

The Western allies ordered train commanders, on principle, not to submit to Soviet control; they were to refuse search and inspection by Red Army soldiers. Beginning April 1, the Russians arbitrarily imposed the restrictions and allied traffic to and from Berlin came to a halt. The Western allies countered by airlifting supplies to the small garrisons of occupation forces stationed by the U.S., U.K., and France in the Western sectors of Berlin. Tensions over the Berlin issue built up rapidly as Soviet harassment and the improvised airlift went on week after week. June came, and as summer began the Berlin crisis came to a head, challenging the West with the cold war's most severe test of will.

Steady progress in taking steps toward European recovery had formed the background of the Berlin developments that clouded the spring of 1948. A key step was currency reform. The Russians had obtained printing plates of the money used when the occupation began; they had been able to flood the Western zones of Germany with currency printed in the East, deliberately fueling the inflation that threatened to block Germany's recovery effort. The plates were changed but the Soviets continued to manipulate the East German currency. On June 17, Congress approved the bill for the European recovery program, and the next day the Western allies announced a currency reform for the Western zones of Germany.

The Soviet and satellite foreign ministers met on June 23. Moscow ordered a currency reform for East Germany and all of Berlin, even though the former German capital was divided into four sectors administered by the four wartime allied powers. The Western allies responded by ordering currency reform in the three Western sectors of Berlin. The next day, June 24, the Russians sealed off all highway, rail, and river traffic into and out of Berlin. They imposed a full blockade not only on the Western allies but on a civilian population of more than 900,000 families, for whom all essential supplies had to come from outside the city.

At first the Soviets took the position that the U.S. never had a legal right to be in Berlin, then later said it had had the right but had forfeited it. But the contest, according to President Truman, was not over legal rights, but over Germany and, in the larger sense, over Europe. The President later observed that the Soviet Union, faced with the Marshall Plan, was trying in Berlin to mislead the people of Europe into believing that America's interest and support would not extend beyond economic matters and that the U.S. would back away from any military risks.

With Berlin blockaded by land and water, General Lucius D. Clay, the U.S. commander in Berlin, made emergency arrangements to have essential supplies flown into the city. On June 26, President Truman directed that this improvised airlift be put on a full-scale, organized basis and that every transport plane available to the European Command be pressed into service. Truman was determined not to let the Berliners be starved into submission or the West forced to abandon the city to the Soviets. But the enormity of the logistical task of supplying the city's needs by air was staggering. Existing food stocks, supplemented by air-lifted supplies, were thought to be sufficient to last approximately 30 days. By introducing dried foods, Berliners might be fed for 60 days. But what then? If the Russians refused to negotiate a peaceful resolution of the blockade, the outcome might be a military conflict that would ignite a world war, or a humiliating Western withdrawal that would turn the citizens of the captive city over to communist control.

The Soviets, having suffered recent setbacks in Italy, France, and Finland since the Marshall Plan proposal, were obviously determined to force the U.S. out of Berlin. Yugoslavia, once regarded as the Soviets' strongest satellite, was beginning to act independently, and the European recovery plan was beginning to succeed. The blockade of Berlin was communism's counterattack. To meet it, the U.S. would have to make a show of strength and determination in Berlin, in spite of the difficulties and the risk that Russian reaction might lead to war.

Instituting a massive airlift accomplished the objective. It was undertaken as a way to stave off political defeat without making a move that would force a military showdown. It meant shouldering a burden of awesome magnitude for an indefinite period, but it would buy time in which to try to negotiate. Little did anyone realize what a protracted crisis it would be.

The airlift at first brought Berlin about 2500 tons of supplies per day, with 52 C-54 and 80 C-47 propeller-driven transport planes making two round trips per day. This was more than enough to handle the food requirements but not enough to bring in the needed amounts of coal for fuel. The minimum needed to sustain the city without extreme hardship was estimated to be 4500 tons per day. For the summer, 3400 tons per day might suffice, but more tonnage would be needed if the blockade extended into the winter. Seventy-five more C-47s could raise the daily total to 3500 tons, and Truman ordered that they be transferred to the Berlin airlift.

Over the objections of the air force chief of staff, Truman gave the airlift top priority and directed that it be given maximum effort, even though this meant a risky concentration of U.S. aircraft. Their destruction in the event of hostilities would adversely affect American capabilities for strategic warfare and the ability to supply U.S. forces and hold bases elsewhere. Transports were relocated and pressed into service nonetheless, taking planes intended for emergency use, disrupting military air transport service, and reducing American air strength elsewhere both in planes and personnel. There was always the possibility that the Russians would attack the American planes. But Truman took the position that the airlift was less risky than an effort to supply Berlin by armed convoys on the ground, which would be far likelier to encounter Russian interference.

Steadily the airlift expanded. More planes were added, the British joined in, and technical improvements and experience increased the results. By the end of the summer, the British-American airlift was bringing Berlin a daily average of 4000 tons and the total continued to climb upward. Stockpiles in Berlin gradually grew to a 25-day reserve of coal and a 30-day reserve of food.

In the meantime, as weeks stretched on into months, Moscow played cat and mouse with American negotiating efforts. The Russians used repeated delays, demands, and foot-dragging tactics to frustrate diplomatic progress. They employed a variety of incidents of threats and harassment behind a background barrage of propaganda attacks. The Communists brought about a split in the Berlin city council, instigated riots, curtailed contacts between the eastern and western portions of the city, disrupted the electric power system, and announced that Soviet fighters would hold air maneuvers in an area that included the air lanes used by the airlifts. But communist subversion and psychological warfare was overshadowed, as was the battle of diplomacy at the UN and in U.S.-Soviet bilateral contacts, by the drama of the air convoys that winged their way to Berlin day after day.

The Airlift Succeeds

Flights continued undaunted through the adverse weather of winter. Spring came, and the airlift's "Easter Parade" broke all tonnage records by flying 13,000 tons of food and coal to Berlin in 24 hours. At last it was clear that time was not on the Soviets' side after all. Russia gave up its waiting game and ended the blockade's war of nerves on May 12, 1949, more than 14 months after the first restrictions had been imposed. It ended the blockade because it was reduc-

ing rather than increasing Russia's power relative to the
West. It was a calculation of power, pure and simple, just as
was the decision to impose the blockade in the first place.
The Soviets considered Germany the key to the balance of
power in Europe and regarded Berlin as the key to Germany. If Germany could not be united under communism,
the Russians wanted it divided and as weak in the western
part as possible.

By cutting overland communications between Berlin and
the western part of Germany, Moscow brought the U.S.
into direct conflict with the Soviet Union. Moscow's action
also placed Berlin's population in a position of having to
choose between East and West. The Soviet aim was to dash ·
hopes for economic recovery in the western part of Germany and block formation of a West German government,
in the process swallowing up Berlin and dealing a blow to
the West that would seriously weaken American prestige
and leadership. In the end, Moscow's gamble backfired.
West Berlin, where a choice existed, chose the West and
freedom; its people were willing to withstand every pressure and endure any hardship rather than fall captive to
Soviet control. The West did not back down, and in the
process dealt a serious defeat to Russia. Instead of impeding
the creation of a stable government and economy in West
Germany, the Berlin blockade promoted and hastened it.

With the Berlin airlift, Truman did much more than get
food and fuel to an isolated city. He demonstrated, both to
the Russians and the Germans, that the Western democracies would stand their ground under extreme pressure and
provocation. Truman also demonstrated, very significantly, his ability to act decisively but with restraint in a
tense situation fraught with the danger of a military clash
that would mean war.

Harry Truman alone, of course, did not defeat the Soviet
assault on Berlin. The blockade was beaten as much by the

Left: "Captain Harry" in his World War I uniform;
above: The Truman family home, where they lived before
and after his presidency, and which they often visited
for brief vacations during his time as President;
below: Truman stands in his Kansas City, Missouri,
men's furnishings store, which he operated with
Edward Jacobson from 1919 to 1922.

Opposite, above: President Roosevelt speaks briefly at the Christopher Columbus statue near Union Station, Nov. 10, 1944, upon his return to Washington. Vice president-elect Truman is at the right; *Opposite, below:* Truman with former British Prime Minister Winston Churchill bound for Fulton, Missouri, where Churchill—at Westminster College—would deliver his famous "Iron Curtain" speech on March 5, 1946; *right:* White House talk with New York's Governor Thomas E. Dewey, who would run for the presidency against Truman in 1948. *below:* Truman enunciates the "Truman Doctrine"—the foreign policy of aiding free peoples resisting aggression—in a joint session of Congress on March 12, 1947.

National Park Service

Wide World Photos

Chase in the *New Orleans States*

United Press International

National Park Service

Opposite, far left: The Democratic Party's concern with Truman's plummeting popularity is expressed by this cartoon of March 12, 1948; *Opposite, right:* The President checks the time as he arrives at a speaking stop; *Opposite, below:* Truman's 1948 "whistle-stop" campaign was aptly named; here Truman and a cowboy exchange greetings during a stop at Sierra Blanca, Texas, on Sept. 28. 1948; *Above:* So sure were most newspapers of Governor Dewey's victory over Truman, some, like the *Chicago Daily Tribune,* announced the fact even though Truman led the balloting from the start; *below:* At White House swearing-in ceremony, Truman stands between George C. Marshall (left) and James F. Byrnes, who are exchanging congratulations as the incoming and outgoing secretary of state.

Left: Truman beams as he rides to the Capitol in Washington on Jan. 20, 1949, to be sworn in as President of the United States; *below:* Truman holds an informal press conference at the Winter White House at Key West, Florida, on March 30, 1950. No other President has had such informal contact with the press; *Opposite, right:* Truman at his White House desk, preparing a message to Congress; *Opposite, below:* Truman and General MacArthur meet for the first time in October, 1950.

Wide World Photos

Wide World Photos

United Press Internatio
U.S. Office of War Informa

Above: President Truman, his wife,
Bess, and his daughter, Margaret,
return to Washington from their
home in Independence, Missouri,
following the election of Dwight
Eisenhower as President on
Nov. 5, 1952; *right:* Observing his
early-morning routine of a brisk
walk, Truman, accompanied by
Secret Service men, strides across
the Washington Monument grounds.

spirit of the people of Berlin. The improvised airlift helped whip up a spirit of resistance. The inspiring sight and sound of the planes coming in every day reassured Berliners that they had powerful friends, or despair might have set in during that long winter. The airlift provided the material basis for resistance, but the strength of will was the Berliners' own. They would not be cowed or blackmailed. Through months of threats and intimidation, knowing their city could be overrun by the Red Army in a matter of hours, the city's people refused to let their spirit and their sense of community be broken. This ability to live with danger — which was to become the West Berliners' way of life — won them admiration throughout the world. The blockade was defeated, too, by the bravery and teamwork of those who flew and maintained the planes. But in the first instance, it was the President who had to make the crucial decision on whether to stay in Berlin and how this was to be done.

Truman clarified U.S. policy toward Berlin as soon as he was briefed on the blockade issue. At a White House meeting, the President considered three possible courses of action in response to the total blockade: (1) decide now to withdraw from Berlin rather than be exposed to repeated crises and humiliation, (2) defend the U.S. position in Berlin by all possible means, including a move to supply the city by force even at the risk of war, and (3) maintain a firm stand in Berlin and try to negotiate with the Russians. When an adviser raised the question of whether the U.S. should stay in Berlin, Truman interrupted. There would be no discussion on that point, the President said. The U.S. would stay. Period. The secretary of the army expressed ''some concern'' as to whether the problem of doing so had been thought out. He did not think the U.S. should be committed to a position under which it might have to fight its way into Berlin unless this possibility was clearly recognized in

advance. Truman replied that the situation would be dealt
with as it developed, but there was to be no doubt that
Americans were in Berlin by terms of an agreement and that
they would remain there.[14]

Truman opted for a diplomatic search for a solution, but
with no retreat. He had two additional squadrons of B-29
bombers sent to Germany to underscore the seriousness of
the U.S. position, and authorized the full-scale airlift to
feed Berlin until the diplomatic deadlock could be broken.

The boldness of the Soviet challenge had demanded an
equally bold response. The total airlift answered the total
blockade of land access effectively. No one knew how
effective it could be over a long haul, for there was no way
of knowing what a prolonged crisis this would be. What
was of crucial importance in coping with the crisis successfully was Truman's promptness and persistence. Any delay
in starting the full-scale airlift, any sign of retreat at the
outset of the blockade might have produced feelings of
defeatism in Berlin that could have tipped the balance. And
once Truman's firm position was taken, it was never dis-
carded in frustration or surrendered in despair. Truman
stayed the course, persistently pursuing the difficult but
prudent path he had chosen between retreat and a greater
risk of war.

New Ties in NATO

Soviet behavior toward Berlin caused the peoples of
Western Europe to close ranks and to identify more closely
with the U.S. It was Moscow's action above all that
mobilized public opinion in the West behind Western cooperation and against Soviet-style communism. And when
Moscow called off the blockade, it seemed to signify the
soundness of the Truman Doctrine. The blockade and airlift

were dramatic evidence of containing Russian aggression by supporting a free people in resisting subjugation. The aggressor was repelled by meeting strength with strength, and pressure with counter-pressure.

The Soviet threat, however, was not diminishing. It was making itself felt elsewhere in Europe all the time the Berlin blockade and airlift were going on. A communist coup in February, 1948, eradicated the last vestige of independence in Czechoslovakia and made it a Soviet satellite. Soviet pressure on Finland produced a mutual assistance pact with Moscow in April. Greece, despite American aid, was still being assaulted by communist guerrillas with support from satellite states across the border. Communists were making new efforts to seize power in France and Italy.

The beginning of the blockade brought home to Western policy makers the stark reality that their military strength in Europe was no match for Russia's. Since the war, the Soviets had kept intact and even strengthened their military force of 175 wartime divisions and 20,000 planes. The Western occupying powers in Germany individually and collectively lacked the armed strength even to parry a Russian blow. The nations of Western Europe represented a military vacuum, with America's atomic bomb providing virtually the only hope for deterring a possible Soviet attack.

A movement in Western Europe for self-protection against the Soviet threat began early in 1948, and in March the Western Union Treaty calling for collective military cooperation was signed at Brussels by Britain, France, Belgium, the Netherlands, and Luxembourg. But this was little more than a sketchy hope for common defense; the arms with which the Union could confront the Red Army were negligible. Western Europe was too weak to make adequate provision for its own security. By 1949 it was only becoming clearer that another American step was needed.

The history of Europe in the postwar years had been one of Soviet aggression and conquest, chiefly through subversion engineered in the direct presence or in the shadow of the Red Army. By 1948, Poland, Hungary, Bulgaria, Romania, and finally Czechoslovakia had been taken over by communist minorities operating under the protection of the Red Army. Western Europe's economic recovery was under way, but had not dispelled the fear of Soviet military moves. There was growing concern that there might be a greater chance of Soviet military aggression as the likelihood of communist internal revolts decreased due to domestic stability.

This collective concern resulted in the North Atlantic Treaty Organization, a collective effort to eliminate the military weakness that would invite Soviet military aggression. Those signing the treaty — Belgium, Britain, Canada, Denmark, France, Iceland, Italy, Luxembourg, the Netherlands, Norway, Portugal, and the U.S. — agreed to resist aggression together. An attack on any one of them would be considered an attack on all. In this way, the Western alliance denied the Soviets the chance to gain cheap military successes by attacking small nations one at a time. In the NATO area, Moscow would have to contend with the combined, coordinated power of all the member countries. Combined military and naval forces would stand ready to back up the treaty.

NATO came into being in August of 1949, with the contracting partners resolving not to permit another inch of Soviet expansion. Czechoslovakia's once-proud capital of Prague would be the last place on the European continent, they vowed, where the Soviets would snuff out the lamp of freedom.

NATO was the military arm of the Marshall Plan, created to protect the economic recovery that the plan was making possible. The military alliance was to serve its purpose well in the ensuing years. There would be more crises and other times of tension, but peace was preserved. And not one inch of European territory did fall under Soviet domination after NATO came into being. The Marshall Plan, though, was at the heart of the fruitful, far-sighted decisions Truman made during this trying postwar period. More than any other effort, it was the Marshall Plan that saved Western Europe. That is a fact attested to by hard statistics. The plan that Truman was careful to have named for someone else but then brought to reality was a plan that Winston Churchill was to describe as "the most unsordid act in history."

The Marshall Plan dramatically reversed the economic and spiritual disintegration of Western Europe. It preserved free and independent governments and put Europe on the road to industrial prosperity. Next to restoring a viable European economy in the first place, the plan's major consequence was to produce the economic unity that has since been projected in the Common Market. And it took less time and cost less money than was expected. Europe's recovery and unity was attained in three years instead of the allotted four, and with an American outlay of $12.6 billion instead of the $16.8 billion originally estimated and approved.

V Winning the Presidency

Harry Truman's greatest personal and political truimph was the election campaign of 1948, when in an epic upset he won the presidency in his own right. Never did he exhibit more dramatically his enthusiasm, determination, and toughness. To say that he was the underdog is an understatement. It was not merely that the odds were against him; they seemed absolutely insurmountable. Yet when his presidential political fortunes appeared to be at their lowest ebb, Truman proved that plain old guts and perserverance could work a miracle.

Looking back many years later, it may seem strange that Truman found himself at such a disadvantage. After all, he had come to grips effectively with unprecedented challenges in international affairs. His foreign policy moves had borne the marks of bold, imaginative statesmanship. He was coping impressively with immense new dangers and responsibilities that America faced abroad, displaying courage and a firm sense of command. But it was not on foreign policy grounds that Truman was in trouble. It was all manner of domestic problems that plagued him. There were bitter divisions in his own party and clashes with Congress. There were complaints from the American people over a variety of economic issues. In some cases the problems were partly of Truman's own making, or were made worse by his handling of them. Much of the criticism he bore, however, was due to circumstances of which he simply had become the victim.

It was Harry Truman's misfortune on domestic issues to

156

suffer an inevitable backlash from being the successor to Roosevelt and facing a Congress controlled by a party that had been out of power for a decade and a half. Republicans, understandably, were feeling their oats. They were basking in their unaccustomed ability to control the legislative process — or to block its control by anybody else. Moreover, Republicans — and the two houses of Congress generally — were eager to stand up to the President. The Congress, and especially its Republican membership, had felt bullied and browbeaten by Roosevelt and relished the chance at long last to push back. Congress was anxious to say no to the President, whomever he was and whatever he said.

The mood of the 80th Congress, then, would have been anything but receptive to the program of any Democratic President. Congress was more inclined to roll back New Deal measures already on the books than to consider enacting anything new. In these circumstances, the fact that Truman was the President and the legislative proposals were his had become almost incidental.

An additional complication was the fact that the coalition that had supported Roosevelt had come apart even before his death. The Democratic Party had held together a few more years largely because of the unifying force of the war effort and because American voters were unwilling to break with the status quo when the nation was at war. Truman was not the architect of that coalition and could not count on it for the backing he so badly needed. Indeed, key groups within it turned their back on him, beginning with the New Dealers. As Truman removed cabinet members to appoint men of his own choosing, as any President would, Roosevelt stalwarts took this to mean that Truman was bent on rooting New Deal adherents out of the government. They were not Truman admirers to begin with, and were not about to close ranks behind him.

This was compounded by inevitable problems in the reconversion of the country's life from war to peace. There was unavoidable confusion and aggravation. Everyone seemed to expect to see the high wages, big profits, and full employment of the war years combined somehow with the low prices and abundant consumer goods of the depression years that preceded the war. It was too tall an order for any President to fill. With these impossible goals, labor, business, farmers, bankers, and housewives began venting all the conflicting animosities and demands that had been repressed during the war years. There was no way to satisfy all the contending forces, and Truman found himself blamed personally for every new problem that came up.

Caught in this cross fire of complaints and impatient demands, with people pulling and tugging at him for special treatment at every turn, Truman often lost his temper. He liked to get things off his chest, and frequently did so by sitting down and dashing off a note. In a flash of anger, he would set forth his feelings in no uncertain terms. This would have been a good way to let off steam, except that Truman too often would immediately drop his sentiments in the mail. By the time he had put the incident out of his mind, the recipient of some intemperate prose would have another critical contribution to make to an uncomplimentary image of the President as hot-headed and sharp-tongued.

Truman was moved at one point in the midst of all the postwar pressures to sit down and write himself a memo. In it he said that what the President really needed was four new cabinet officers. First he needed a Secretary for Inflation, to convince people there was no real problem no matter how high prices rose or how low wages fell. He should have a Secretary of Reaction, to abolish "flying machines" and "restore oxcarts, oar boats and sailing ships." He also needed a Secretary for Columnists, who would read them all and thus be able to tell the President just how the country and the world should be run. Finally he should have a Secretary of Semantics, to furnish fancy words that would enable him to keep quiet and say everything at the same time and be against inflation in one city and for it in another.[1]

Controversy and Division

There was plenty of justification for such an outburst of sarcasm. Harry Truman did get more than his share of harsh criticism from the press. Almost any incident was used to portray him in the worst possible light. When, for example, he announced plans to build a balcony leading off his second-floor White House study, several newspapers drew attention to the fact that Adolf Hitler and Italy's fascist dictator Mussolini had also liked balconies. Truman was not to be put off; the south portico had been designed by Thomas Jefferson, he insisted, who intended to have a balcony. Truman had it done, and could not resist remarking that all additions to the White House had faced resistance — like gaslights and cooking stoves. They almost lynched Millard Fillmore's wife, Truman observed, for putting in the first bathtubs.[2] Truman accepted much of the criticism, however unfair, with philosophical resignation. "If you can't take the heat," he liked to say, "you should stay out of the kitchen." The heat nevertheless could make Truman testy. He was not always content to suffer in silence, and was rarely at a loss for a waspish comeback.

Many of Truman's detractors simply disliked his style. Roosevelt had always been careful not to depart in public from his aristocratic image. Truman was very different from Roosevelt anyway, and was the same person in public that he was in private. Critics had a field day looking down their nose at Truman for being inelegant and unsophisticated because of his unbashed enjoyment of such things as loud sport shirts, a hand of poker, and an American Legion parade. He was entirely unpretentious; if his tastes seemed earthy or corny they were nonetheless genuine. He was convinced that his declining popularity resulted from persistent efforts by the press to misrepresent him, his program, policies, and staff. And he had a point; most newspaper publishers were staunch Republicans, and their news columns, editorials, and editorial cartoons were always receptive to jibes at Truman.

Almost as if to accommodate his critics, Truman seemed to have a knack for controversy. He made some mistakes that were politically costly. One example was the heavy-handed manner in which he forced an end to a railway workers' strike. A long series of vexing strikes had plagued the country since the end of the war. With dogged determination, Truman got settlements negotiated. Major disputes in the steel and auto industries finally were resolved, but just when it seemed that the siege of strikes had ended, more than 300,000 railway workers walked off the job. Only two out of 20 railway unions refused to accept a settlement formula Truman proposed, whereupon he called the two union leaders to the White House and read them the riot act. "If you think I'm going to sit here and let you tie up this country, you're crazy as hell," said the President. "I am going to protect the public and we are going to run these railroads and you can put that in your pipe and smoke it!"

The two union leaders involved had worked hard for Truman's reelection to the Senate in 1940. Truman was no ingrate, but prior political support carried no weight with him when he saw an issue as a matter of principle. He was now thoroughly incensed, and issued an order for the government to seize the railroads. When railway workers still stayed off the job the next day, Truman made a nationwide speech announcing that he would ask Congress to authorize the army to run the railroads. "The crisis of Pearl Harbor was the result of action by a foreign enemy," the President intoned. "The crisis tonight is caused by a group of men within our country who place their private interests above the welfare of the nation." The next day, Truman had actually begun speaking from the rostrum of the House of Representatives, asking that striking workers be drafted into the armed forces, when word came that the strike had ended. It was a controversial episode, one that saw Truman widely condemned for overreacting in anger. He did so on principle, but in the process seriously jeopardized his political standing with organized labor.

Another controversial incident was his firing of Henry Wallace, the remaining high priest of the New Dealers, who had stayed on as Truman's secretary of commerce. Truman dropped him from the cabinet amid a furor that came after Wallace had made a speech attacking Secretary of State Byrnes, on the eve of a foreign ministers' meeting, for not being sufficiently conciliatory toward the Soviet Union. The President was perfectly justified in dropping Wallace, and probably should have done so sooner. But he bungled the handling of it when he did. He delayed the dismissal and surrounded it and its policy implications with confusion and indecision. By the time he acted, the whole awkward affair made Truman look most inept. Most of his mistakes were not such whoppers. But any of them, even relatively harmless slips or unguarded statements, were apt to be trumpeted as evidence of his unfitness for the presidency. "To err is Truman" became a common quip of the day.

The year 1948 got off to a bad start for Truman. Just a few days before it began, Henry Wallace announced the formation of a third party. It was called the Progressive Party, and its obvious purpose was to pull from the Democratic Party

as many New Dealers and liberals as possible. At the end of
the first week in January, Truman delivered his State of the
Union message to Congress, and his listeners sat on their
hands. The President paused several times during his address, allowing for expected applause, only to suffer em-
barassed silence when nobody clapped. One of Truman's
proposals was a tax cut of $40 for every taxpayer. In
response, one congressman remarked that ol' Tom
Pendergast paid only two bucks a vote and now ol' Harry is
offering $40! Truman's next personnel move was to drop
the head of the Civil Aeronautics Board, an old friend of
Roosevelt's, and replace him with a Republican. The reaction within his party made clear that this was not an auspi-
cious beginning for an election year.

Early in February, the President's political fortunes declined further. Truman tended to be impatient with problems, and wanted something done at once to get them
solved. A case in point was his belief that blacks were long
overdue for fair treatment. During the war, they were always segregated into separate units in the armed forces.
When the war ended, Truman ordered the armed forces to
integrate. Generals and admirals objected, but to no avail.
The Constitution makes the President the commander in
chief of the armed forces, and by executive order Truman
simply commanded that segregation in these forces be
ended, and it was. He also named a civil rights committee to
help him plan a program of action in the civilian sphere. On
February 2, 1948, without conferring with his congressional leaders, Truman sent Congress a 10-point civil rights
message. Among other things, the President called for a
federal law against lynching, a federal Fair Employment
Practices Committee, protection of the right of all citizens
to vote, the elimination of the Oriental Exclusion Act of
1924, and an end to segregation laws in any activity —
restaurants and hotel and motel accommodations, for ex-

ample — related to interstate transportation, which was subject to federal regulation.

However noble the ideal behind it, Truman's timing and the way he took Congress by surprise — not to mention some of his advisers and cabinet members — with his civil rights program demonstrated his enormous knack for stirring controversy in the Democratic Party. Southern congressmen were outraged. Fifty-two of them issued a statement that they would not support Truman for President. A Southern senator reserved a table for 10 at the Democrats' annual Jefferson-Jackson Day fund-raising dinner in Washington on February 19, but kept the table empty. He told reporters that he feared his wife would be forced to sit with a "Nigra." A member of the Democratic National Committee from Alabama insisted at a White House luncheon that the President send a message to the people of the South, telling them integration would not be rammed down their throats. Truman refused. "I'm everybody's President," he said. "I take back nothing of what I propose and make no excuse for it." A black White House waiter got so excited at the verbal exchange that he knocked a cup of coffee out of Truman's hands.[3] The fat was in the fire. Southern Democrats genuinely feared that Truman's civil rights stand would keep them from being reelected and that they must disassociate themselves from it and from him.

All this domestic political turmoil in the spring of 1948 sent Truman's prospects plunging further downhill in a hurry. The Democratic Party was rent asunder. There was Wallace's third party on the one hand, and the southern revolt over civil rights on the other. There was New Deal and labor disenchantment in between. A Gallup poll published in May indicated that only 36 percent of the population thought Truman was doing a good job. In the President's own party it was no longer just a matter of dwindling support. There were active efforts to ditch him as a candidate. *Time* magazine, calling the President awkward and above all mediocre, observed that the country appeared to be ready to drop the whole Truman administration.

Notions of dropping the whole thing were probably entertained by Truman, too, during those difficult times. He confided in the spring of 1948 that on the day three years earlier when victory was won in Europe he had felt sure he could make durable arrangements for peace. He therefore had made up his mind to retire in January of 1949, when he had served out the remainder of Roosevelt's fourth term. "But I was wrong," Truman told an interviewer. "The worst mistake we made was to demobilize," Truman said, "and I helped make it." "Now there are measures for peace under way which I must see through. I am not a quitter."[4] Not only that, Truman's dander was up. He was determined to show a thing or two to the Democratic leaders who opposed making him the party nominee.

As if defections by the southern bloc and by the Progessives would not offer challenges enough, Truman's nomination was also opposed by a third movement within the Democratic ranks. Persons Truman referred to with scorn as "professional liberals" were promoting General Dwight D. Eisenhower to be the Democratic standard-bearer. As a national war hero, Eisenhower was being touted as an ideal dark-horse candidate to substitute for Truman. Despite many rumors and much talk, an Eisenhower boom never developed, largely because Ike stubbornly maintained that he wanted to have nothing to do with politics. With that potentially formidable obstacle at last removed on the eve of the Democratic National Convention, when Ike reiterated his insistence that his name not be presented, Truman was not to be denied. Even so, Truman approached his party's convention with his popularity at its lowest point. Politicians of his own party from James Roosevelt, who headed the California delegation, to William O'Dwyer, Mayor of New York, publicly had urged the President not to run, and a prominent Republican Congresswoman was dismissing him as ''a gone goose.''

Shifting Gears

Harsh attacks from the opposition, however, did not send Truman to the showers. Neither did the humiliation of having leading figures and sizeable segments of his own party turning their backs on him. There can be no doubt that the stinging criticism and the betrayals hurt, although Truman would be the last to let on that they did. He must have been dismayed, discouraged, and at times deeply wounded by what he felt to be unfair attacks on his policies and on him personally. Yet he never sank into self-pity. If his spirits were low, he preferred not to bother his friends or give his detractors the satisfaction of letting it be known. He did not go into hiding at every opportunity, or retreat from contacts with the public and his regular encounters with the press.

If anything, being under fire made Truman dig in his heels. Set upon from all sides by critics eager to drive him out of the political picture, President Truman would not retreat. He was not going to resign himself to the forecasts of inevitable defeat. He had no intention of running from a fight, and the more embattled he became the more determined he was to stay the course.

Truman's mounting political troubles did not alter his conviction that he was doing the right thing and that he was doing his best. In fact, it is very likely that whatever chance there might have been that Truman would choose to retire from the demands of the presidency and not run for election was eliminated by the efforts of those who were most eager to see him make that very choice. Perhaps at no other time in Truman's life did he display more spunk than during the period from the spring of 1948 into the autumn of that year. Perhaps at no other time did he show more vividly his immense reservoir of courage and determination, as well as his appetite for a knock-down, drag-out political battle.

It can also be said that at no time did Truman display more realism. As always, he saw his circumstances for what they were. He was not going to kid himself, or let himself be misled by well-intentioned advisers about the rocky, uphill road he had made up his mind to travel. Truman was in a desperate position. He and his trusted political counselors knew it and accepted it as nothing less than that.

Truman wanted desperately to be elected President in his own right, to win on his own the office he had inherited from Roosevelt. He did not want his time in the White House to be only an interlude that was an accident of history. He wanted to prove himself and his policies and leadership, all the more so in the face of a shrill chorus of criticism. Truman was unwavering in his faith that the ordinary people of his country would endorse his efforts. To obtain the endorsement now, however, with so much going against him, called for a superhuman effort. It also called for a different approach, and a dramatic change of tactics. It required more than just guts and determination. It meant shifting gears to go for votes. Truman was willing to alter accordingly the ideological stance that had characterized his presidency up to that time.

For his three years in office before the campaign, Truman had not played the role of a liberal President. He had pursued a foreign policy that happened to please most conservatives, which is why he could win support for it from a mostly conservative Congress. But on domestic matters, Truman had been a consensus politician in search of compromise and the middle ground. As often happens in seeking compromise, no one is really satisfied. Conflicting sides have to settle for less, and are less than happy with the settlement. The postwar reconversion was marked by un-realistic expectations and unreasonable demands. It was a time of economic dislocation and disruptive transition in American life. As a result, it was inevitably a time that was unusually lacking in consensus. People were not inclined to compromise, and almost everyone was displeased at the way things were going.

There would be no percentage in stubbornly seeking compromise throughout the upcoming political campaign. For one thing, Truman believed that the democratic politi-cal system requires public combat as part of the electoral process. Truman's presidential efforts to reconcile compet-ing interests and to strike a pose above the political fray would have to be abandoned, he felt, when it came time for serious electioneering. Leading his party in combat would require it. But the main thing was that his situation now demanded it, if he was even going to have the opportunity to lead his party. He would have to fight for his own survival. He would have to do battle in his own behalf, to sell himself to his party and the people.

To do so, Truman would have to have an issue. He could not stand pat and wait for the prize to be delivered to him. The Republicans were taking this position, but Truman could not afford to. He needed instead to hoist some banner aloft. He would have to seize some viewpoint and carry it forward. It could not be foreign policy, which from the beginning he had cast as a bipartisan, national policy that was to be set apart from the arena of party politics. There was no issue he could make there. So Truman found one. He settled on the appeal his domestic legislative program had to those segments of the population most hurt by infla-tion — which happened to include large blocs of voters that had made up Roosevelt's remarkable New Deal coalition.

There was no way of reconciling the emotional offshoots represented by Wallace's Progressives and the South's conservatives. In that sense there was no way of putting Humpty Dumpty together again. But farmers, consumers generally, and the labor and ethnic vote in the cities represented potent political forces to which Truman could appeal. On their behalf he had bombarded the Republican Congress ever since it convened in January with a series of liberal legislative proposals. Truman asked for continued high price supports for farmers, public housing projects, urban redevelopment, anti-inflation legislation, national health insurance, and higher minimum wage and social security benefits, plus his civil rights program.

The legislators would have none of it. The Republican Congress instead voted overwhelmingly for a Displaced Persons Act that tended to discriminate against Catholics and Jews. It enacted the Taft-Hartley Act — intended to curb labor's power in collective bargaining — over Truman's veto and labor's charges that this was a "slave labor law." Congress simply was dead set against legislation of a New Deal nature. Truman would no sooner serve up a proposal than Congress would knock it down, water it down, or ignore it entirely. Frustrated by the Congress, the President concluded that his best bet — perhaps his only chance — was to take his domestic program to key blocs of the voting public.

His decision to make his bid in earnest on this basis came in late spring of 1948, when it became apparent to Truman that he did not need to fight for the middle ground. That is the territory that is customarily at a premium in American politics. It was Truman's natural battleground. Yet no one else seemed to want it. Wallace's communist-dominated Progressive Party was a radical fringe occupying a distant left field. The so-called Dixiecrats were an anti-civil rights splinter group based only in the Deep South and not, in

Truman's view, really representing the true feelings of the people of that region. The Republican position was to sit tight and do and say as little as possible, in the certain belief that by not rocking the boat they could expect the tide of events to bring them victory in a few brief months as a matter of course. With the center thus uncontested, Truman was obligated neither to seek it nor defend it. So he went on the offensive as a liberal.

The occasion he chose for launching this offensive was a train trip to the West Coast and back, ostensibly for the sole purpose of accepting an honorary degree from the University of California. Since Truman was not yet his party's candidate, he was not officially campaigning, and his aides billed the trip as ''nonpolitical.'' The distinction had little meaning, of course, and no effect on the nature of the trip. Truman's special train stopped for dozens of speeches en route to and from the California commencement exercises. People would flock to the railroad station and the President would speak to them from the train. In every speech, the President dredged up fears of the depression and recalled New Deal programs that struck responsive chords. There was a new fire in the speeches, many of them delivered off the cuff, and a new rapport between Truman and his audience. As news spread of Truman's scrappiness in waging his uphill fight, the crowds grew larger and more demonstrative.

It is not entirely certain whether it was by cunning or by accident that this strategy was chosen, but that does not really matter. The important thing is that Truman tried it and saw it as his salvation. The experimental June offensive was, by and large, a smashing success. The informal, small-towney, trainside style suited Truman perfectly. Some people, at least, began to sit up and take notice — among them some of the Democratic faithful that were despairing over the party's prospects.

He was by no means home free, but Harry Truman now knew not only what he had to do but how he would go about doing it. He was convinced he could make it work. As the presidential train headed back into Washington's Union Station early that summer, Truman must have done a lot of smiling to himself. At sixty-four, this veteran political warrior knew he had some new tricks.

The "professional liberals" Truman deplored turned out indeed to have underestimated him. Truman wanted the nomination and went after it. He managed in spite of everything going against him to control the nominating convention after all, and he made no bones about doing so. The Democratic leaders who opposed him were, in Truman's view, evidently not familiar with the history and procedure of political conventions. The President is in a position to control the choice of the chairman of the convention, Truman observed. No matter how many detractors there may be, the chairman controlled the organization of the convention. The convention, Truman said, will operate in the manner in which the chairman and the President want it to.

"When I had made up my mind to run, those in the party who turned against me could do nothing to prevent it," Truman said. "Presidential control of the convention is a political principle which has not been violated in political history."[5] In Truman's view, the politicians opposing his nomination were naive and foolish. Even if they nominated someone else, Truman knew that person would have to run on the President's record. This would put the party hopelessly on the defensive after having rejected the maker of that record. Truman stood by his record, and let his detractors defect. He refused to trade principle for votes by trying to appease any faction.

In the end, the "dump Truman" efforts came to naught. Members of the Americans for Democratic Action, the organization of the Democratic left wing that had spearheaded the movement to draft Ike, were unable to build up sentiment for Supreme Court Justice William O. Douglas, who also turned them down. When Georgia Senator Richard Russell failed to win the nomination, and his backers also failed to defeat the strong civil rights plank Truman wanted in the party platform, some members of the anti-Truman southern bloc walked out of the convention. These rebellious southern Democrats, officially calling themselves States Rights Democrats but more commonly known as Dixiecrats because of their regional base, met later in Birmingham and drew up their own ticket to run against Truman. Their hope was that, with the Progressive Party also in the race, they could force the presidential election into the House of Representatives by preventing either major party from winning a majority of the electoral votes. In the House, the seniority system had bestowed powerful committee chairmanships on several of these southerners, whose bargaining position would be a strong one.

The Democratic Party's vice-presidential nomination went to the Senate minority leader, Alben W. Barkley of Kentucky. A good many of the convention delegates doubtless considered it a worthless nomination, generally believing that Truman was certain to be beaten. Barkley had long wanted a vice-presidential nomination, and the dispirited gathering looked upon him as a worthy caretaker for the party in defeat — and as too old, at 70, to have political ambitions when the next election came around.

Now that the ball was his, Truman was ready to run with it. He was hell-bent on dispelling the gloom that seemed to hang over the weary, wilted delegates sweltering in Philadelphia's convention hall on the hot, humid night of July 14. It was actually after 2 A.M. of the next day when Truman, now officially nominated for President, strode

briskly to the speaker's platform to deliver his acceptance
speech.

Masterful Tactic

The picture of vitality in a crisp white linen suit, Truman
proceeded to set the tone of his presidential campaign. He
came out fighting. He was taking up where his California
train trip of the month before had left off. There was no
mistaking the style and strategy. Truman was seizing the
initiative, and serving notice that he would wage a no-
holds-barred, hell-for-leather battle.

For the faithful seeing the convention through in
Philadelphia that hour, Truman began to turn the tide of
emotion with the positive character of his opening words.
"Senator Barkley and I will win this election and make
those Republicans like it — don't you forget that!" He was
on the attack, and the effect was electric. For 20 minutes
Truman blistered the opposition with one of the toughest
speeches a presidential candidate ever made. Time and
again he brought the crowd roaring to its feet.

At the climax of his hard-hitting speech, Truman delivered the master stroke. The Republican convention had
been held earlier, producing the usual kind of political party
platform replete with promises and platitudes. The
Republican-controlled 80th Congress had adjourned for the
summer. Now Truman threw down the gauntlet in daring
fashion. He challenged the Republicans to translate their
party platform into action and announced that he would give
them just the opportunity they would need. In two weeks,
he told them, he would exercise his power as President to
call the Congress into special session. He would ask the
Republican Congress to pass laws to halt rising prices and to

meet the housing crisis — things the Republicans' platform said should be done. Truman went on down the list:

> I shall ask them to act upon other vitally needed measures, such as aid to education, which they say they are for; a national health program; civil rights legislation, which they say they are for; an increase in the minimum wage, which I doubt very much they are for; extension of the Social Security coverage and increased benefits, which they say they are for; funds for projects needed in our program to provide public power and cheap electricity.
>
> I shall ask for adequate and decent laws for displaced persons in place of this anti-Semitic, anti-Catholic law which this 80th Congress passed.
>
> Now my friends, if there is any reality behind that Republican platform, we ought to get some action from a short session of the 80th Congress. They can do this job in 15 days, if they want to do it. They will still have time to go out and run for office.[6]

Truman called it his trump card. By any description it was a masterful tactic. The expectant Republicans, having chosen Governor Thomas E. Dewey of New York and Governor Earl Warren of California to head their ticket, had been exuding confidence. The election campaign appeared to be little more than a formal prelude to inauguration. Now Truman's rousing acceptance speech put them squarely on the spot. Republican spokesmen screamed foul, squirmed, and stammered about "cheap politics." But Truman had them. The special session came and went and accomplished nothing. Its Republican leaders were awaiting what seemed to them a certain Dewey victory in November. They had no desire to give the credit for legislation to Truman that might better go to Dewey.

The fact that the Republican-controlled Congress would do nothing to enact the Republican party pledges gave Truman all the campaign ammunition he needed. It would become, in his every campaign reference, that "do-nothing" Congress.

Summoning that special session was an original, bold move that has gone down in the annals of American politics as a stroke of sheer genius. It not only showed Truman's daring, it showed his shrewdness. It had always been a fact of political life than an incumbent President was on the spot. He was in the position of having to defend his record, and the opposition was free to attack him for all the worthwhile objectives he had failed to accomplish. Truman turned the tables. It was now the President who was demanding action on behalf of the people, and blaming the opposition for not producing it. The opposition was thus in the position of having to defend itself, and Truman was free to attack. Time and time again he would denounce "that no-good, do-nothing 80th Congress."

With the Progressives having broken off in one direction and the Dixiecrats stomping way in another, the President seemed to be left as the head of a rather small army. He was nonetheless determined that it would not lack for spirited leadership and tireless effort on his part. He went straight to Washington from his acceptance speech at the nominating convention, arriving at the White House at 5:30 A.M., the time he usually got up. He went to bed at 6:00, listened to the news, slept until 9:15, ordered breakfast, and at 10:00 was in his office, from which he immediately made good on his pledge to call the special session of Congress.

Soon Truman assembled his White House aides to inject a winning spirit and provide a much-needed dose of confidence. He had sensed a mood of discouragement bordering on defeatism in comments made by staffers as they discussed details of the coming campaign. Some had suggested that the best that could be hoped for was to go down fighting.

Not so, Truman insisted, in a locker-room type of pep talk. "We are going to win," he maintained. "I expect to travel all over the country and talk at every whistle-stop.

We are going to be on the road most of the time from Labor Day to the end of the campaign. It's going to be tough on everybody, but that's the way it's got to be. I know I can take it. I'm only afraid that I'll kill some of my staff — and I like you all very much and I don't want to do that.''[7] Press Secretary Charlie Ross liked to say the election was won that day in the President's oval office. The President's boyhood chum may have overstated the case, but Truman at least was off and running with a loyal band of believers behind him.

Ironically, both Truman's rival candidates from out of Democratic Party ranks quite inadvertently gave the President's credibility a healthy boost long before the campaign's stretch run began. The first came from Senator Strom Thurmond, the Dixiecrats' candidate for President, who was asked why he had broken with the Democrats over Truman's civil rights stand. Had not President Roosevelt campaigned with similar promises of justice and equal opportunity for America's black citizens? That was so, Thurmond agreed grimly, ''But Truman really means it.''

The other unexpected — and equally unintentional — break for Truman came when the Progressive Party convened its nominating convention. It got the full light of national publicity right after the Democrats left Philadelphia. Truman was again fully absorbed in Washington with the rigors and responsibilities of the presidency. He was, in fact, standing firm in the test of iron wills over the Berlin Blockade. At this moment Henry Wallace, apparently believing there was a rich vein of votes in being pro-Soviet, devoted his acceptance speech to the theme that America should abandon Berlin if this would please the Russians. This astonishing approach prompted one political columnist present to dub Wallace ''Old Bubblehead.'' To most Americans it was an apt description. There could scarcely have been a more striking contrast. On the one hand, there was Wallace's fuzzy-minded maneuver. On the other, there was the President's strong posture in facing an international challenge of unprecedented implications. Truman's foes were discrediting themselves even as he began scoring blows of his own.

By the end of July, Truman got another lift. Arriving in New York for a speech, he received a warm reception headed by Mayor O'Dwyer. That was a first. Always before, Truman's appearance in the city would find O'Dwyer sick, out of town, or too busy to be on hand. Welcoming him in such friendly fashion now, as Truman the party's candidate, struck the President as a particularly good sign because he had New York's mayor pegged as "a bandwagon boy."[8] The greeting indicated that the party was closing ranks. For Truman, it was encouraging evidence that he was getting somewhere in dispelling some of the Democrats' defeatism.

Republican Overconfidence

One could also count as help coming from unexpected quarters the arrogance that the Republicans displayed. If a single word described Truman's major opposition, "smug" was the word. The Republicans were going once again with Governor Dewey, aptly characterized during his earlier campaign for the presidency in 1944 as resembling the plastic groom on a wedding cake. The description applied equally well in 1948. He seemed stiff and completely lacking in personality. Repeatedly assured by opinion pollsters, his campaign strategists, and the press that he was a sure winner, Dewey conducted an aloof campaign that avoided issues. He was cold and distant with reporters. His contacts with the public always came off as forced and contrived. There seemed to him and his advisers to be every reason for Truman to lose and thus no reason why the Republicans should not expect to win.

From Labor Day on, Truman was campaigning with a vengeance, blaming the Republicans for nearly all the ills of mankind. In the meantime Dewey, in what now seems an almost comic contrast, exuded supreme confidence. It was not merely that Dewey miscalculated by never ceasing to believe that his victory was inevitable. He grew increasingly arrogant about it. He acted as if he were perfectly justified in being impatient with Truman for taking up precious time until the rightful occupant was in the White House. Dewey seemed genuinely annoyed by the President's conduct of the country's business, but not necessarily because of differences with Truman over a particular issue. Rather it was as if Dewey was upset that Truman was bothering to tend to the nation's affairs at all. It was as if it were somehow quite improper for Truman to be doing this when everyone knew that he, Dewey, should be. Truman, for example, was attempting to negotiate with the Soviets during the Berlin blockade. This prompted Dewey to complain bitterly, with unmitigated gall, that Truman ought to keep his hands off foreign affairs so as not to disturb things in the few months he had left in office.

Dewey was not alone, of course, in his belief that the outcome of the election was a foregone conclusion. Almost everybody thought so. Some pollsters became so sure of it that they simply decided not to take any more polls. When Dewey appeared during the campaign, bands often would play "Hail to the Chief," music reserved for the President alone. It must have begun to rub some people the wrong way. At the least, it helped make Truman's down-to-earth approach a welcome, refreshing change of style.

The spontaneous, personal touch that came so naturally to Truman was something that Dewey could never bring off. Truman could usually toss in a local reference or a personal observation wherever he went. In Clarksburg, West Virginia, for instance, he mentioned that, as a student of the War Between the States, he always had a warm spot in his heart for Clarksburg as the birthplace of Stonewall Jackson. In Hammond, Indiana, he recalled the production there of many tanks for the war effort and told his listeners that American soldiers all over the world were grateful for the high quality of their work. In Iowa, Truman won over many farm votes by relating how, behind a team of Missouri mules, he used to "sow a 160-acre wheatfield without a skip place showing in it." He could plow a straight furrow, he said, and a prejudiced witness would vouch for it — "my mother."[9]

Governor Warren, Dewey's running mate, was so bothered by the meaningless pap he was required to dispense that he complained to Dewey's campaign strategists of being bored to death with his own speeches. It was no use. "Don't rock the boat," they told him. "We've got this election won, so don't try to change the strategy."[10] Warren dutifully complied. Dewey stiffly and impatiently went through his campaign motions. They were merely marking time. Dewey obviously viewed the campaign with an air of boredom. To him it was strictly a formality, and in fact an exasperating waste of time.

Giving 'em Hell

The "little" man from Missouri was, in the meantime, using his time to the fullest. He stuck with his whistle-stop campaign, so named because it featured appearances in so many small towns, including places too small to be a regular railroad stop. Only when a signal was set would a train stop in such a spot, and the engineer would toot the train whistle to call attention to the arrival. The campaign bore some similarities to that ragtag race Truman ran in Missouri in 1940 to be sent back to the Senate. He put his presidential bid together with much the same quality of cut and paste and sheer bravado, which may be why he knew all along that it could be done.

The long trek had its discouraging moments. The campaign reportedly came close to folding one night late in September, when the railroad refused to move the "Truman Special" out of the Oklahoma City station until overdue charges were paid. Only a hasty passing of the hat among some oil-rich Oklahoma Democrats — Oklahoma's governor, Roy Turner, was chairman of the national Truman-Barkley Club — averted a humiliating disaster. Then, two weeks later, *Newsweek* magazine published a high-powered poll in which 50 leading political writers from around the nation predicted unanimously — *unanimously* — that Dewey would be President. It was Dewey 50, Truman zero. But Truman was undaunted. He took a deep breath, squared his shoulders, and kept going strong.

Firmly believing that his was a crusade for the common man, Truman chose his homespun, hard-hitting rhetoric accordingly. While Dewey droned his polished generalities, virtually ignoring his opponent, Truman fired away with both barrels, straight from the shoulder. Everywhere he went he left the impression of the game underdog, and Dewey unwittingly was helping him create it. Dewey's well-paced, efficient, carefully arranged appearances went off like clockwork. Truman's whistle-stop campaign went from dawn to dusk, and seemed to be a helter-skelter struggle all the way. While Dewey behaved as if he had it in the bag, Truman was playing catch-up with furious effort.

The President's campaign followed a formula that varied little from day to day. It began with his train picking up a clutch of local politicians usually featuring the governor, senators, and a congressman or two — if they happened to be Democrats — or the Democratic candidates for these and other major offices. There would also be the state and local party chairmen and a few important contributors to the campaign coffers. Some of them might stay aboard throughout the day. They would go along to introduce the President at various stops, or just to be seen with the country's "first family" and to gain whatever advantage might come from being in the presidential presence. Usually there was an outdoor rally or two or a major speech each day, complete with a motorcade to transport the President's party from the train and back. Then the "Truman Special" would roll across the countryside again, pausing at station after station where waiting crowds had assembled.

Men, women, and children would surge close to the observation platform on the rear car of the train, and there were always a few who had climbed onto nearby rooftops or signal towers. A school or community band would struggle through the "Missouri Waltz." For the rest of his life, "Missouri Waltz" was invariably played when Truman appeared, and someone always suggested that he play it whenever a piano was available, as if it were his theme song. Much later Truman would confess that he had never liked the song; with its incalculable repetition, he doubtless came to hate it. For Truman it was one of those prices a politician has to pay — over and over. To cheers and applause the beaming, unpretentious President would appear after the local introduction, make his remarks tied to that particular locale, and launch into his broadsides at the opposition.

The usual theme was that the Republicans running the Congress were turning a deaf ear to the voice of the people. The Republican villains instead did the bidding of the "bloodsuckers of Wall Street" who financed them and from whom only the "special interests" were benefitting. Truman appealed for help from his listeners in order to put things right; only with their votes would he be able to stand up for their interests.

It was said to have been in Albuquerque, New Mexico, that the incident occurred that gave Truman's campaign its enduring label. As the President warmed to his subject, lighting into the Republican Congress for refusing to pass his legislation, a listener suddenly yelled out, "Lay it on, Harry! Give 'em hell!" Truman shot back, "I will! I intend to!" The shout of "give 'em hell" became a battle cry repeated wherever the "Truman Special" went.

At each of the train's frequent stops, the President would deliver still another plain-talking, hard-hitting speech. "And now," he would say when it ended, "I want you to meet the boss." Truman would turn to the doorway of the car and proudly lead his wife out onto the rear platform beside him. As the plump and motherly Bess acknowledged the applause with a smile and a wave, Truman would announce, "And here's the one who bosses her!" That would bring out his daughter Margaret, then a radiant 24 years old, usually carrying a bouquet of roses as she stepped out to join her parents and always drawing a loud response that included a few wolf whistles. As Margaret threw a rose or two to the crowd, the President would reach over the railing to clasp as many outstretched hands as he could. The train whistle sounded, the band struck up another number, and the "Truman Special" began to pull slowly away. The entire event would not have lasted longer than 20 minutes, but it would have made a red-letter day for the memory book of Wenatchee, Washington; Dexter, Iowa, or Kearney, Nebraska.

These whistle-stop appearances, the heart of his campaign, were repeated time and again across the land as Truman went to the people in an unprecedented political odyssey. There were no coast-to-coast television extravaganzas; television was only in its infancy and there was not enough money to use it in the campaign anyway. Not many of Truman's campaign speeches were even broadcast on radio. His approach was coast-to-coast travel, meeting the people where they lived, looking them in the eye, and talking to them in language he — and they — understood. No big productions, no fancy speeches from prepared texts. Truman gave it to them straight, and invited questions. A lot of it was corny, but it was working.

At first, the President's audiences had been attentive but generally undemonstrative. Now the crowds began to grow, in size and friendliness. Throughout the month of October, the "Truman Special" pulled into town after town, the President kept plugging away, and the crucial momentum began to build. When corn prices dropped sharply just a few weeks before the election, Truman quickly blamed the opposition. The Republicans, he said, had stuck a pitchfork in the farmer's back. Truman was singling out farmers and workers especially, telling them that if they did not do their duty by the Democratic Party, they were the most ungrateful people in the world.

As a matter of good party politics, a couple of key Democrats did join efforts with the President — Chicago Democratic boss Jake Arvey and Walter Reuther, head of the United Auto Workers. Labor unions did not back Truman enthusiastically, laregly because they shared the widespread belief that he was going to lose. They did work hard, however, to elect pro-labor Democratic senators and congressmen, and getting out the labor vote worked to Truman's benefit as the head of the ticket. By throwing the Chicago organization into the election battle, Arvey helped Truman carry Illinois.

Needing all the allies he could muster, Truman welcomed assistance. He was getting even more help from his running mate. The 70-year-old Barkley campaigned energetically, making 250 speeches in 36 states. But nothing in the incredible, come-from-behind campaign was as remarkable as Truman's own efforts. Counting his June trip to the West Coast before the convention, Truman by Election Day had covered nearly 32,000 miles by train and made an astounding total of 355 speeches. After Labor Day, his major campaign trips included a second swing to the West Coast in September, a journey through the Midwest in mid-October, and a final, Sunday-punch tour through the industrial North in the last week of October. In the two months from Labor Day to Election Day, Truman delivered 278 speeches.

Through it all, Truman never faltered, seeming to draw fresh energy from the direct and jovial give-and-take he established with the people along the way. He gave as many as 16 speeches in a day. He began to draw some amazing turnouts, but still they were explained away, even by reporters traveling with the "Truman Special" as indicating nothing more than curiosity about seeing the President. As the election date drew near, the mild response to Truman had given way to the cheering of large, enthusiastic throngs.

Eleventh-Hour Triumph

Five nights before the election, the President addressed a crowd of 16,000 in New York's Madison Square Garden. The state's Democrats having despaired of Truman's chances, it was left to the Liberal Party — a labor-led group that voted Democratic in national elections — to pitch in and rent the Garden. It was a climactic bid for the state that then had the largest package of electoral votes, but it fell short. Truman would lose New York State to Dewey, largely because 509,559 New York City voters would cast their ballots for Wallace's Progressives. As a result, Dewey was going to squeak by in his home state by some 61,000 votes.

Truman brought his exhaustive campaign trail to an end by heading home to Missouri. The day after a tumultuous rally in St. Louis, the President on election eve made only two more speeches — one in Kansas City and a final radio appeal to the nation broadcast from the living room of his home in Independence. In the meantime, Dewey was taking a special train back to New York. In a rare instance of informal contact with reporters, he strolled back to the press car to discuss some of the men he intended to name to his cabinet. He talked confidently and casually of plans for a post-victory holiday to make preparations for the new administration.

Darkness settled as Election Day drew to a close on November 2, 1948, with poor Dewey still believing — with plenty of high-powered company — that his victory was assured. Truman, seeming to be the solitary exception to that belief, stepped out of the voting booth early in the day in Independence, and cheerfully told waiting reporters that he expected to win — a prediction that brought gales of laughter.

That afternoon, Truman slipped away with the two men who headed his Secret Service detail. They drove with him to the Elms Hotel at Excelsior Springs, Missouri, a resort about 30 miles northeast of Kansas City, where he could hope to get a good night's sleep. The President took a Turkish bath, ate a ham sandwich, and drank a glass of milk. After listening to some early election returns on the radio, he did go to sleep — as astonishing as that seems, with his furture hanging on the reports that were now coming in from throughout the nation. Truman was never behind, but it seemed incredible that he could hold his lead through the night — incredible, evidently, to everyone but him. He was said to be irked at being awakened around midnight to be told of a late bulletin. The President stayed awake long enough, though, to listen to a leading radio commentator, H. V. Kaltenborn — whom Truman delighted in mimicking for years afterward — give his famous analysis that the President was running ahead only because most of the returns were from cities. When the returns came in from the country, the national radio audience was assured, the results would show Dewey winning overwhelmingly.

It was this stubborn disbelief that Truman's stunning lead would hold up that led the *Chicago Daily Tribune* to print the first edition of its newspaper for the day after the election with the banner headline that proclaimed: "DEWEY DEFEATS TRUMAN."

The President was not irked when he was awakened again. It was 4 A.M. this time, and the news was that he was leading by 2,000,000 votes. Although Kaltenborn was still saying in his broadcast at that hour that he didn't see how Truman could be elected, the President knew the outcome was clear. Late vote-counting at last gave California and Ohio, where the returns had fluctuated through the night, to Truman, assuring his election. He told his two Secret Service companions they had all better be going back now, because it looked as if he was in for another four years. The President arrived with them in Kansas City at six o'clock on Wednesday morning to join a celebration by his campaign staff. At 10:30, Dewey conceded that Truman had won.

The final figures showed the President polling 24,105,695 votes to Dewey's 21,969,170. Despite the Dixiecrats, who took away four southern states, and the Progressives, who cost him New York, Truman carried 28 states to 16 for Dewey. The President carried the country's 13 largest cities, and the seven large agricultural states of California, Illinois, Iowa, Minnesota, Missouri, Texas and Wisconsin. Truman's majority in the electoral college ended up being a one-sided total of 303, to 189 for Dewey, and 39 for Thurmond.

It was a triumphant return to Washington for the "Truman Special," renamed the "Victory Special" for the trip back to the nation's capital. En route, Truman enjoyed an immense demonstration in the railroad station at St. Louis, where he was given a copy of the now-famous *Chicago Daily Tribune* with the headline prematurely announcing his political demise. "That's one for the books," he grinned, holding the newspaper up for all to see. In Washington, an unprecedented crush of people estimated to number more than three-quarters of a million jammed Union Station and the streets to the White House upon Truman's return.

The shock wave of Truman's unbelievable upset was followed immediately by the spectacle of a stampede to make excuses or make amends. Before Truman was back at his desk in the Oval Office he was being besieged by johnnie-come-lately backers, all too eager to say, "Gee, Mr. President, we were with ya all the way!" There was a flood of back-dated campaign contributions. There were many sheepish figures — in leading party and even cabinet positions — that were notably absent or silent during the campaign who now were saying how glad they were that "we" won.

Truman could not fail to notice, as his motorcade passed the cheering throngs on Pennsylvania Avenue, the huge sign draped on the front of the *Washington Post* building which said, "Mr. President, we are ready to eat crow whenever you are ready to serve it." The President had no such menu in mind, for the press or anyone else. For the pollsters and other "experts," the 1948 election was a huge goof from which they would not soon regain respectability. Truman couldn't resist a joking reference from time to time about Kaltenborn, the *Chicago Daily Tribune*, and similar forecasts, but he did not rub it in. There were many who had discredited themselves so openly that neither they nor the public needed to be reminded.

The President probably felt some satisfaction in having held Dewey to a smaller proportion of the total vote than Dewey received in running against Roosevelt. Certainly there was a fulfillment for Truman in having won the presidency on his own. But he was not one to gloat. The fact that only now was there a crowd on the bandwagon did not cause him to bear grudges or be vindictive. He felt he had gone to the grass roots. He had given the voters a clear view of the choice they were free to make, and they had made that choice.

The people wanted him to keep on being President; it was as simple as that. He had a job to do, and he'd best get on with it. His only mixed feelings had to do with what was now guaranteed for him and his family for the next four years — the unique demands and restrictions that life in the White House imposes. Upon his return that triumphant day in November, Truman referred privately to being back in the "great white jail."

VI The "Loss" of China

The glow of electoral triumph can dim quickly in the policy arena of a democracy. The brilliance of his miraculous victory did not stay with President Truman for long. Ironically, it really was not a falling out over his program for America that took the luster from the later years of his presidency. Nothing tarnished the grand design that was taking shape in Western Europe. The clouds formed instead from America's involvement in Asia. By the end of Truman's full term as an elected President, disillusionment and recrimination would cast a shadow over his accomplishments. This all began with the so-called "loss" of China — Truman's failure somehow to keep China from going communist.

If it had not been for China, the U.S. might have resisted a direct, active role aimed at influencing developments in Asia after Japan's defeat in World War II. With all that was going on in Europe and the eastern Mediterranean, the U.S. would have had its hands full enough in Asia occupying Japan and helping the Philippines and other war-torn Pacific territories get to their feet. But America already was very much a part of what was happening in China, and could not neatly separate itself from it. Since one cannot lose something that one does not have, America could not have kept a China it never controlled in the first place. But no matter that it was beyond the capability of Truman or anyone or any country to control what happened in China. The fact is that Truman, no matter how unjustly, was to suffer for it. It became the turning point in his presidency.

What happened in China would have much to do with Truman's reaction to later developments in Korea. The frustration that grew out of America's inability to deal satisfactorily with the chain of events in China would grow into a deeper frustration over America's involvement in Korea. These far-reaching events in Asia ultimately would turn the tide of public sentiment against Truman. They made his policy record vulnerable where it had always been strongest — in his foreign policy that defended the interests of the Free World.

The "loss" of China, seen by many as a conspicuous blemish on Truman's record of containing communist expansion, would be turned into an open wound by unscrupulous political foes who charged that something sinister must be behind it. The "loss" would crack the political armor of the President's otherwise carefully constructed, bipartisan foreign policy, and his opponents would exploit that opening to the fullest. By the time his term expired, the fruit of tragic events in Asia would sour Truman's White House tenure as surely as they would later destroy the presidencies of Lyndon Johnson and Richard Nixon.

China's central government was that of the Kuomintang, or Nationalist, Party headed by Generalissimo Chiang Kai-shek. With help from the Soviet Union, Chiang in the 1920's had militarized the Kuomintang and imposed at least a loose unity on the vast Chinese nation. The Kuomintang broke with the Communists in 1927, however, and from that time on had faced a challenge for authority in China from the Chinese Communist Party headed by Mao Tse-tung. A decade of disunity and unrest had left China weak and vulnerable when the Japanese invaded in 1937.

Japan's military forces moved into China with such ease that it was apparent the Chinese could not indefinitely resist conquest alone. The outbreak of war in Europe after September of 1939, however, made it unlikely that any European powers that might be friendly to China could spare arms and other assistance. China's government approached the U.S., which granted loans for purchasing civilian supplies and, in 1941, gave some Lend-Lease aid. When Japan attacked Pearl Harbor and the U.S. entered the war, it became vital to U.S. strategy to fight with China. Together they could at least tie down Japanese forces on a second front while the American island-hopping campaign took place in the Pacific. China suddenly became a major American ally and a major theater in the far-flung conflict with Japan.

The war against Japan did not, however, diminish the hostility between Chiang's Kuomintang and the peasant army commanded by Mao and operating from Chinese territory controlled by the Communists. It became increasingly apparent to the U.S., in fact, that the rival Chinese leaders were as concerned with their own struggle as they were with waging war against the Japanese.

U.S. activities in China during World War II were directed toward the defeat of Japanese military forces there. U.S. policy was to promote a coordinated military effort by China's opposing political factions so the combined power of Chinese arms could be brought to bear upon the common enemy, Japan. This objective was never realized, however, and a combined war effort by the U.S. and China never fully materialized. Relations between the two countries were colored by the same internal Chinese political complications that hamstrung the conduct of the fighting and rendered ineffective the China theater of operations. The U.S. was inextricably involved in these complications because of its predominant role in the war against Japan. Throughout the war, the American government followed in its political involvement with China what seemed to be the only reasonable course. In the interests of a successful war effort and postwar peace and stability, the U.S. tried to convert China's central government into one representing a peaceful union of China's feuding political factions.

Then the sudden surrender of Japan caught the U.S. by surprise. Orders were hastily issued to halt the movement of American forces from Europe to East Asia, and to disperse the vast expeditionary force which had been gathering for the expected invasion of Japan. With equal haste, the U.S. had to confront an increasingly chaotic situation in China. Whatever interlude Japan's eight-year occupation of Chinese territory had provided in China's civil conflict, the Kuomintang-Communist power struggle flared with renewed vigor with Japan's defeat.

No sooner had Japan announced its surrender than Chiang Kai-shek demanded greater and prolonged American assistance. The Nationalist government would need the aid in order to disarm Japanese forces still in China and to seize control over northern China and Manchuria, the scene both of Japanese military concentrations and the ambitions of the Chinese Communists. America was faced with the perplexing prospect of virtually assuring a divided China if assistance was refused. Yet there was no assurance that if America gave what Chiang asked that there would be an end to its involvement.

The situation was further complicated by the clamor immediately raised in the U.S. to bring America's fighting men home. Congress was deluged with baby shoes attached to postcards that read, "I want my daddy back." It was an organized campaign that an investigation later found was communist-inspired. But the fact was that the American military organization was fast dissolving, its forces being demobilized and headed homeward as fast as possible. It did not seem realistic, in this ebb tide of America's military effort, to contemplate any course of action in China which might require the active employment of substantial American forces for an indefinite period of time. Few indeed were the people who should have spoken up for prolonging military service in order to try to affect the outcome of the struggle in China, or even to prevent the extension of Soviet control in Manchuria.

Postwar Dilemma

China, of course, was only one of a host of complex and critical situations Truman was facing in his first few months after assuming the presidency. He saw nevertheless that the problem of communism in China differed from political problems elsewhere. The Nationalist government was confronted not by a militant and scattered minority, but by a rival government controlling approximately a quarter of the country's population, within a definite portion of its territory. Because nearly 3,000,000 Japanese — over 1,000,000 of them military personnel — remained in China at war's end, Truman felt there really was little choice as to the course the U.S. could pursue. His advisers expressed fear that, even in defeat, the Japanese might be able to control China because of their ability to tip the scales in China's internal contest for power. The U.S. could leave the Chinese open to the possibility, and wash its own hands of the situation. It could, by throwing huge resources and a vast number of American troops into China, move by force to eliminate the Japanese from the mainland and compel the withdrawal of the Soviet Union from Manchuria. Truman did not regard either of these alternatives as practicable. He did not believe the U.S., given the circumstances, could turn its back on China's appeals. Truman would not permit — nor would the American public have been likely to permit — a massive commitment of American men and resources. The President therefore decided the U.S. could best contribute to peace in China by supporting Chiang's Nationalists politically, economically, and, within limits, militarily.

Within 48 hours of the Japanese surrender, civil war was raging in China, and the U.S., long entangled as arbiter of the dispute between China's two contending parties, was now caught up in the impossible task of trying to support the government of Chiang Kai-shek and at the same time to avoid deeper involvement in Chinese internal affairs. The one precluded the other. Attempts at arbitration having come to naught, the U.S. could act only as a partisan — however reluctantly — and try to save Chiang Kai-shek. Moscow took up the cause of the Chinese Communists, giving them the support that probably turned the tide in China's civil war.

American China policy was briefly brought into focus when in November, 1945, Patrick Hurley — whom Roosevelt had sent as ambassador to China — announced his resignation from that post. To Truman's surprise, Hurley charged that the President and secretary of state had failed to make public the intents and purposes of their China policy. Hurley's outburst undoubtedly reflected his years of frustration over the lack of improvement in conditions in China. Nonetheless, the dissatisfaction he expressed prompted an inquiry by the Senate Foreign Relations Committee.

Hurley made clear in appearing before the committee that he did not regard the Chinese Communists as a part of an international communist movement. At a Foreign Relations Committee hearing on December 6, 1945 — ten days after his resignation — Hurley asked the senators to distinguish between the Chinese Communists and the Soviets. Not only did Hurley emphasize that the two were different, he said that in his opinion Russia did not recognize the Chinese Communists as Communists at all, that Russia was not supporting them, and that Russia did not desire civil war in China.[1] The solution seemed to lie in getting the Nationalists and Communists to come to terms and get together. Sharing the view that some such accommodation among the feuding Chinese appeared to be the only way out was the U.S. Commander of the China Theater, General Albert Wedemeyer. In a report sent to Washington in November, 1945, Wedemeyer said Chiang Kai-shek would be unable to stabilize the situation in China for months or even years without a satisfactory settlement with the Communists, but that such an understanding seemed remote.[2]

Secretary of State Byrnes spoke to clarify the subject on the day after Hurley expressed his views to the Senate committee. According to Byrnes, the long-range goal of American China policy was simply an extension of that pursued during the war: the development of a strong, united, and democratic China. As to how this was to be achieved, Brynes merely urged the dissident elements in China to be willing to compromise in order to settle their differences. He said Chiang Kai-shek's government offered the most satisfactory base for democratic government in China, but that it should be broadened to include representatives of many large groups in China which had no voice in their government.

The Senate Foreign Relations Committee, after Byrnes promised to review the management of China policy by the State Department, voted to discontinue the hearing and dispense with a report. This was all there was to the raising of the China issue. It called attention to America's dilemma there, and Truman decided to launch a major diplomatic initiative to resolve it. To carry out the initiative, the President appointed George Marshall, who at the time had just retired as General of the Army and Chief of Staff, to be his special representative in China, with ambassadorial rank.

Truman directed Marshall, as his personal emissary, to use America's influence — on the scene — to help unify China through peaceful, democratic methods. Specifically, Truman on December 15, 1945, urged that a national conference of major Chinese political units be convened in China. Its purpose would be to broach a solution that would end the civil strife and unify China in a manner which would provide fair representation for the main political elements. The President promised American assistance in rebuilding the Chinese economy, but promised also that there would be no American military intervention.

Marshall was to go to China and do whatever could be done — by encouragement, mediation, and negotiation — to achieve unity by settling peacefully the disputes between China's Communists and Nationalists. The President, with these instructions, sent Marshall on his mission and virtually turned over to Marshall the conduct of American China policy. In so doing, however, the President emphasized that the detailed steps to peace and political unity in China would have to be worked out by the Chinese themselves.

The degree to which Truman delegated full authority to Marshall is revealed by letters the President sent to heads of departments and agencies whose officials might be dealing in China with representatives of the Chinese government. The recipients included the secretaries of commerce, the treasury, agriculture, and interior; and the chairman of the board of the Export-Import Bank. In the letters, dated December 18, 1945, Truman stressed the fact that he had authorized Marshall to inform Chiang Kai-shek and other Chinese leaders that a China disunited and torn by civil strife could not be considered realistically as a proper place for American assistance. Truman also said he wanted all conversations with Chinese officials regarding economic or financial aid suspended. No member of the staffs of any

American agency was to engage in talks with Chinese
officials which might encourage the Chinese to hope that
the U.S. was contemplating the extension of any type of
assistance except in accordance with the recommendations
of General Marshall.[3]

Marshall immediately set to work to secure a cessation of
hostilities. At his urging, a committee composed of one
representative each from the National government and the
Chinese Communist Party, with Marshall as chairman, was
convened on January 7, 1946. Despite obvious distrust
between the two Chinese groups, Marshall succeeded in
persuading them to sign a cease-fire agreement. The next
month, they agreed to a plan for reorganizing China's
armed forces and integrating communist units into the National Army. In March, an executive headquarters was
established — including Chinese Nationalist, Chinese
Communist, and American personnel — to plan and super-
vise the execution of the military unification plan.

On March 11, 1946, some three months after the mission
began, Truman recalled Marshall for further consultation.
Marshall reported on the efforts being made toward peace
and unity. In his view, their success depended on the
rehabilitation of China and a general improvement in
economic conditions. He believed American economic assistance would be necessary to help this process along.
Truman agreed, but the efforts toward peace and unity to
which Marshall referred were soon rent asunder. As he
returned to China in mid-April, the Chinese Communists
violated the cease-fire agreement by attacking and seizing
the city of Changchun, Manchuria. It was the first of many
incidents of bad faith from both sides which dashed
Marshall's hopes and eventually caused his mission to end
in frustration.

Almost as if it were trying to enhance the Communists'
claims to be bringing democratic reforms, China's

Nationalist government was ruling by terror. With dictatorial efficiency, Chinese liberals and democrats were killed, imprisoned, or silenced out of fear. Newspapers were suppressed; intellectuals and those the Kuomintang labelled as "thinkers" were registered by government police and required to carry special identification cards. Corruption was rampant in Kuomintang officialdom. Coupled with ruthless rule it contributed, along with communist battle successes and propaganda appeals, to growing demoralization in the Nationalist ranks. Defections from its forces became widespread. Meanwhile the communist forces being equipped by the Soviets increased in number and effectiveness, and steadily gained both territory and popular acceptance.

Truman Losing Patience

His patience growing thin, Truman sent a strongly worded message to Chiang Kai-shek in August of 1946. The President expressed concern with the "rapidly deteriorating political situation in China." Truman told Chiang that, "while it is the continued hope of the United States that an influential and democratic China can still be achieved under your leadership, I would be less than honest if I did not point out that latest developments have forced me to the conclusion that the selfish interests of extremist elements, both in the Kuomintang and the Communist Party, are obstructing the aspirations of the people of China."[4]

Truman also told Chiang of growing sentiment in Washington for a review of American China policy in the light of increasing strife in China, especially the spreading suppression by Chiang's government of democratic views and of freedom of the press. The President cited in particular recent assassinations of distinguished Chinese liberals, which, he said, had "not been ignored" by the United States. "Regardless of where responsibility may lie for these cruel murders," said Truman, "there is increasing belief that an attempt is being made to resort to force, military or secret police rather than democratic processes to settle major social issues." Truman closed by candidly advising Chaing Kai-shek not to expect American opinion to "continue in its generous attitude toward your nation unless convincing proof is shortly forthcoming that genuine progress is being made toward a peaceful settlement of China's internal problems."[5]

In a bland reply, Chiang could only blame all China's ills on the Communists. This and the continued lack of progress toward a peaceful settlement in China prompted President Truman to send another message to Chiang in which he stated tersely his hope that it would be feasible to provide further U.S. aid for Chinese industry and agriculture. Such a feasibility, he made clear, was contingent upon a prompt removal of the threat of civil war.

Although China was on the brink of economic collapse, Chiang Kai-shek continued to wage war on a constantly expanding scale throughout the fall of 1946. Military operations were negating proposals for peace talks, and were consuming some 70 percent of the Nationalist government's budget at the same time Marshall was being pressured to recommend large loans from the U.S. Marshall emphatically told one senior Chinese official urging more American aid that it was useless to expect the U.S. to pour money into the vacuum being created by the determination of Chinese military leaders to settle matters by force. Marshall also said it was useless to expect America to contribute a steady flow of money to a government dominated by a completely reactionary clique bent on exclusive control of political power. When another

Chinese official questioned the rejection of certain loan requests by the Export-Import Bank, Marshall indicated that the open corruption of the National government, as well as its military policy, had influenced the decision.[6]

In a conference with Marshall on December 1, 1946, Chiang discounted any dangers of economic collapse and said he was confident the communist forces could be destroyed in eight to ten months. Marshall at this point firmly replied that a group as large as the Chinese Communists could not be ignored, and that the Kuomintang was not capable of destroying them before being confronted with a complete economic collapse.

The intransigence of both the Kuomintang and the Chinese Communists had brought the Marshall mission to an impasse. Marshall concluded that the Nationalists sought American mediation merely as a shield for military campaigns. He concluded that the Communists were no longer interested in mediation; they wanted only to avoid being blamed for rejecting it. Unwilling to let himself be used by either side or to serve as a battlefield umpire, Marshall felt it was futile to continue his efforts. The Chinese themselves, of their own volition, would have to take the steps he had tried to take.

In a statement issued on December 18, 1946, President Truman reaffirmed U.S. China policy as he had set it forth a year earlier. After reviewing the course of events in China, he said the U.S. still believed in the importance of a united and democratic China, and that China would come nearer realizing this goal if the base of the Chinese Nationalist government were broadened to make it representative of the Chinese people. Truman also restated the view that peace and stability in China required putting an end to armed conflict, which the Chinese themselves must decide to do. He said the U.S. intended to continue to help the Chinese people bring about peace and economic recovery, but again stressed his determination to avoid U.S. involvement in China's civil war.[7]

On January 6, 1947, Truman announced the recall of Marshall and the end of American mediation in China. This was followed by a frank public statement by Marshall of the personal impressions he had gained on the scene. In it, he cited the almost overwhelming suspicion with which the Nationalists and the Communists viewed each other as the chief obstacle to peace in China. Other factors he blamed for obstructing negotiations included the unyielding opposition of a dominant group of reactionaries in the Kuomintang, "dyed-in-the-wool Communists" who were willing to wreck China's economy to facilitate the government's collapse, and the dominant influence of the military. The next day, Truman nominated Marshall as secretary of state. Soon after he was in that office, the U.S. announced the withdrawal of American personnel from the executive headquarters Marshall had created in China, and the return of American Marines stationed in the northern part of that country.

Confronted after World War II ended with nothing but undesirable alternatives in China, Truman had decided on the Marshall mission as the best approach he could take. Doing nothing would only perpetuate the bloodshed. Trying to enforce a cease-fire with American military forces was out of the question, but Truman was anxious to do what could be done to encourage peace and stability. The Marshall mission was his answer. Marshall had given it his best. He had brought the opposing sides together, and set up conferences and other mechanisms for building cooperation. He had done everything constructive that he could manage to do. Even as he did, the conditions grew worse, the suffering went on, and armed conflict continued, yet neither side would budge.

No sooner had Marshall left China than the civil war spread and grew even more intense. Having become secretary of state, Marshall recommended avoiding commitments that might involve the U.S. more deeply. Truman agreed. It was better, the President believed, to let the "dust settle," to wait and see what would happen.

In the meantime, the situation was closely followed. The U.S. ambassador in China continued to relay to Chiang Kai-shek Washington's warnings about the seriousness of his difficulties and advice regarding corrective measures. The Truman administration was perturbed about the economic deterioration that continued unabated in China as hostilities spread. But the President shared with his secretary of state the belief that, in the final analysis, the fundamental and lasting solution of China's problems would have to come from the Chinese themselves. The U.S. could not initiate and carry out the solution of those problems. That much was confirmed by the Marshall mission. The U.S. could only assist as conditions developed which game some beneficial results. Unfortunately, no such promising turn would appear.

The circumstances in China which worried the administration most were the persistent signs of spiritual bankruptcy. The Nationalist leaders seemed psychologically dependent on outside aid as the only means of meeting China's problems. They showed little awareness of the realities of the situation, and of the critical need to adopt measures for self-help. China's Nationalist government appeared incapable of acting, or unwilling to act, to alleviate the pressing problems that surrounded it.

In the summer of 1947, the President sent General Wedemeyer, the former commander of the China Theater, on a fact-finding mission to China. Truman had Wedemeyer appraise the current and projected political, economic, psychological, and military situation.

Wedemeyer reported that he had found apathy, lethargy, and "abject defeatism" in many quarters. According to Wedemeyer, China possessed most of the physical resources needed for its own recovery. What China needed was inspirational leadership and a resurgence of spirit that could come only from within. It could not be ordered up in Washington and shipped from America's shores. It was the general's opinion that the Nationalists still could gain the confidence of the Chinese people by rooting out corrupt and incompetent officials and by immediately effecting far-reaching reforms. Military force in itself, Wedemeyer warned, would not eliminate communism. Promises of reform would no longer suffice. The government could save itself only through performance.[8]

Wedemeyer submitted a confidential report to the President, which stirred some controversy because it was not published at the time. Its contents, however, differed little from Marshall's analysis of the China situation, or from the reports made by the American Embassy. It was not published chiefly because it contained a suggestion that the UN immediately put Manchuria under a trusteeship, or guardianship of five powers that would include the Soviet Union. Truman deemed it inadvisable to make public a recommendation that would be highly offensive to the Chinese as an infringement on their sovereignty. Moreover, such a suggestion would surely be rejected by China, since it would provide for a partial alienation of Chinese territory. The President and the secretary of state considered it an impractical proposal. They also thought the future of the UN, confronted with other immediate and serious problems, would be jeopardized if such a burden were to be placed upon it. Wedemeyer did urge some increased aid to the Nationalists, but stipulated that first the Chinese must (1) effectively utilize their own resources in a program of economic construction, (2) initiate sound fiscal policies leading to the reduction of budgetary deficits, (3) give evidence that urgent political and military reforms are being carried out, and (4) accept American advisers to assist them in employing American aid in the intended manner.[9]

Truman's Program of Aid

Throughout the fall of 1947, while the U.S. ambassador in China tried to persuade the Kuomintang to launch basic reforms, the State Department drafted a program of further aid to China. Intensive studies were made. The program to be recommended was not to be one that could put the U.S. in the unwanted position of virtually taking over China's government and administering its economic and military affairs. Limitations on what could be drawn from the resources of America's economy had to be carefully considered, because of preparations for the European Recovery Program.

During congressional hearings the next spring, Secretary Marshall said he could not sanction an attempt to underwrite China's economy or conduct China's fighting. Such a course would constitute too great a burden on the American economy and too great a military commitment. Truman explained in a message to Congress on February 19, 1948, that "ever since the return of General Marshall from China, the problem of assistance to the Chinese has been under continuous study. We have hoped for conditions in China that would make possible the effective and constructive use of American assistance in reconstruction and rehabilitation. Conditions have not developed as we had hoped, and we can only do what is feasible under circumstances as they exist."[10]

The President recommended $570 million in aid to China. As he did, he emphasized again that the aid could not, even in small measure, be a substitute for necessary action that could be taken only by the Nationalist government itself. Truman described his aid program as one that could "accomplish the important purpose of giving the Chinese government a respite from rapid economic deterioration, during which it can move to establish more stable conditions. Without this respite," he said, "the ability of the Chinese government to establish such conditions at all would be doubtful."[11] It was a very limited objective, but important enough in Truman's view to justify passage of the proposed program of assistance.

Congress approved the China aid measure as part of an omnibus foreign assistance act which also provided, among other things, for the European Recovery Program and further aid to Greece and Turkey. Truman's request for China aid was reduced by more than $100 million, however, to $338 million for economic and rehabilitation assistance, and $125 million for additional aid through grants, on such terms as the President might determine. Despite Congress' reduced funding for China, the Bureau of the Budget, the military services, and the civilian departments concerned (State, Commerce, and Agriculture) endorsed the appropriation, so Truman accepted it, too.

Owing to the uncertainty of the situation in China in 1949, Congress in that year granted only $75 million, plus the use of economic aid appropriations which remained unobligated (amounting to slightly more than $50 million). But the 1949 appropriation brought to well over $2 billion the total American aid extended to China, through grants and credits, under the Truman administration in the four years following the surrender of Japan. In addition, American civilian and military surplus property worth another $1 billion was sold to the Nationalist government for less than a quarter of that amount, much of which could be repaid on credit. Altogether, wartime and postwar American aid to China amounted to more than $3.5 billion in grants and credits, plus the value of the excess and surplus property that was provided to China on bargain terms.

The effect of the aid was necessarily dependent, of course, upon how well the Chinese utilized it. Truman, for his part, made sure that it got there in a hurry. In the summer of 1948, his secretary of defense reported that, in compliance with Truman's request, prompt action was being taken to help China's government acquire the military supplies Congress had authorized. Early that fall, Truman called for an interim report on the status of expenditures. The report, which was made public, revealed that as of October 3, exactly six months after the enactment of the China Aid Act, a total of more than $88 million (some 70 percent) of the $125 million authorized as additional aid to China had been extended to the Nationalists as grants for military purposes. As for economic assistance, the value of supplies actually delivered to China represented 90 percent of the target figure for the first six months of the program.[12]

In August of 1948, the American embassy in China transmitted to Washington a gloomy report that the Chinese Communists were scoring one military victory after another. China's government, instead of grasping for a way to stem the tide, was ignoring military opportunities and competent military advice. The Nationalists' political and military leadership was continuing to go downhill. Important posts were being filled on the basis of personal loyalty and political reliability rather than competence. A spirit of defeatism had set in, reaching even men of cabinet rank. The U.S. embassy observed that no longer was there evidence of faith on the part of the Chinese people that the existing government could bring a return to even a bearable standard of living without some radical reorganization.

With this frame of mind prevailing, the ambassador reported, a cessation of hostilities was desired at almost any price.[13]

Anticipating that such a price might be a Kuomintang-Communist deal that would mean a regional breakup of China, the American ambassador asked the state department for guidance. He noted that there was violent popular agitation against Chiang and his government, and observed that it was already so close to collapsing that it might already be too late for the U.S. to do anything to change the course of events.[14]

The guidance that came in reply was that deeper involvement and further commitments were to be avoided. The ambassador was told not to imply support or encouragement for a coalition government with communist participation.[15] The pattern of communist exploitation of coalition governments in Eastern Europe was by that time all too clear, and the Truman administration hoped the Chinese would not now be lured into the same kind of trap. Neither did the administration want the U.S. to be trapped in the middle of any political dealings in China. The ambassador was told that the U.S. had no intention of again trying to be the mediator in China.

Secretary Marshall explained in a dispatch to the embassy later in the summer that the administration was unlikely to be drawing up any rigid plans for future American policy in China. The situation in China at that juncture simply didn't lend itself to firm plans. Developments were obviously entering a period of extreme flux and confusion, Secretary Marshall said, in which it was impossible with surety to perceive clearly, well in advance, the pattern of things to come. Truman plainly felt the U.S. must preserve maximum freedom of action.

Several times during the autumn of 1948 the American ambassador in China called attention to the continuing deterioration there. Few Chinese, the embassy reports now said, continued with conviction to support Chiang. The reports said it was difficult to see how any American efforts, short of large-scale armed intervention, could head off military disaster. American military advisers in China felt that losses in manpower, materials, and morale already suffered by the Nationalists were probably too great to make any such effort successful anyway. There was no will to fight left in Chiang's forces. The ambassador asked if, in the face of this, he should adopt a different stance. The answer was "no."[16] The Chinese Communists might be gaining the upper hand, but Truman knew that an attempt to remove them forcibly from the picture would require an undertaking of such magnitude that there was no estimating what its final cost to the U.S. would be. Not only that, American military intervention would make China an arena of international conflict that could involve grave consequences for the U.S.

The Truman administration never wavered in the fundamental nature of its instructions to the embassy in China during this turbulent period. American aid was being delivered to China with dispatch. But the guidance to the embassy was emphatic in the judgment that foreign aid could not correct the fundamental weaknesses of the Chinese Nationalist government. Because of prior commitments to that government, the administration concluded that America should support it as long as it remained "an important factor on the Chinese scene." But the hope that could be placed in that government was faint indeed. There was little reason to believe that any amount of American assistance would enable it to reestablish and then maintain its control throughout all China. Nonetheless, what faint hope there was would not be entirely abandoned. What course the U.S. would take if the Nationalist government gave up its capital at Nanking, collapsed, disappeared, or

merged into a coalition with the Chinese Communists
would be decided when the time came. For its part, the U.S.
— hoping things would somehow take a turn for the better
— would play out the string and try not to get further
entwined.

European events were uppermost in America's international concern. The outlook there was grim enough. The
Berlin blockade, an electrifying, full-blown international
crisis, was dominating the headlines. At the same time, the
American election campaign was in full swing. Truman
was battling for the presidency and his political life. He was
encountering no problems in that campaign from the absence of any hard-and-fast policy for coming to grips with
the quicksilver of China's domestic upheaval.

The Collapse Comes

George Marshall, 68 years old and in poor health, resigned as secretary of state and was succeeded by Dean
Acheson — his extremely able and experienced second in
command — on January 20, 1949. By February, the collapse of Chiang Kai-shek appeared to be merely a matter of
time. Truman called a White House conference of
Acheson, Vice-President Barkley, and Senator Vandenberg, the former chairman and now the ranking Republican
on the Senate Foreign Relations Committee. Vandenberg
strongly opposed deserting Chiang Kai-shek. He expressed
no hope that a communist conquest of China could be
prevented, but wanted America to avoid responsibility for
what might be viewed as the last push that made the
takeover possible. He recommended waiting until the fall of
Chiang was settled by China and in China, and not by the
U.S. government in Washington. This was the tack Truman
took.

Throughout the first half of 1949, the Truman administration cautiously endeavored to keep a free hand in China.
The U.S. extended only token aid aimed at ameliorating the
severe economic conditions under Chiang's government.
Circumstances in China had become so chaotic as to pre-
clude any further crystallization of American China policy.
When, in the summer of 1949, the final collapse of the
Nationalist regime was imminent, Truman felt a comprehensive public accounting should be made of American
efforts and the U.S. role in the situation that had evolved.

In August the State Department released a voluminous
document entitled *United States Relations with China* —
the so-called China White Paper. In more than 1000 pages,
it presented a detailed record of Chinese-American relations, with special emphasis on the period 1944–1949. The
primary purpose in having such a "frank and factual record" published, according to a statement Truman made
upon its release, was to insure that American policy toward
China, and the Far East as a whole, "be based on informed
and intelligent public opinion."[17]

America's foreign policy, Truman said, was not made by
the decisions of a few, but was a product of the people, and
representative of their collective judgment. "Misrepresen-
tation, distortion, and misunderstanding" of the role of the
U.S. in its relations with China had occurred, however, and
must be dispelled. What Truman also meant, of course, was
that his administration was going to be the target of partisan
brickbats hurled the moment the Chinese Communists
came out on top.

The time had now come, in the President's view, when
the mutual interests of the U.S. and China required full and
frank discussion of the facts. Only in this way could the
American people and their representatives in Congress have
the understanding necessary to the sound evolution of U.S.
foreign policy in the Far East. What Truman wanted under-

stood was spelled out clearly in the conclusion the White
Paper reached. It was "the unfortunate but inescapable
fact" that the ominous result of the civil war in China was
beyond U.S. control. Nothing America did or could have
done within the reasonable limits of its capabilities, according to the White Paper, could have changed that result.
Nothing America left undone had contributed to it; it was
the product of internal Chinese forces, forces which the
U.S. tried to influence but could not.

The final demise of the Chinese Nationalists came with
astonishing quickness and finality. Before the summer of
1949 they had surrendered their capital at Nanking and
China's chief port of Shanghai. On October 1, 1949, the
confident Communists, firmly in control of most of the
mainland, proclaimed the establishment of the People's
Republic. In the same month, the Nationalist armies surrendered in Canton, the historic home of the Kuomintang
and the principal city of South China. Chiang and the
remnants of his forces attempted resistance on the run, but
by the end of the year were forced to take refuge on the
island of Formosa.

At the beginning of 1950, amid assertions by the Com-
munists that, having become the "legal" government of
China, they were entitled to take control of Formosa,
Truman explicitly disclaimed American involvement. The
U.S., he said, had no intention of utilizing its armed forces
to interfere in the situation, and would not pursue a course
that would lead to involvement in the civil conflict in China.
Truman said his administration would follow through with
economic assistance under existing legislative authority.
He said the U.S. would not, however, provide military aid
or advice to Chinese forces on Formosa which, in his view,
were adequate to defend the island.[18]

Six months later, the communist invasion of Korea
would nullify the President's position on Formosa. To help

prevent the spread of hostilities and to protect the flank of United Nations military operations in Korea, the U.S. Seventh Fleet would be stationed off the coast of China to guard Formosa, and Chiang's forces there would be given American military assistance.

Even before the stroke of communist aggression in Korea altered the American position, U.S. opposition to Red China was hardening. Flagrant disregard of the rights of Americans in China was accompanied by torrents of virulently abusive anti-American propaganda. American consular officials in China were mistreated — some were incarcerated, for example, and held incommunicado nearly a month. They were then humiliatingly deported after a "people's court" declared them guilty, without judicial process, of unspecified "crimes."

Americans were outraged at seeing their country's diplomatic representatives made victims of official conduct of this sort. They were shocked by photographs and news reports of mass executions and other violent actions by China's new rulers. The Truman administration, having presided over the period that saw the culmination of the Communists' rise to power, now found itself rocked by resentment and partisan recriminations as America reacted to the nature of China's new masters.

China and the American Public

Harry Truman had not tried to disguise or gloss over the futility of his attempt to negotiate peace and stability in China through the Marshall mission. He publicly acknowledged the failure upon Marshall's recall, and called a halt to American efforts to mediate the clash of arms in China. Truman's move was widely approved, according to an analysis of press and radio comment by the Public Opinion

Studies Staff of the State Department, which periodically provided U.S. foreign policy-makers with assessments of public attitudes on pertinent issues. The withdrawal was reportedly favored "almost unanimously" as a "logical and inevitable step." Most commentators endorsed a "hands-off" policy. They shared the President's conviction that the U.S. could not run China's affairs, and that the Chinese themselves would have to determine their destiny.

After the Marshall mission, the central feature of Truman's China policy was noninvolvement in China's civil war. Truman chose to let the Chinese run their own government. He did so both as a matter of principle and because he felt the U.S. in any event could not pay the price of a full-scale attempt to decide the outcome of China's internal chaos. A second aspect of Truman's policy was to give American counsel and substantial quantities of aid to the established Chinese government, in a manner consistent with China's independence. He hoped in vain that the assistance would enable the recognized government of China to put its own house in order. A third aspect of American China policy under Truman was an increasingly intransigent opposition to the Chinese Communists.

Confidential polls of a national cross section of the American public, taken for the Public Opinion Studies Staff, indicated that in 1948 — the year Truman proposed a China aid program of $570 million — some six out of ten Americans agreed with the idea of continuing to help the Nationalist government. When the collapse of Nationalist China was increasingly imminent, in the spring of 1949, the Public Opinion Studies Staff assessed the way the public viewed the likelihood of a Communist China. The staff reported that such a turn of events was increasingly considered of serious consequence, but that no clear indication was being given of what course the U.S. should follow. It found "most editors and observers" supporting the

President's decision to stand by for a dust-settling before making a policy move. Public opinion polls in the summer of 1949 revealed that fewer than one out of every four Americans polled felt the U.S. should send help to keep China from the Communists.

In August of 1949, when the so-called China White Paper set forth a detailed record of Sino-American relations, studies revealed no shifts of opinion as a result of the report. Most commentators continued to concur with the administration's view that the debacle had been brought on by the inability of China's government to halt its own deterioration. There was general agreement with the report's conclusion that the outcome of the civil war was beyond American control.

Following the announced formation of the People's Republic of China in the fall of 1949, a comprehensive study of American opinion on possible U.S. diplomatic recognition of the communist regime revealed widespread reluctance on the part of commentators to commit themselves one way or the other. The strongest reaction reported to the communist takeover was a feeling that the U.S. should move slowly and cautiously in formulating its China policy. This feeling was deepened by the series of incidents involving American consular officials in China. Popular opinion was found to oppose recognition by a two-to-one margin, but some 40 percent of those polled either had no opinion or said they were not familiar with the situation.

Polls taken late in the spring of 1950, months after the establishment of communist rule in China, indicated that fewer than a third of those polled felt past American policy had been wrong and that, had some different policy been pursued, the communist seizure of China might have been prevented.

Given his experience in capturing the 1948 election, one wonders how much stock Truman would have put in these

opinion polls on China issues. At any rate, the results of
these polls of a national cross section of the American
public reveal clearly that most people who expressed any
knowledge of the President's China policy approved of it.
Although by late summer of 1949 two out of three Americans who gave an opinion felt China would become a
communist state, scarcely more than one American in four
felt Truman's China policy had been unsound.

If Truman's China policy deviated at all from the tenor of
public sentiment, it probably was in the degree to which he
extended American aid to Chiang Kai-shek. Public attitudes, as ascertained by the Public Opinion Studies Staff,
showed neither overwhelming support nor strong opposition to American aid. Sentiment behind it did not amount to
60 percent of the public at its highest level. At the time
Truman proposed his $570 million China aid program, 55
percent of the respondents in a national poll approved
sending aid, with no specific amount indicated. As for the
recipient of the help, little more than a third of the American
public ever felt favorably toward Chiang Kai-shek. Ironically, it was on this ground that Truman was to come under
fire — for not doing enough to prop up Chiang and somehow keep the Chinese Communists out of power.

The American public had at least generally recognized
the obstacles the Truman administration ran into in China,
and generally agreed that the U.S. could do only so much.
Truman's approach was so generally endorsed that the
conclusion is inescapable that later controversies about his
conduct of China policy — after the "loss" and especially
with the Korean War — were inspired by partisan motives.
It seems clear that Truman actually did more in assisting the
non-communist forces in China than the American public
expected. What the American public also expected, of
course, was success. Despite convincing evidence that the
public generally went along with Truman on China policy,

it is also evident that there was a widespread lack of concern about it. Such a large "don't know" or "no opinion" category on a subject can be converted into strong feeling when suddenly the subject is perceived as a very unfavorable turn of events. The ultimate collapse of China's long-tottering government was that way; it could be seen coming, but it still arrived with a jolt. The impact evoked a sense of failure, a feeling that something that should not have happened had happened anyway. It was the kind of feeling that intensifies frustration and produces a natural inclination to look for a scapegoat on which to put the blame.

Such feelings can be played on very easily, and in this case a partisan faction was eager to do just that. The China "defeat" was seized upon as something that could be the Truman administration's Achilles' heel. Republican frustration with Truman's upset victory in 1948 had already found expression in reckless allegations by some — very definitely a minority — about communist influence in the government. The "loss" of China fit these unfounded charges very nicely for those who were not above insinuating that some sinister manipulation might well have played a part.

A shrill chorus was raised, led by the ambitious Republican Congressman Richard M. Nixon and fed by the free-wheeling Republican anti-Communist in the Senate, Joseph McCarthy. It found ready backing in the well-heeled "China Lobby" in Congress and others with considerable wealth tied up in China and in the fate of the Nationalist government. It picked right up with an anti-communist theme that, in the mood of the time, was striking a responsive chord with a broader audience than the hard core of fanatics who imagined a "Commie" in every closet and behind every bush.

Anti-communism was a staple in the American political diet long before Harry Truman became President. From the beginning of the New Deal, some conservatives in both parties contended that social legislation was nothing more than Communism disguised as democracy. Now the communist menace throughout the world was making gray areas out of so much that had always seemed black and white, and the tensions of the cold war were making many Americans wonder how else to explain so much that was going wrong in the world. There was plenty of objective evidence of Communism on the march in many places in the very visible form of governments toppled, resistance crushed, and countries occupied by Red Army soldiers. But there were also the new, pervasive, more insidious forces of propaganda warfare, infiltration, and subterfuge. Extraordinary events such as the communist seizure of China seemed to defy ordinary explanations.

The unspoken implication now was that the "loss" of China could not entirely be attributed to ordinary incompetence in the administration's conduct of China policy. It was alleged to be evidence of that, to be sure; but might there not be more to it than met the eye? The insinuation was that perhaps there were hidden in key places some unspecified persons of questionable loyalty and uncertain motives who managed somehow to help the communist takeover come about. The suspicion was planted that the "loss" of China reflected a lack of will, and that perhaps this calamity did not just happen.

VII Drawing the Line

In January, 1949, Truman had begun the new year and his new term with good spirits and noble objectives. In his State of the Union address he again had called on Congress to enact the domestic measures that the perplexed special session had failed to act on the previous summer. "Every segment of our population and every individual has the right," he declared, "to expect from our government a fair deal." The "Fair Deal" was picked up as the shorthand name for his legislative program.

The President had gone along with plans for a full-blown inaugural celebration, figuring the party was entitled to one after wresting a hard-fought victory from a predicted disaster. Truman had begun the Inauguration Day with a breakfast for 97 veterans of his old Battery D. He still insisted that, instead of "Mr. President," they please just call him "Captain Harry" as they had 30 years before. He had them march alongside his car in the inaugural later that day. The President's rather portly, distinctly aging, former comrades in arms made an odd-looking honor guard, but the President did not see it that way. Appearances did not matter to Harry Truman, but loyalty mattered a great deal. He had grown to be elected President of the United States, but he never outgrew old friends.

Before the inauguration ceremony the President and his family, with Vice-President-elect Barkley and Chief Justice Vinson, who would administer the oath of office, had driven from the White House around Lafayette Park to attend a service at St. John's Episcopal Church. Soon afterward, Truman raised his hand and repeated the same words he had spoken in the hushed presence of a handful of persons assembled so unexpectedly in the White House three years and nine months earlier. Now he addressed an estimated 100,000 gathered outside the Capitol building.

Foreign policy was the main subject of Truman's inaugural address. He used it to introduce a proposal for sharing America's vast scientific and industrial experience with the many underdeveloped nations emerging from colonialism into freedom. He summed up the plan — which was shortened to Point Four because it was the fourth point in the foreign program he outlined — with these words: "I believe we should make available to peace-loving peoples the benefits of our store of technical knowledge, in order to help them realize their aspirations for a better life."

Point Four captured the imagination of peoples in the underdeveloped world, and 35 nations eventually signed up for technical assistance. Much good was accomplished. Point Four projects dried up malarial swamps in many villages of Asia and Latin America, and brought the first pure drinking water to scores of others. Point Four wiped out a typhus epidemic in Iran, and supplied the tractors and technicians with which Egypt made farmland from 3,000,000 acres of desert. Point Four built a hydroelectric plant in Mexico, developed irrigation projects in Jordan and Haiti, and introduced a modern system of money and banking to Saudi Arabia.

Truman saw Point Four as a continuing program of helping the less-developed nations help themselves through the sharing of technical information already tested and proved in the U.S. By the time Truman left office, Point Four would have a budget of $155.6 million, with nearly 2500 U.S. technicians scattered abroad putting its programs into effect.[1] It was enabling participating countries to send an even larger number of their most promising young

specialists to study abroad, mostly in the U.S., so they —
and the technicians they trained in turn — could release
America's technical missionaries for pioneer work in other
fields.

In later years Truman spoke with special fondness of
Point Four as a peace program that improved living standards for millions and saved millions of lives. "To call the
undertaking a 'bold new program' was no exaggeration,"
he said later. "It was an adventurous idea such as had never
before been proposed by any country in the history of the
world."[2] Be that as it may, Point Four could not compete
for headlines with the other events of Truman's full term as
President. Unfortunately, the exaggeration was more likely
in his hopes for the program. Point Four did foster highly
useful projects. It set a pattern of technical assistance that
remained a lasting feature of foreign aid, embellished years
later as the highly publicized Peace Corps.

As a humanitarian program, however, it did not live up to
the billing Truman gave it. When Point Four came along,
Congress was preoccupied with the North Atlantic Treaty,
and the public was wondering where the country's overseas
obligations would ever end. Both Point Four and Truman's
domestic program suffered, as did the President's relations
with Congress generally, from the attention focused on the
threat of communist infiltration at home.

The communist victory proclaimed in China on
October 1, 1949 carried greater impact because it came
right on the heels of the announcement in September of a
Soviet atomic explosion. These events, combined with
revelations in the Alger Hiss case, were offered — and
accepted by a great many — as evidence that the Truman
administration was "soft on Communism." Now the
enemy had nuclear secrets and the enemy had China; both
these coveted possessions, the reasoning could go, had
been obtained from the U.S. It was the U.S. government,

after all, that was responsible for protecting nuclear secrets and U.S. interests in China, which meant that federal emp- loyees were in a position to betray these to others.

Alger Hiss had been such an employee, a former State Department officer who was convicted of perjury in 1949 after testimony at his trial alleged his involvement in giving classified information to Soviet agents. This and similar charges involving other federal employees aroused de- mands for tougher screening procedures for government workers and a crackdown on communist and leftist organi- zations. The President objected to "witch-hunting" by congressional inquiries, but did tighten up loyalty and se- curity provisions for keeping Communists and subversives out of government jobs.

Truman was never entirely convinced that the nature of these measures was in the American tradition. He con- tended that the kind of programs Congress was calling for would give government officials vast powers to harass citizens in the exercise of their right of free speech. It was with this concern in mind that the President vetoed the Internal Security Act of 1950, a law designed to curb and punish "subversive" political expression. His vice- president and the Democratic leadership in Congress had urged Truman to relent and sign the bill. The political climate demanded it, they argued, and a veto was certain to be overridden.

They were right on both counts. Truman's veto was courageous, but ineffective; Congress overrode it within 24 hours by an overwhelming margin. It had been a typically Truman type of tangle with Congress. The fur flew. The chips could fall where they may. Truman stood his ground for what he believed to be right. He lost, and his enemies gloated over his defeat.

Worries about internal security preoccupied congress- men and the public for the remainder of Truman's time in office. They became acute when the Republican senator from Wisconsin, Joe McCarthy, raked the raw nerves of neurosis with his charges that "card-carrying Communists" infested the State Department and that the administration was "soft" on Communist Party members and sympathizers in its midst.

Truman was hardly "soft" on Communists, but neither was he "soft" on McCarthy, whom he scorned as a demagogue. Truman was especially angered at McCarthy's leading role in blaming George Marshall and Dean Acheson, for whom Truman felt abiding loyalty and respect, for "selling Chiang Kai-shek down the river" and "turning China over to the Communists." Knowing they had stung Truman with the charges was all the encouragement his opponents needed. The madness held sway, to such an extent that in December of 1949, the Republicans in both houses of Congress voted overwhelmingly to ask Truman to dismiss Acheson.

The request was refused with as much scorn as Truman could muster, which was a great deal. But the furor would not go away altogether. The President had a running battle with "Red-baiters" for the rest of his term over the "loss" of China and being "soft" on Communism. Beset on the home front, Truman was soon fatefully involved with Asian events again. This time, what seemed to be one of the lesser trouble spots of many on the world map exploded into the biggest crisis the President and the country would face in the postwar years.

Background to Korea

The line of containment had not been drawn in China. It could not have been; the situation there was too blurred from the beginning. The choices could be made only between undesirable alternatives. The ground kept shifting, and the direction was unclear. The U.S. had to play by ear rather than by note. Unlike the case with countries in Western Europe, the Chinese government's intentions and capabilities were always in question. The key quality of being willing and able to help itself was always in doubt if not lacking entirely. The Chinese Nationalists and their well-meaning American ally were never quite able to get on the same wave length and establish mutual trust and confidence. The administration simply could not get a firm reading of the situation from which to draw up a blueprint — such as it did with the Marshall Plan in Europe — to which congressional support could be rallied.

There may well have been no way to avoid doing so, but Truman contributed to his own problems by abandoning in the case of China the bipartisan policy approach he had so carefully maintained in dealing with Russia. As former senators, both Truman as the new President and Byrnes as his new secretary of state had been well qualified to appeal for congressional tolerance and support while endeavoring to keep up with rapid developments involving the Soviets.

The bipartisan approach was carried through the foreign minister's meetings and into the peace treaty negotiations involving Europe. As Truman developed his foreign policy in the face of the Soviet threat there, he was at pains to construct it as a national policy. He sent the Republican chairman and the ranking Democrat on the Senate Foreign Relations Committee to sit at either side of Secretary Byrnes at the negotiating table. By associating the senators with treaty negotiations, Truman lessened the risk of Senate rejection of the treaties. The bipartisan approach to Europe worked well and was successful in preventing any serious Republican criticism of America's uncomfortable postwar position there.

Whatever accounts for the failure to make a similar effort with China policy, it turned out to be a most damaging omission. Bipartisan cooperation was never established, and once China policy was embroiled in partisan controversy, it was too late. Perhaps the pent-up pressure from suppressing partisan division on other foreign policy fronts helps explain the intensity with which it burst forth over policies pursued in Asia. At any rate, the breakdown of bipartisanship in dealing with China was a grave liability for Truman. It made him politically vulnerable in his policy approach to Korea as well.

In the early months of 1950, it would have been impossible in the climate of controversy over China to construct a bipartisan blueprint for Korea, which did not loom in America's consciousness as a place that cried out for one. The joint chiefs of staff had dismissed Korea as being of little military concern in terms of America's broad defensive strategy in the Pacific. As General Douglas MacArthur, the U.S. commander in the Pacific, had put it, America's postwar line of defense, previously based on its own West Coast, now ran "through the chain of islands fringing the coast of Asia. It starts from the Philippines and continues through the Ryukyu Archipelago . . . back through Japan and the Aleutian Island chain to Alaska."[3] It did not include Korea. In fact by mid-1949, in accordance with UN resolutions sponsored by the U.S. in keeping with the wishes of the joint chiefs to get remaining U.S. divisions out of Korea,[4] Soviet and American forces had been withdrawn from that country.

With its defeat in World War II, Japan's decades of steel-booted control of Korea came to an end, but tens of thousands of Japanese occupation troops still had to be disarmed and repatriated. To do this, the Russians sent an occupation force into the northern part of Korea from Manchuria, and U.S. troops landed at a port in the south. To simplify the job, which included setting up some kind of civilian government in place of the Japanese, it was decided that, simply as a matter of convenience, the Russians would take care of things north of the 38th parallel and the Americans would operate to the south. The geographer's line was chosen simply because it divided the country into two approximately equal parts.

The Soviets, however, did not see it simply as a demarcation. They interpreted it as a partitioning of the country, and clearly had no interest in reunifying it. They cut off traffic across the 38th parallel, halting the flow of electrical power and the movement of goods southward, and set up a communist government. The U.S. took the issue to the UN, and the General Assembly created a mission on unifying Korea to oversee general elections there the next year. The Soviets and their North Korean puppet regime refused to allow the UN election commissioners to enter their territory, so an election was held only in the south. The next year, acting in rare accord, the U.S. and the Soviets pulled out their occupation forces, leaving behind only training cadres for the native armies — in the U.S. case, an advisory group of about 500 officers and men. What also remained were two autonomous Koreas, mutually suspicious and hostile.

In the spring of 1950 the Truman administration, wishing to boost South Korean morale with some economic aid, asked for a small appropriation of $60 million for the 1950–51 budget, but Congress turned it down. Truman has acknowledged that he also was receiving intelligence reports that spring about North Korean hit-and-run raids across the 38th parallel, and a continuing build-up of the Soviet-led North Korean forces. He said he received reports the North Koreans might at any time decide to change from isolated raids to full-scale attack. There was no clue, however, as to whether an attack was certain or when it was likely to come. And Korea was scarcely alone as a subject of intelligence warnings; there were any number of places around the world where the Soviets "possessed the capability" to attack.[5]

The Communists Invade

On Saturday, June 24, 1950, the President's wife and daughter were already enjoying a vacation visit to the family home in Independence. Truman flew to Missouri that afternoon to join them for the weekend, after dedicating the new Friendship International Airport in Baltimore. It was after ten o'clock that night when the telephone rang at 219 North Delaware in Independence, and Secretary of State Acheson, calling from his home in Maryland, told Truman the news. North Korean tanks, spearheading columns of infantry and barrages of artillery, had rolled across the 38th parallel in the pre-dawn darkness of June 25, Korean time. Communist forces had launched an all-out offensive, and were attacking at a number of points all across the Korean peninsula.

Although caught off guard as much as anyone by the stunning news, Truman reacted swiftly. He instructed Acheson to request an immediate special meeting of the United Nations Security Council and to seek from it a declaration that the invasion was an act of aggression under the United Nations Charter. Truman said he would return to Washington at once, but Acheson advised him to wait until he could provide more information on what was happening in Korea and at the UN. The next call came late Sunday morning as Truman sat down for an early dinner. Acheson had additional reports on the invasion, and word that the UN Security Council would meet in emergency session.

The challenge had come. Anticipating that the UN would call for a cease-fire and that North Korea and its allies would ignore it, Truman knew a decision would have to be made at once as to what the U.S. was willing to do in South Korea's behalf. He directed that his top diplomatic and military advisers prepare recommendations to consider in a meeting with him later that day. Truman flew back to the capital, and that evening conferred with the group, which included the secretary of defense, the service secretaries, the joint chiefs of staff, and the secretary of state and his senior aides.

Each person there realized the nation faced a major crisis, perhaps as great as any it had ever confronted. For Truman's containment policy, it was the first challenge by force of arms. The responsibility for deciding what course of action to take rested squarely with the President alone. Truman made certain that each of his advisers had a chance to speak up, and apparently everyone did. There were differences over what might be needed militarily, but the feeling was unanimous that whatever had to be done to meet this aggression would be done. There was no thought of backing down. The U.S. must stick by South Korea and stand firm, whatever the cost, if a third world war was to be prevented.

"This was the test," Truman said, "of all the talk of the last five years of collective security." General Omar Bradley, chairman of the joint chiefs, expressed the view that Russia was not yet ready for war but in Korea obviously was testing the U.S. The line ought to be drawn now. Truman agreed emphatically. The line, he told his advisers, will have to be drawn.[6]

As Truman and his chief State and Defense department officials were meeting, the UN Security Council — which Moscow had boycotted since January, protesting the UN's refusal to seat Communist China — approved by a vote of 9 to 0 a resolution ordering North Korea to halt its invasion and withdraw its forces. As expected, the North Koreans disregarded the UN resolution. Their forces were advancing rapidly, making clear that the United Nations would have to apply force if it wanted its orders obeyed.

For South Korea, time was running out. Almost by the hour, the outlook for its survival grew more and more alarming. South Korean troops were no match for the well-equipped invading force with its Russian tanks and fighter planes; the South Koreans had no tanks or planes at all, and resistance was crumbling. Seoul, the South Korean capital located less than 50 miles below the 38th parallel, appeared doomed and was being evacuated. The government was forced to relocate; North Korea's fighters were strafing the capital, and its tanks were entering the city's outskirts. Refugees were fleeing in panic. Reports flashed to Washington from Korea left no doubt that help must come at once if the country was not to be overrun.

Again Truman convened his national security advisers. He told them that Korea seemed to him to be a repetition on a larger scale of what had happened in Berlin. The Communists were probing for a weakness; somehow the U.S. must parry the thrust without getting embroiled in a chain of events that would result in world war. The President listened to more reports of the rapid deterioration in Korea. Seoul had fallen, and South Korea's army had been all but destroyed. General MacArthur had radioed from his headquarters in Japan that Korea's complete collapse was imminent. In return, Truman directed his secretary of defense to call MacArthur on the scrambler phone and authorize immediate use of American air and naval assistance to South Korea. Simultaneously the UN Security Council, with U.S. backing, called on all members of the United Nations to help South Korea.

A nominal United Nations command was established with General MacArthur at its head, and American ground troops headed into the Korean conflict. Sixteen other nations, in time, would make tangible contributions, but the

U.S. would bear 90 percent of the burden of helping South
Korea defend itself. The decision to intervene, Truman said
later, was probably the most important he made in his years
as President. It would prove politically troublesome for him
in part because of a label given to the U.S. action at a press
conference Truman held during that first difficult week of
decision. Asked if the U.S. was at war, the President
summed up his view with characteristic bluntness: "The
Republic of Korea was set up with United Nations help. It
was unlawfully attacked by a bunch of bandits which are
neighbors, in North Korea. The United Nations held a
meeting and asked the members to go to the relief of the
Korean Republic, and the members of the United Nations
are going to the relief of the Korean Republic to suppress a
bandit raid on the Republic of Korea. That is all there is to
it."

"Would it be correct," a reporter asked, "to call it a
police action under the United Nations?"

"Yes," said Truman, "that is exactly what it amounts
to."[7]

It was not his label, but Truman accepted it because the
analogy fit and its meaning conveyed a crucial distinction
about limited U.S. objectives, something which later would
be bitterly debated.

What had happened with dizzying swiftness was that in
one short, agonizing week a U.S. President for the first time
in history had taken the country into a shooting war.
Truman had demonstrated that the U.S. meant what it so
often had said about containing communist aggression. He
kept congressional leaders fully briefed, but did not ask
Congress for a declaration of war because he did not see it
that way. From the beginning, the President saw it as an
armed struggle clearly confined to repelling aggression.
During the months that Truman was immersed in the conflict and its incessant demands for decisions that only he

could make, he said he made every one with one aim in mind: to prevent a larger war.

Strategies at Odds

At first the American-led effort in Korea went badly, and Truman must share some of the blame. His bold foreign policy demanded more military strength than budget-consciousness had allowed. After many years of built-in deficits, Truman succeeded in balancing the federal budget. In so doing, he may have become almost too economy-minded. He approved cutbacks that weakened U.S. military forces considerably. As a result, the Korean conflict caught the U.S. under strength. The first American troops, sent from Japan to fight in Korea, had to face modern Soviet-supplied tanks without any tanks of their own or even antitank weapons, and they took a beating. The U.S. soon plunged into a speedy military build-up, but for a time its soldiers were at a disadvantage as they fought desperate rear-guard struggles just to get a foothold on the Korean battleground.

Differences between Washington policy-makers and the U.S. commander in the field surfaced early in the war. MacArthur was undeniably a clever military strategist, but his downfall was a colossal ego that inclined him to try political strategy as well. Unlike other outstanding American generals with better judgment, MacArthur actively cultivated strong ties with partisan political circles. He counted among his closest friends and supporters certain Republicans who were the President's severest critics, and MacArthur kept in touch with them.

MacArthur would have taken a back seat to no one as an expert on national security in general or on the Far East in particular. He had spent most of his life in Asia, and in fact had not been back in the U.S. for nearly 14 years. MacArthur was by no means a modest individual, and undoubtedly did not believe the combined intellect of his peers on the joint chiefs could offer him any enlightenment on any subject, least of all how to fight a war in Asia.

Truman was better versed than MacArthur turned out to be on the subject of the Constitution of the United States, which ultimately decided the outcome of their differing views. The Constitution is quite clear on the subject of the President being the commander in chief of the armed forces, and the principle of civilian control of the military is quite deeply ingrained in America's political culture. Truman was better versed than MacArthur, too, on the big picture that a national policy-maker must endeavor to see.

Truman and his advisers, including of course the military leaders who made up the joint chiefs of staff, were dealing at all times with far more than the battleground in Korea. They assumed that Moscow was masterminding the North Korean war effort. That was not an unreasonable assumption, given the fact that Moscow had set up the North Korean Communst government and trained and equipped its military forces. Russia's involvement raised several serious questions that had to be weighed in Washington. Would Soviet forces at some point enter the fighting in Korea? Did the Soviets by now have an operational nuclear weapon they could use there — or in Europe — where the stakes for the Soviets were higher? Had Moscow fostered the Korean conflict merely to tie down U.S. forces and divert attention from a move to be made in Berlin or elsewhere in Europe?

MacArthur almost seemed to be wearing blinders, as did certain critics at home. He saw everything in terms of Korea, as if there were not a larger picture of worldwide commitments, dangers, and major imponderables that had to be considered simultaneously.

MacArthur publicly advanced, and would not abandon, the view that the Chinese Communists were unlikely to get involved in the Korean conflict. Therefore he urged that Chiang Kai-shek's Chinese Nationalists be brought into the fray from Formosa. Truman and his advisers were of one mind in regarding this as an unwisely provocative move. The President was emphatic in his belief that, wholly aside from whatever short-term military value it might have in Korea, it ran too great a risk of widening the war. It might bring a Soviet countermove, for example, or encourage the Chinese Communists either to enter the war or to retaliate with an attack against Formosa. The U.S. Seventh Fleet in fact was stationed off Formosa and the coast of mainland China as much to keep Chiang reined in as to keep the Communists at bay.

By late summer, as a front was stabilized and the North Korean's advance was slowed with almost the whole country in their grasp, MacArthur executed one of the most daring maneuvers in military history. The U.S. landed a large amphibious force at Inchon, well up Korea's west coast and about 150 miles behind the enemy's lines. The North Korean invaders were outflanked, cut off from their supply sources, and forced to flee northward. By early October, American forces had the initiative. They had been authorized to cross the 38th parallel for tactical military purposes, and now were sweeping up the neck of the peninsula deep into North Korea.

The tide seemed to have turned. It struck the President as a good time to impress on his commanding general in the field the wisdom of moving prudently in the north so as not to give China undue cause for alarm. Truman decided that a face-to-face talk would be the best way to try to get MacArthur to see eye to eye on how to proceed. On October 15, the two men met for the first time on Wake Island in the Pacific. General MacArthur was optimistic.

He predicted to the President that the Chinese Communists would not enter the war and that the fighting would be over by Thanksgiving. Truman was pleased. Again he stressed that this "police action" had strictly limited objectives, a prime one being to confine the fighting to Korea.

Upon his return to Korea, MacArthur gave his armies free rein and they raced toward the Yalu River, the border between North Korea and China's province of Manchuria. Only ten days after MacArthur expressed such optimism to his commander in chief, China did enter the conflict. Suddenly an overwhelming force of 200,000 well-equipped and suicidally determined Chinese troops poured into North Korea and sent the UN forces reeling backward with heavy losses. A ghastly reversal had begun.

The combined communist force battered the Americans and their allies back below the 38th parallel. In the process of falling back, the U.S. and UN forces had to struggle again across the rugged Korean landscape, this time in the depths of an incredibly cold winter. This time the conflict settled into a virtual standoff — a seesaw struggle in which weeks stretched into agonizing months and then even into years of unrelenting, tough, bloody, and frustrating combat.

Confronted with Chinese intervention, Truman held fast to the policy of limiting the fighting to Korea. He was determined to avoid further escalation, a policy with which the other members of the United Nations force agreed. China's enlargement of the war did not sit well with the President and his advisers, but neither did General MacArthur's persistent and increasingly political agitation in opposition to the President's policy. Truman, for his part, did not give a hoot what Douglas MacArthur thought of Harry Truman as a person. But Truman insisted with every essence of his being that the presidency — as a political institution, as an office under the U.S. Constitution — be absolutely respected as he himself never ceased to respect it.

General MacArthur was now making a pitch for direct air attacks on Chinese territory across the Yalu River. It was another case of disputing the tactical boundaries established by his superiors, and MacArthur increasingly chose to do this by airing his grievances so they could be picked up and debated in the political arena. Truman would respond by dispatching a suitable diplomatic or military intermediary to reemphasize patiently and politely to MacArthur what the President's policy was. In so many words, he told the general time and again that he sympathized with his problems in the field but that he had plenty of his own which were at least as great. Truman in fact showed remarkable restraint in the face of repeated instances of MacArthur's insolence. But Truman's patience was not inexhaustible, and MacArthur's conduct became even more flagrant.

Firing General MacArthur

MacArthur brought matters to a head and sealed his own fate with his actions in March of 1951. Three months earlier, Lieutenant General Matthew Ridgway had taken over the U.S. Eighth Army, the backbone of the UN fighting force, after a jeep accident took the life of the previous commander. Ridgway was an imaginative and decisive leader who revived the Eighth Army's battered morale, to the evident pique and surprise of General MacArthur. By mid-March, Ridgway had recaptured South Korea's capital, now a burned-out shell of a city. It was very difficult going, but the UN force gradually was gaining ground and had fought back to where the 38th parallel was within reach.

On March 15, MacArthur took a step that went beyond being difficult; he openly defied an order from the President forbidding military commanders to make unauthorized statements to the press. MacArthur issued just such a statement, objecting to stopping the UN advance at the 38th parallel or short of accomplishing "our mission in the unification of Korea."[8] MacArthur knew good and well, of course, that the unification of North and South Korea was not his military mission.

Nine days later, MacArthur went even further. America's allies, especially in NATO, were eager to see the Korean conflict end. It was becoming apparent in Washington that a clear-cut military victory was unlikely. Undoubtedly the Communists now saw that they could not win either. It therefore seemed to be a reasonably good time to take some diplomatic soundings about a negotiated settlement.

Carefully worded drafts of a proposed statement to be made by the President were sent for comments to each of the 14 allied governments participating with troops in Korea. The draft statement was to the effect that, with the aggressors repulsed, the UN side would be receptive to a cease-fire and negotiations. A copy was sent to MacArthur, so the commander in the field would know that his chief executive was conducting diplomacy at the highest and most sensitive level.

A few days after receiving this background message, MacArthur — without warning or authority — made a public announcement that *he* was prepared to negotiate. His statement contained praise and some self-pity for his command's brilliant success despite having to labor under inhibitions and restrictions. MacArthur then declared himself ready to confer with the enemy commander to find military means of realizing the UN's political objectives in Korea. MacArthur pointed out, however, that the enemy should be painfully aware that if the UN chose to depart from its tolerant effort to keep the war in the area of

Korea, all of China would be doomed to imminent military collapse.[9]

It was an extraordinary statement for a field commander to issue. Coming when it did, it constituted a major act of diplomatic sabotage. In a single public declaration, the UN commander had threatened — completely counter to UN strategy — to carry the war to China; he had again defied his commander in chief, and he had cut the ground out from under the President in the midst of delicate diplomatic maneuvers. This was the last straw. Truman concluded that he had no choice but to relieve MacArthur of his command.

As if further justification were needed, MacArthur promptly provided it. On March 20, he had written a letter to Representative Joseph W. Martin, the House Republican leader, that made a broadside attack on the President's policy. Martin had asked MacArthur if he wanted these views to be off the record; the general put no restriction on their use, so Martin rounded up an audience and on April 5 read the letter in the House of Representatives.

After again endorsing the idea of using in Korea the Chinese Nationalist forces on Formosa, MacArthur's letter expressed disdain for the inability of "some" — obviously meaning Truman — to see things his way. "It seems strangely difficult for some," MacArthur wrote, "to realize that here in Asia is where the Communist conspirators have elected to make their play for global conquest, and that we have joined the issue thus raised on the battlefield; that here we fight Europe's war with arms, while the diplomats there still fight it with words; that if we lose this war to Communism in Asia the fall of Europe is inevitable; win it and Europe most probably would avoid war and yet preserve freedom." MacArthur concluded with the stirring words, "There is no substitute for victory."[10]

This was more than just another case of MacArthur licking his wounds in public. He had acted to provide, in fact to participate in, a direct, partisan attack on the President. Truman believed in victory, but neither his best judgment nor the best counsel available from his national security advisers supported MacArthur's definition that victory, in the context of repelling aggression in Korea, meant embroiling Chiang Kai-shek, bombing Chinese cities, and expanding the war to all of China. What was at issue between MacArthur and Truman, however, was no longer a policy debate. For several weeks it had been a clear-cut issue of insubordination. The President vows in his oath of office to uphold the Constitution of the United States. If Truman were to uphold the Constitution, MacArthur had to go.

Before acting, Truman sounded out his senior advisers. Soon after the Korean conflict began, Truman had persuaded George Marshall to come out of retirement and serve as his secretary of defense. Marshall expressed concern about the effect MacArthur's dismissal might have on congressional passage of urgently needed defense appropriations. Secretary of State Acheson warned that the President was headed for the biggest fight of his administration. Both, however, recommended relieving MacArthur of his command and removing him from the Far East, with the concurrence of the joint chiefs. General Bradley believed that on grounds of military discipline, MacArthur should be relieved. Bradley consulted the other members of the joint chiefs, and reported their unanimous agreement.

The President wanted to carry out the dismissal properly. Efforts were made to contact Secretary of the Army Pace, who was in Korea touring the battlefield with General Ridgway. The plan was to have Pace go to Tokyo and deliver to MacArthur in person the order relieving him of command and designating Ridgway as his successor. It did not work out that way. General Bradley brought Truman the news that the plan had leaked out. If the story were published before the official orders were delivered, MacArthur would probably try to beat the President to the punch by resigning. "He's not going to be allowed to quit on me," Truman exploded. "He's going to be fired!" The orders were hastily conveyed to MacArthur by cable.

The deed was done, and now Truman would take the heat he knew was in store. He was secure in the knowledge that he could not have acted otherwise. As he told a friend in a letter written on April 10, 1951, the day he signed the order relieving MacArthur of his command, "It will undoubtedly create a great furor but under the circumstances I could do nothing else and still be President of the United States. Even the Chiefs of Staff came to the conclusion that civilian control of the military was at stake and I didn't let it stay at stake very long."[11]

It was not long, either, before the furor hit with a ferocity equalled by few political events in American history. General MacArthur's World War II exploits as the U.S. commander in the Pacific had forged an heroic image in the public mind. He was an almost legendary figure with a great many admirers. His dismissal, and the abrupt way it appeared to be done, caused an explosion of outrage.

Across the country, civic groups and PTA's passed heated resolutions, and thousands of angrily worded letters were fired off to congressmen and newspapers. Figures of Truman and Acheson were burned in effigy on college campuses. Congressmen were in a rage, many of them vying with each other and the searing outbursts from their constituents to see who could express the most indignation. Senator Jenner of Indiana shouted on the Senate floor that the country was in the hands of a secret inner coterie directed by Soviet agents and that the only choice was to impeach President Truman. The House Republican leader telephoned an invitation to MacArthur to come to Washington immediately to address a joint session of Congress.

Whatever pleasure he felt in the fury being directed at
Truman, it was the offer of such an extraordinary speaking
engagement that struck MacArthur's fancy the most. The
opportunity to have such a forum, to stand at the hallowed
rostrum of the nation's Capitol, speaking to both houses of
Congress and an adoring national audience, suited
MacArthur's taste perfectly. He was nothing if not a master
showman, with a keen sense for image building and a rare
gift of eloquence. He could make the most of his considerable intellect when it came to rhetoric and dramatic style.

MacArthur made a triumphant return. His performance
in addressing the assembled congressmen and an enthralled
national audience was a masterpiece. It was a moving
display of a great general's sense of honor, love of country,
and devotion to duty. MacArthur's delivery was flawless.
His words were carefully chosen to impart with quiet dignity the unmistakable implication that he, an innocent warrior motivated solely by patriotism, was being persecuted
by an ignorant and ignoble political hack.

Some people bought it, some didn't. In the end, Truman
weathered the storm. He had given a speech of his own,
explaining again, in detail, the strategy adopted in Korea
and the policy he had pursued from the beginning. Then he
had let MacArthur have his day. Truman took no cheap
shots. He did not attack or degrade MacArthur.

A congressional inquiry was launched in an expectant
aura of confrontation. But as the hearings dragged on and
the facts were laid out, it gradually became apparent that
General MacArthur was not larger than life after all. His
own appearances and testimony at the hearing could not
conceal his arrogance and the fallibility of his judgment.
Regardless of the merits of his views on military tactics,
there could be little doubt that MacArthur's conduct had
been out of line. And *that* was the real issue; it was his
conduct that got him fired. The public learned there was

much more to the record than had met the eye, and when the record came out the furor subsided.

The Use of Power

Truman's actions in handling the Korean crisis and in dealing with MacArthur embodied the blend of courage and restraint that is so critical in the use of power. Whatever frailties marred Truman's manner — and he was far from faultless — he had the strength of character to exercise power responsibly in a world of unprecedented challenges and dangers.

There were missteps, such as his threat to draft striking railroad workers in his first term, and his second-term seizure of the nation's steel mills to avert a strike and a price rise. In domestic crises Truman could get carried away with his inclination to act decisively and forcefully. He had little patience with problems at home that badly needed solving. He saw that the means for solving them were right at hand, but that one side or the other just would not get on with it. In such cases Truman could be forthright to a fault, and too inclined to tackle things head on. More than once he took his lumps in popularity and political standing as a result. Yet in the uncharted depths of international affairs, Truman applied leadership with sophistication and strength.

In conducting the affairs of state, Truman excelled when the chips were down. He was at his best in steering a steady course despite unprecedented challenges and dangers. He had the courage to act when action was required, and the restraint not to overreact or to carry his actions too far.

His unhappy experience with China undoubtedly affected Truman's reaction to Korea. He was still smarting from accusations that the "loss" of China suggested softness on Communism and questioned his decisiveness, strength of commitment, and sense of direction concerning events in Asia. When the Communists invaded South Korea, Truman probably felt he had no choice but to act swiftly and with a show of force. All the same, what Truman accomplished cannot be explained solely in terms of eagerness to avoid another "loss" to Communism. He may have been predisposed to meet the next challenge in Asia more directly, but that did not mean it could be done easily. Korea was a difficult and different kind of challenge. The backlash from the China experience certainly influenced if it did not predetermine Truman's readiness to draw the line in Korea, but it did not give him the ability to do it and to do it so wisely. Truman has to receive credit for the courage and capacity to act with speed and wisdom in a grave, fast-moving military crisis.

It was a brilliant stroke of political foresight and diplomatic savvy to join the battle in Korea under the flag of the United Nations. It was a far cry from the bitter diplomatic and political experience America would have in Southeast Asia not many years later. Being in Vietnam to defend America's national security was to be an assertion that would fall on deaf ears in most places abroad, and an explanation that would soon have a hollow ring for many at home. In Korea, even though Americans furnished almost all of the UN force and its equipment, the intervention was truly a collective action. The UN aegis made it thoroughly defensible. It was a matter of repelling aggression in order to uphold the UN Charter and its protective role over South Korea. That imparted a different character to the American role, and its political wisdom has stood the test of time.

Perhaps most significant was the fact that Truman did not overreact in drawing the line in Korea. He did not yield to the temptation to show his nation's enemies abroad or his detractors at home how tough he could be. Despite tremendous pressure on him to escalate and expand the war after China intervened, he remained true to the limits declared at the beginning. He would not allow himself to be panicked, pressured, or baited into relinquishing that restraint, no matter how frustrating it was militarily or how unpopular it was politically.

In the case of MacArthur, too, the "little" man from Missouri summoned up a mountain of both courage and restraint. On his White House desk, President Truman kept a sign that read, "THE BUCK STOPS HERE." The little sign said a lot about the nature of the presidency and about Truman's acceptance of the full responsibility that goes with it. When the really tough decisions come along, the ones that can be made nowhere else, they come to the President. This was one of the toughest. As with others, Truman did not try to pass the buck. He knew the job was his.

There are many examples of momentous decisions Truman made as President that point up the loneliness of speaking the last word on a critical issue — among them the decision to use the atomic bomb, to launch the Truman Doctrine and contain communist expansion, to defy the Berlin blockade, and to intervene in Korea. Perhaps none more vividly illustrates the personal courage these decisions require than the fateful decision to depose a general who had become a popular idol.

In the process, the President displayed abundant restraint toward outrageous provocations. He did not have someone else give MacArthur a dressing-down, when he could easily have ordered that done. Instead of summoning MacArthur to Washington to stand before his commander in chief, Truman had gone to MacArthur, flying halfway around the world to talk things over. Truman repeatedly went a second mile with the haughty general, providing one patient explanation after another.

When at last he knew he must draw the line on MacArthur, Truman's popularity was at a low ebb, and he knew his decision would be unpopular in the extreme. His ad-

ministration did not need to be any more embattled than it
was already, and firing MacArthur was sure to make things
worse than ever before. There was no telling what the
controversy would lead to. It could have grave consequences for Truman's ability to serve effectively. It could
even threaten his continuation as President. But Truman
perceived the issue that had been raised by MacArthur as
one that transcended its personal impact on Harry Truman.
It was nothing less than a challenge to the American constitutional system. Once again, Truman rose to the occasion
and did what he believed must be done.

There was no love lost between Truman and MacArthur
by the time the President signed the order relieving the
general of command. Even so, Truman resisted the impulse
to rub MacArthur's nose in what the general had done.
Truman stood apart from the frenzy the firing set in motion.
He did not heap abuse on MacArthur any more than he tried
to obliterate North Korea or China in order to draw the line
in Asia. There were limits. As Truman saw it, you try to do
the right thing. You also try to do it the right way. Both are
important. Truman distinguished himself as President by
drawing the line, and also by how he drew it.

Stalemates Home and Abroad

The Truman administration by no means ended in a blaze
of glory. It did not end in disgrace, either, but rather in a
kind of stalemate. In Korea, the war settled along the 38th
parallel into a bitterly contested standoff that would last
until a truce in 1953. At home, the Fair Deal never really got
off the ground. When his second term began in 1949, a
confident Truman had hoped for a vigorous advancement of
his program to aid the underprivileged. He believed his
dramatic election victory and the return of Congress to

Democratic control meant there was a mandate for domestic reform. Congress did not see it that way. It could get excited over charges about Communists in government, and over Truman's conduct of the war in Korea, but not about the Fair Deal.

In Truman's second term, as in his first, there was greater harmony between President and Congress on foreign policy — especially economic and military aid to Europe — than on domestic affairs. Except for the Housing Act of 1949 and the Social Security Act of 1950, which increased by almost ten million the number of persons who could benefit from old-age insurance, only a small part of Truman's Fair Deal was enacted into law. He managed to persuade Congress to spend on foreign aid but found it reluctant to provide funds for education and social legislation. In part this reluctance stemmed from discontent over dislocations — such as higher taxes and rising living costs — that the Korean conflict caused.

Truman strove to keep the economy stable, a determination dramatized in April of 1952, when he took over the steel industry to head off a strike and price hike in that basic commodity. Late the previous year, the steelworkers had said they would go on strike unless the industry raised their wages substantially and improved working conditions. The steel industry refused to negotiate, so Truman ordered a fact-finding study by the federal Wage Stabilization Board. It recommended a wage boost of 26 cents an hour, which the steel industry refused to accept unless granted an increase of $12 a ton in the price of steel.

Truman was outraged. "If the steel companies absorbed every penny of the wage increase," he said, "they would still be making profits of seventeen or eighteen dollars a ton. During the three years before the Korean outbreak, steel profits averaged a little better than eleven dollars a ton. The companies could absorb this wage increase entirely out of the profits and still be making much higher profits than they made in the three prosperous years before Korea.''[12] In Truman's view, you could say goodbye to economic stability if the steel companies got their way. Knuckling under on this issue would remove the lid, and prices would jump up all around. It would not be limited to things using steel, but would drive up the cost of many commodities, including grocery items.

His conviction about the far-reaching impact this issue would have on the nation's economy led Truman to act. Invoking emergency powers because of the Korean conflict, Truman put the steel industry under government operation. The stunning move aroused the ire of the business community and especially, of course, the steel industry. It waged all-out war against the President's action on two fronts — with advertising dollars in the communications media and with legal briefs in the federal courts. In the end, the Supreme Court upheld steel's challenge on the ground that Truman had exceeded his constitutional authority. He was obliged to approve a price rise.

Truman never doubted that he had done the right thing, of course, and also never ceased to insist that he had acted legally. He recalled past presidential actions such as Thomas Jefferson's Louisiana Purchase, Abraham Lincoln's response to the outbreak of the Civil War, James Polk's annexation of territory after the Mexican War, and Franklin Roosevelt's moves during the depression and World War II, contending they demonstrated the same inherent powers he had invoked under conditions of national emergency. Truman's move was nevertheless unpopular with many and was ultimately unproductive.

There were reasons other than the high cost of living and a high-handed effort to deal with it that caused disenchantment with Harry Truman during the second half of his presidency. An obvious one was Korea, which for Americans was an exceptionally difficult experience. It came such a short time after World War II had dominated their lives, involving anxieties and inconveniences for everybody and, for a multitude of Americans, the pain of separation and the loss of loved ones. They were not ready for more of this. Neither were they prepared for an insolent, pipsqueak half of a country to push around the United States of America, the triumphant conqueror of the Axis powers and now the acknowledged supreme power of the world.

Little North Korea had behaved like a bully, and America had stepped in heroically to administer the whipping the North Koreans deserved. It was all supposed to be done with dispatch. The fact that the North Koreans could not quickly be whipped was more than many Americans could bear. It was a blow to the ego — always the hardest kind of blow to take. When North Korea's Chinese allies joined the battle against America and its allies, it added injury to insult. American frustration deepened as the fighting was drawn out, so bitterly but inconclusively, for such a long time. It became easy to vent one's frustration by blaming Truman for expecting the hero to pull his punches.

The sad fact was that in the waning months of his administration, Truman lost the confidence of much of the country. It was more than Korea. Truman himself was partially to blame. He had a remarkable grasp of the big picture, and could organize and digest a vast array of detail, but his faith in others was not always repaid. His managerial style was to trust those to whom he delegated responsibility. He took their integrity and competence for granted, and did not look over their shoulder to see how they were doing their jobs. A few, it turned out, were not up to it. In some instances, it was Truman's old friends who did not fully merit the trust and independent authority he gave them as government officials. These instances were gleefully magnified in the press, which, with the help of Truman's political enemies, delighted in discrediting him with exaggerated reports about his "cronies" and "the mess in Washington."

Some people felt that Truman, although likeable, just never gripped the public's heartstrings — that somehow he lacked that magnetism that arouses and inspires the nation. Perhaps it was that the "little" man from Missouri was simply too ordinary in his manner and appearance to be pictured as a knight in shining armor astride a white horse. The very middle-class tastes, the flashes of temper, the plainness, and homespun qualities of the President were so ordinary that many could not see his extraordinary qualities.

Both the nature of the Congress he confronted and the office he held worked against Truman's program for domestic reform. Even when Democrats won majorities in Congress, these turned out to be paper majorities whenever a coalition of Republicans and antiadministration Democrats got together. The forces of deadlock that had appeared in Congress toward the end of Roosevelt's New Deal had become institutionalized by the time Truman was pushing his Fair Deal. Frustrated by Truman's victory in 1948, Republican congressmen were determined to build a winning case against ineffective Democratic leadership by 1952. Joining forces with them were a number of conservative Democrats, mostly from southern, rural constituencies, who because of the prevailing seniority system were entrenched in important committee chairmanships. These Democrats were prepared to take part in a coalition to thwart enactment of Fair Deal measures which they looked upon as catering to the urban, liberal, North. Truman was up against this throughout his presidency.

Progress in his domestic program was also made more difficult by the fact that Truman was the first to conduct a "dual presidency." The developing cold war, with the new problems and unprecedented foreign responsibilities it thrust upon the U.S., was relentlessly competing for attention with peacetime domestic legislation. The same conservative coalition that worked against domestic reform was an integral part of the internationalist coalition in Congress that supported Truman's foreign policy. As a result, there were many times when he could not push too hard for a domestic program for fear of alienating support for a key foreign policy move.

Ultimately, China and Korea just about ended Truman's chances for passage of his domestic programs. Events in Asia — the communist threats they raised and the military demands they made — became the major concern for Congress and much of the American public.

An Uncertain Succession

As the Korean conflict dragged on, Truman came to one of the last momentous steps of his presidency — the decision not to run for another term. It was not a sudden decision. In the fall of 1951, Truman had confided to members of his staff that he had already made up his mind on the subject. But he surprised the country when he announced his decision during a Jefferson-Jackson Day speech in Washington on March 29, 1952. "I shall not be a candidate for reelection," Truman told the stunned gathering of 5300 Democrats. "I have served my country long and I think efficiently and honestly. I shall not accept a renomination. I do not feel that it is my duty to spend another four years in the White House."[13]

Soon after that speech, Truman told his 300th press conference as President that "My reason for not running is based on the fact that I don't think any man — I don't care how good he is — is indispensable in this job."[14] Eight

years, Truman said, provided sufficient time for a President
to make all the contributions he could. By then he had either
done it well or not well. Truman sensed, as did the country,
that it was time for a change. He had had his time. Before
the next election campaign got under way he would have
spent 30 years in public office. When his term expired, he
would have served almost all of two terms as President.
That was enough for Truman. Besides, the job, he
confessed privately, was a killer; he'd rather not ''be carried out of the White House in a pine box.''[15] So he also
drew the line on his own ambitions.

The Trumans in fact looked forward to returning to the
peace and quiet of small-town life in Missouri. They had no
taste for high society, and did not bask in the glamour that
tends to go with the presidency. For Truman, the office
amounted to a demanding job that had to be done, an
awesome burden he was called upon to bear, and nothing
more. He could do without the trappings. He and his family
were never comfortable with the constant restrictions of
security and the glare of publicity that the presidency imposed on them.

Truman was not going to be indifferent, of course, to the
question of who would be the next occupant of the White
House. He intended to have a say in the matter. His first
choice was the Chief Justice of the Supreme Court, Fred
Vinson. The distinguished Georgian was an old friend
Truman greatly admired; he had a long record of government experience spanning the legislative, executive, and
judicial branches. After much thought, Vinson declined, on
grounds of health, to resign and take on a grueling campaign for nomination and election. Truman was deeply
disappointed. After a few months, he turned to Governor
Adlai E. Stevenson of Illinois, who was highly recommended to him and who had been elected in 1948 by an
impressively large vote.

Stevenson at first said no, but following several months of uncertainty decided at last to seek the nomination. Truman helped him get it, and stumped for him vigorously during the campaign. The President did so because he was a loyal party man and because he was worried about what would happen to American foreign policy if Dwight Eisenhower became President. This was Truman's primary concern — that key features of his foreign policy be carried forward without interruption or letup. They included perfecting the NATO alliance, rebuilding free nations with economic aid and Point Four programs, and pursuing the difficult challenge of Korea. He knew General Eisenhower agreed with these policies; in fact, as NATO commander, he was helping carry some of them out. But now that Ike had let himself be talked into being the Republican nominee for President, Truman had grave misgivings. No matter how well-intentioned, the general was totally inexperienced in politics. Truman was fearful Ike would never be master of the Republican household. He was afraid Ike would soon come under the influence of powerful Republican isolationists who tended to oppose an active American role in world affairs.

Stevenson disappointed Truman with his ineffectual campaign, and the President was not greatly astonished when Eisenhower won. As a candidate, the Illinois intellectual had confirmed Truman's worst fears about an "egghead" in politics. Stevenson's wit was elegant. His vocabulary was most impressive. His speech was polished and unfailingly articulate. But much of what Stevenson said sailed over his listeners' heads. He was given to couching every position he stated in tedious, cautious, carefully qualified rationalizations. His approach was no match for the shy grin and "aw shucks" folksiness of the war hero he was running against. In Truman's view, an election campaign was a power struggle, not an educational process. He campaigned for Stevenson to the end, but was further disillusioned as Stevenson struggled to disassociate himself from Truman's record.

A shift by Truman on an issue concerning Korea helped seal Stevenson's defeat. Talks to arrange a truce were underway in Korea, and one of the points under discussion was the repatriation of prisoners taken by both sides. Truman felt that North Korean prisoners who wished to remain in the South after an armistice was signed should not be forced to go back. The President therefore told his negotiators there must be no compromise on the subject of exchanging prisoners of war. Each prisoner must be left free to choose to be repatriated. The principle Truman stood on so firmly was an admirable one, but on this issue the Korean negotiations stalled for the remainder of his term. This assured the continued existence of the Korean War as a major issue throughout the campaign. The continued stalemate and mounting U.S. casualties enabled Eisenhower — the number one national hero of World War II, untarnished by all the domestic difficulties of the postwar years — to clinch the election by announcing to a war-weary American public that he would go to Korea to obtain peace. Eventually there would be an armistice, one that has been described as "a poor substitute for victory but a tolerable substitute for war." Ike's political victory at home was more clear-cut; he buried Stevenson in a landslide.

After the election, Truman made elaborate arrangements to smooth the transition to a new administration and to acquaint the President-elect with pending problems. But a White House meeting between the two was stiff and unproductive. Truman felt the general was still smarting from the partisanship of the campaign. Truman was troubled by the meeting, and Eisenhower's apparent belief that the President should operate like a general. The first thing he had done in their White House session was to demand to know who the chief of staff was. Truman did not have one. Eisenhower gave the impression that he had no interest in hearing about any problems until his staff had worked on them, and that he did not expect his staff to bring him any problems unless they also brought along solutions. The approach was alien to Truman's way of doing things, and it did not make him happy. He was sure Ike was going to be very frustrated to discover that the presidency was not like the army.

Qualms gave way to animosity when the President-elect went to Korea. Bess Truman's mother had died in the White House, and the President had accompanied his wife to Independence for the funeral. From Korea, Eisenhower wired MacArthur that he would meet with him to discuss MacArthur's ideas for ending the struggle. Truman was returning to Washington when he read in a newspaper of the Eisenhower-MacArthur exchange. Truman bristled. If MacArthur had a solution — which Truman doubted — he should present it to his President now rather than save it for his successor. Back in Washington, Truman strode into a press conference and hotly dismissed Eisenhower's trip to Korea as "a piece of demagoguery."[16]

Eisenhower and Truman did not meet again until they rode together in the back of an open car in the ceremonial procession to the Capitol for Eisenhower's inauguration. It was a chilly ride, and not only because of the January weather. The two had little to say to each other — that day or later.

Home to Missouri

No public send-off had been planned. The Trumans expected to leave Washington quietly and all but unnoticed in the turmoil of the Republican's celebration. The inaugural parade was passing by the Eisenhower reviewing stand back at the White House, and downtown Washington was a monstrous traffic jam when the Trumans reached Union Station to board the train that would take them home. To their dismay, the station was jammed with thousands of cheering, singing well-wishers who had come to bid the Trumans farewell. It was a tribute that moved Truman as few experiences had done during all the time he was President. And there was more to come. An estimated 10,000 persons greeted the train at the Independence railroad station, and some 5000 more managed to cram themselves in front of the Truman home. The touching outpouring of affection for the outgoing President was a precursor of how his stature as President would grow with the years.

The clean break Truman made when he left the exalted office of President was one of the most remarkable things about him. He had none of the Potomac fever that almost invariably lingers in those who have tasted power. When Truman left Washington, he left for good. He brought with him no illusions about returning to the life of private citizen. No one understood better than he that the privileges and powers had belonged to the office of President, not to Harry Truman. He had occupied that office; he did not try to hang on.

On the eve of the President's final departure from the White House, a reporter asked him, "What are you going to do when you get back to Independence?" It never occurred to Truman that his questioner was probing for a hint of some grandiose plans. Truman was a little startled by the question. "Well," he replied, "I guess I'll carry the suitcases up to the attic."[17] There was no hint here of further ambitions. There was no desire in this man to seek a prestigious appointment, to hold another position or title that might put his hand on some rein of political power and give him a prominent role in national or party affairs. "I have had all of

Washington that I want,'' Truman said in retirement. ''I never had the complex of being a big shot. I prefer my life in Missouri and I prefer to live the way I do.''[18]

For Truman, retirement did not mean sleeping late and loafing. He enjoyed more than ever his morning ritual of long, brisk walks. He was delighted that after years of being surrounded by servants and aides and Secret Service men he could again do things for himself like carrying his own suitcases and driving his own car. He continued to take a half dozen newspapers, and he plunged into the preparation of a long, factual account of his presidency that would be published as his *Memoirs*.

Above all, Truman achieved a dream that became the joy of the last years of his life — establishing a library where his papers and other material pertaining to the presidency could be stored and studied. He was justly proud that it did not cost the country's taxpayers one cent to build the Truman Library — the people of Independence gave the site and Truman raised the money entirely from private donations. He was immensely pleased, as this writer knows firsthand, to have researchers use the library's materials. Truman's keen sense of history had prompted him to have every scrap of paper that crossed his White House desk saved as part of the record of his presidency. He believed the office belonged to the people, and that they should know more about it. He wanted to be sure that a visit to his library would be an educational experience, and he instilled in its staff a spirit of openness and helpfulness.

Content in the judgment that he had done the best he could, Truman was willing to let the record speak for itself. He was not one to dwell on his achievements or brood about his failures. Truman himself may have summed it up best in his own simple, direct style: ''I have tried my best to give the nation everything I have in me. There are a great many people — I suppose a million in this country — who could have done the job better than I did it. But I had the job and I had to do it.''

Truman always liked to quote an epitaph, reputed to be in a cemetery at Tombstone, Arizona, which says, ''He done his damnedest.''

''I think that is the greatest epitaph a man can have,'' Truman said, ''when he gives everything that is in him to the job he had before him. That is all that you can ask of him and that is what I have tried to do.''

VIII The Verdict of History

A lot of people hated Harry Truman. Others hailed him. Not many were neutral. He had a way of inspiring admiration or provoking wrath. His popularity soared or plummeted. The Gallup poll has obtained popularity scores for incumbent Presidents since the Roosevelt years, and more than two decades after leaving office Harry Truman still held the record high (87 percent) and the record low (23 percent). A contemporary of Truman's remarked that one sure way to start an argument is to say that Harry Truman was a good President, and another sure way is to say that he wasn't.

Reviewing his actions as his presidency drew to a close, Truman said "The presidents who have done things, who were not afraid to act, have been the most abused . . . and I have topped them all in the amount of abuse I have received." He helped create much of the partisan furor, of course, with his own partisan combative style. And it was often his own statements that gave critics a field day. Press conferences were a continuing problem. Truman deserves credit for holding them so often, but his natural inclination to be forthright and helpful made him all too eager to respond to questions without a word of qualification or a moment's hesitation. The answers came too quickly and too surely. Retractions were a common follow-up to a Truman press conference, and would provide another round of ammunition for an army of columnists, cartoonists, editorial writers, and political adversaries.

In the heat of developing issues, the pages of the periodical press throughout Truman's presidency abounded with verbal fireworks. They provide a mixed commentary on his day-to-day performance as it was reported and reacted to at the time. But when he left office, there was a dramatic change of tune in much of the news media. It was more than a case of the potshots ceasing simply because the target was no longer there. There seemed to be a general recognition that the good about the Truman presidency far outweighed the bad. For many, the scars would stay and the bitterness toward Truman would not quickly disappear. Truman was no less controversial and would remain so. Nevertheless, most commentators conceded that the man who had just stepped out of the White House had been a hard-working, devoted servant of the people.

Truman's Contemporaries

Throughout Truman's presidency, partisan viewpoints tended inevitably to color accounts of his performance. A reading of the commentaries of the day shows him alternately praised and roundly condemned, depending largely on the issue of the moment and how it happened to affect certain viewpoints and interest groups. Overall, the chorus of contemporary reaction was discordant. Truman was that kind of person — in the thick of things, taking sides and doing battle. He was almost always dealing with that kind of problem — the volatile ones where the lines were drawn sharply, the feelings ran deep, and the sparks flew. He was not one for sitting on the fence. He could be lauded as a crusader for all that was noble and good, and he could be scorned as the devil incarnate. The times were unusually trying, and the topics unusually tough. Truman was forever grappling with the "gut issues" that hit closest to home — the bread-and-butter issues that hit the pocketbook, and the emotional ones that touched the quick of fear and suspicion.

Even so, some early impressions of him in the presidency revealed insight into qualities of Truman's which would transcend and outlast the issues of the day. These were traits he brought with him and which stayed with him. They were characteristics of him as a person as well as the President, and they persisted through the trials of office. They were perceived in those first demanding months of Truman's presidency by the trained eye of an artist and author who observed Truman as he went about his work in the Oval Office.

The portrait that emerged in words shows a man whose straightforward affability was unaltered by pomp and circumstance. Truman was determined that the office would not change him. The man who dealt firsthand at Potsdam with such giant figures as Churchill and Stalin was no self-important statesman. One day while strolling on the south lawn of the White House, the spectators at a ball game going on across the road spotted him and began heading for the iron fence. Truman beat a hasty retreat. Even the President, he said, should not interfere with a ball game.[1]

The close observer of Truman as President was struck by the strong streak of sentiment in his makeup, and by his old-fashioned tastes. He was devoted to family and friends. He did not mind being called old-fashioned because he admired the King James version of the Bible and Shakespeare, and because Bach, Beethoven, Brahms, and Chopin still sounded good to his ears. He was gregarious by nature, and continually irked by the restrictions that being President imposed on his freedom. After a long day of meetings and reports he would have loved to go down to the Senate office building for a gab session with his old cronies there, but that would mean being accompanied by Secret Service men and that in turn would attract attention. He showed himself in his work as a great believer in the personal equation. He had confidence that much could be accomplished by sitting

down and "thrashing things out." He was willing to take
advice, to listen to others. And anyone who observed him at
work could not help but be impressed by the rapidity with
which he made decisions and the finality with which he
announced them.[2]

No one was better placed to observe Truman tackling the
great issues of his time than was Dean Acheson. As undersecretary of state and later as secretary of state he worked at
close quarters with Truman throughout his administration.
Acheson marveled at Truman's inexhaustible supply of
vitality and good spirits. "He could, and did, outwork us
all," Acheson wrote later, "with no need for papers pre-
digested into one-page pellets of pablum." When things
went wrong, Truman took the blame, and when things went
right he gave someone else the credit. These are the qualities of a leader who builds spirit and boosts morale, Acheson noted, and they were characteristic of the private side of
the President. There was the public figure — the peppery,
sometimes belligerent, "give-'em hell" Harry — and there
was the patient, modest, considerate, and appreciative
boss. He inspired loyalty by being helpful and understanding not only in official matters but equally so in any private
worry or sorrow.[3] Once when Acheson was in Europe,
involved in negotiations, his daughter had to be hos-
pitalized in Washington. Truman — himself the doting
father of a daughter — checked on her condition every day,
and each night telephoned Acheson with a personal report
on how she was doing.

George Marshall, another distinguished contemporary
whose association with Truman was long and close, called
the capacity for decision the rarest gift given to man, and
often said that Truman had it to a high degree. Acheson
agreed, observing that Truman was able to decide and act
without being beset by second thoughts, self-doubt, and
"that most enfeebling of emotions, regret." Acheson

praised Truman for more than that, noting that the capacity for decision does not of itself guarantee wise ones. A President, according to Acheson, is not merely coping; he is called upon to influence and move to some degree his own country and the world around it to a purpose he envisions. The former secretary of state felt that when Truman found his footing in foreign affairs, his policies showed a sweep, a breadth of conception and boldness of action that were new in America's history. It had been seen in the early domestic policies of the New Deal and in the military effort of World War II, but not before in foreign policy. "The 1947 assumption of responsibility in the eastern Mediterranean, the 1948 grandeur of the Marshall Plan, the response to the blockade of Berlin, the NATO defense of Europe in 1949, and the intervention in Korea in 1950 — all those constituted expanding action in truly heroic mold," Acheson wrote in assessing Truman's performance from the perspective of a decade and a half later. "All of them were dangerous. All of them required rare capacity to decide and act. All of them were decided rightly, and vigorously followed through."[4]

The contemporary portrait of Truman was not so much a clear picture as a montage. One observer could relate how President Truman was guided by devout and uncomplicated moral precepts, cherishing Solomon as the model of a public man and seeking to govern his own conduct in office by a biblical passage about the Old Testament king.[5] Another observer could characterize Truman as being as corny as they come. Enjoying himself at an American Legion convention in Missouri, the President, it was said, "did everything except have himself shot from the mouth of a cannon."[6] A contemporary biographer, writing while Truman was President, described him as both the product and the embodiment of the American faith, which he spoke in the language of his countrymen. "Moscow understands what he says, as well as Independence and Iowa, the steel towns, the Carolinas, and Wall Street."[7]

No less a personage than Winston Churchill, generally regarded as the supreme statesman of his day, paid Truman one of the highest compliments that one world leader ever gave another. Shortly after Truman left office, Churchill confessed to Truman that when he had inherited the presidency and come to Potsdam, he had held him in very low regard. In fact, Churchill said, "I loathed your taking the place of Franklin Roosevelt." Then Churchill said, "I misjudged you badly. Since that time, you, more than any other man, have saved Western Civilization."[8]

"Free of the greatest vice in a leader, his ego never came between him and his job," said Acheson of Truman.[9] Marshall once tried to assess Truman while he was still in office. "The full measure of this man," Marshall said, "will only be proved by history. But I want to say here and now that there never has been a decision made under this man's Administration . . . that has not been made in the best interest of his country. It is not only the courage of these decisions that will live, but the integrity of them." It was characteristic of Truman that when he thought of great men, he never thought of himself. He considered Marshall the great man. And it was characteristic of Harry Truman that, as he listened to Marshall's words of praise, tears ran down his cheeks.[10]

Seeing the Forest

Once the political hubbub he loved to help create had died down, it was easier to render a balanced judgment of Truman. The controversy around him lingered, but did not greatly overheat the emotions — except about once every four years, around presidential election time, when in certain Republicans a certain amount of Truman-hating would surface. Truman had expected, as he put it, to be "cussed and discussed" for a long time to come, and probably was taken aback at the general growth of good will and esteem that came his way the longer he was out of office. The chronicles of political combat gave way to reflections and appraisals that benefitted in perspective from the passage of time. Those who wrote neither to attack nor defend Truman's presidency but to evaluate it were able, beginning a decade later, to see the forest come into focus and not have their vision blurred by the trees of particular issues, events, and clashing personalities.

Alfred Steinberg noted, in *The Man from Missouri,* that there were still some prudish souls appalled by Truman's language. There were a few ultraconservatives who held that Truman promoted radicalism while in office, and a few McCarthy die-hards who contended that he was "soft on Communism." There were academicians who questioned Truman's grasp of public affairs, and New Dealers who still disliked him because his name was not Franklin Roosevelt. But when the veneer of his tumultuous era in office was stripped away, and Truman's frank language and excessive loyalty were forgotten, what remained was a man of strength and patriotism who made great and courageous decisions. "He can already be called the most underrated President," Steinberg wrote, "in his country's entire history."[11]

In what may well be the most readable and the best account of Truman's presidency, written by Cabell Phillips, Truman is commended especially for refusing to let presidential initiative be eroded by Congress. Truman was a man of Congress himself, of course, having spent ten years in the Senate. He venerated it as an institution and loved it for its excitement, its companionship, and the sense of personal fulfillment it provided. But Truman also knew its frailties — its parochial shortsightedness and its tendency to yield to the whims and prejudices of a handful in positions of power — and occasionally to demagogues. He knew Congress could be a partner in governing with a strong executive in the White House, but he knew Congress could not govern and it could not lead. As President, Truman did battle with Congress almost constantly. At times the conflict rose to heights of fury. He lost many skirmishes, but the sum of his victories was seen by Phillips as reaffirming against heavy odds what Jackson, Lincoln, and the two Roosevelts had asserted before him — that in America's government of divided powers the President is "first among equals."[12]

Phillips suggests measuring the greatness of a President by asking if he actively used the potentialities of his position to advance the national interest. His conclusion is that, in Truman's case, the answer is an emphatic "yes." Emerging from the humbling shadow of Franklin Roosevelt, he pushed the nation steadily toward new goals of national welfare and international security. Although Truman's gains on the domestic front were, in the end, modest, his achievements in foreign policy were acclaimed as monumental. His two terms were overshadowed at all times by a danger no other President ever had to face — the rebalancing of world power between two hostile and incompatible forces, each capable of utterly destroying the other. Truman met that danger with bold, imaginative, and durable countermeasures. The Truman Doctrine, the Marshall Plan, NATO, the Berlin airlift, and the Korean intervention stand as landmarks of historic proportions along the road of national maturity. Phillips wrote that they have profoundly and permanently affected the destiny of the American people and of the world.[13]

In a biographical collection of five American leaders and how they coped with crises, the Pulitzer prize-winning author William S. White saw Truman demonstrating a "subtlety of thought and action in the crisis arenas of world affairs which was so improbable a part of his leadership qualities, given all his background and experience." Truman, in his view, ranks as "one of the very great Presidents," as "one of the finest masters of grand affairs and one of the most inept handlers of petty affairs and problems within the lifetime . . . of this republic." White credits Truman with being "an abler President, when things really and enduringly mattered . . . than his patron and chief, Franklin D. Roosevelt, had ever been." White, in fact, portrays Truman in even broader, bolder strokes than that. In what some would consider extravagant characterization, he describes Harry Truman as "an Abraham Lincoln utterly without the melancholy grandeur of his prairie predecessor and totally lacking in the mystical quality of that gaunt, richly neurotic figure. And yet where Lincoln saved a nation, Truman saved a world."[14]

The yardstick White used in measuring such giant stature for the "little" man from Missouri was the ability to tell the indispensable from the merely desirable objective. To White, history's verdict would rest on this vital distinction. Truman, he believed, knew when to commit himself, and all he had, to a political aim and when not to do so. The questions he had to answer were these: Is the objective big enough to justify risking much? Is it truly national in scope and meaning, or is it parochial or regional? Is it an objective that truly engages the national safety, honor, or welfare? Or is it something that, in an ideal world, ought to be settled but yet can really be deferred without vast harm to the republic? Different times will give differing answers to these critical questions. In White's judgment, Truman had the quality of knowing what the right answers were for his time.

Circumstances put Truman in the presidency at a time when not extending domestic welfarism but rather coping with and containing the vast enigmas of the cold war in a new age called "atomic" became the mission of the U.S. and thus of its leader. To accomplish that mission, Truman accepted domestic defeats that left most of his 21-point program right where it began in 1945, as proposals. He accepted unpopularity, leaving office scorned by millions in his own country but valued by more millions abroad who had little concern for what Truman had not done in the U.S. but respect bordering on reverence for his achievements across the world. White believes Truman conceded the contest in home affairs and forfeited all chance for reelection in 1952 by putting first things first. He carried out his obligations as a responsible leader while lesser men with larger vocabularies and more polished manners were pleading with him to "bend a little" to domestic outcries.

White cites the example of Truman resolutely keeping in office the most maligned secretary of state in history, Dean Acheson, fully knowing that doing Acheson in would instantly improve his own standing in the polls and with his fellow Democratic politicians. Why did he do it? Not because Truman had a death wish or a martyr complex but simply because he knew Acheson to be honorable and competent. He knew, too, that sacrificing Acheson to know-nothings would stain an institution that had been lent to Truman's trust — the presidency of the United States.

The point White makes is that Truman knew the crucial difference between being instantly responsive to public pressure where the issue was domestic comfort, and being utterly resistant to pressure where the matter concerned was deeper and more vast — such as national safety or the integrity of national institutions or traditions. He could be as partisan as the next fellow, or even more so, when partisanship could do his party some good and the national interest no great or lasting harm. He did not mind demagoguing it up, as the political pros put it, when it was only a question of doing minor damage on a comparatively minor matter. But he would not retreat an inch to public pressure or partisan necessity when he knew his last, unalterable duty was to stand firm upon a course, no matter who or how many did not like it. Truman knew how to discriminate between objectives and understood their relative values. This, White contends, is where Truman's greatness lay. He had an instinct for making the critical choices.[15]

Similar if less laudatory appraisals of Truman's decision-making qualities began as years passed to come from some of the most unexpected quarters. As the distance from the emotions and personalities entwined in earlier issues grew greater, even Truman's former enemies perceived virtue where they had seen only evil at the time. None was a more dramatic reversal of form than the praise bestowed as President by Richard Nixon, who had been quick to take the lead in abusing Truman when he was President. Twenty years later Nixon, too, paid tribute to Truman, acknowledging the toughness and rightness of his decisions to use the atomic bomb, to launch the Truman Doctrine, and to intervene in Korea. "The little man from Missouri had that indefinable quality, or character," Nixon said, "that made him a man capable of making tough decisions."[16]

Although not the Truman-baiter Nixon was, Earl Warren was the Missourian's partisan adversary as the Republicans' vice-presidential candidate in 1948. Later, as chief justice of the Supreme Court, Warren served on the board of directors of the Truman Library. After Truman's death, Warren described him as "a great, great President. As time goes on the greatness of his personality and his actions will become more apparent to the nation and the world." Senator Barry Goldwater, a Republican spokesman and partisan of the first order, and his party's presidential candidate in 1964, later rated Truman as "possibly the best

President of this century.'' Goldwater explained that
''What the Presidents we remember are remembered for is
leadership in time of peril. Washington led us in the peril of
birth; Jefferson in the peril of an emerging government . . .
Lincoln guided us through . . . desperate times in our
history; Teddy [Roosevelt] did the same; and that brings us
to Truman.'' Goldwater said, ''I didn't agree with much
that Truman did, but one thing I could always say: I knew
where he stood and I didn't have to wait around for a press
conference, a television show, or a group of press agents to
tell me what it was he said or what he was supposed to have
said.''[17]

Revisionists at Work

America's involvement in the Vietnam War was to have
an impact on every aspect of American politics and on
American thinking about politics. There was a questioning
of the meaning and purpose of American involvement there
and of the underlying assumptions upon which American
foreign policy rested. It is no wonder, then, that this in turn
led to a questioning of assumptions about the early years of
the cold war. As sentiment in the U.S. against an American
role in Vietnam became more emotional, grew more widespread, and gained more momentum, it set in motion a
pendulum of criticism.

It is the nature of a pendulum to keep swinging until it
carries to the other extreme, and this one was no exception.
It soon became rather popular to suppose that if America
being involved in Vietnam was wrong, that perhaps
America being involved anywhere was wrong, that perhaps
America was just wrong, period, and it probably wasn't
wrong just now, but had been all along. So it went. It
became popular for Americans to question their country's

intentions and conduct during the post-World War II era. This trend soon spawned a school of critics of the cold war who have been variously labeled the revisionist historians, or the left revisionists. Given the freedom in America to express these views, a literature of revisionist history came into being. Beginning in 1961, this school of thought became a full-fledged effort to rewrite the recent history of the U.S. in international affairs. Naturally the same cast of characters was involved, but assigning the part of the villain was quite different.

Some left-revisionist academicians brought to their work an almost Calvinistic concept of original sin. They zealously advanced the view that America was rotten to the core, that America's inhuman capitalism and U.S. expansionism in the 19th century inevitably produced the cold war and then Vietnam. Revisionists took the position that, after World War II, it was America's aggressive plans and actions that threatened the Soviet Union and thus set off the string of crises that came to be known as the cold war. The frightened Russians had been forced into it by American evil doing.

A leading example of this line of thinking is found in Joyce and Gabriel Kolko's *The Limits of Power,* published in 1972. The authors argue, for example, that Truman invented the Berlin blockade and airlift in order to frighten Congress into accepting his administration's warlike views. It is not clear just how the airlift, as a response to a blockade that the other side instituted, makes the crisis the creation of the U.S. President. It apparently is clear to the authors, however, who contend that Truman saw the blockade as a manageable crisis that was useful for conjuring up an ominous Soviet threat whenever it served his legislative purposes.

The roots of revisionism actually predate Vietnam, although it was that national trauma that gave the approach

special impetus. The roots go back to the 1950s and the
writings of William Appelman Williams, who described
American diplomacy as nothing but expansionism, engaged in for solely economic reasons. It was America's
conduct, according to Williams, that caused U.S. and
Soviet interests to clash. The U.S. was entirely to blame
and the Soviets were entirely blameless. Many historians
took issue with the way in which this one-dimensional,
pro-Soviet thesis was advanced. They saw it as a very
oversimplified and one-sided explanation of foreign policy,
and thought that there was much in Williams' writings that
simply did not meet normal standards of scholarship. He
seemed less interested in well-reasoned analysis than in
arguing a cause. He simply ignored too much evidence if it
did not fit his thesis. His writing was in the nature of an
ideological polemic. It created a bit of a sensation, though,
and Williams and some others who were so inclined obviously liked that. In their view, the stir was not over quality
or credibility, but because theirs was a bold and provocative
approach that challenged conventional assumptions.

Those who are taken with the idea of challenging conventional assumptions in this Williams style of questionable
objectivity have been active in disputing Truman's decision
to use atomic bombs. In the lead was Gar Alperowitz,
whose *Atomic Diplomacy,* written in 1965, charged that
Truman used atomic bombs on the Japanese not to end the
war and save lives in the long run, but to put political
pressure on the Russians. The Alperowitz argument
launched the controversy, still unresolved, between those
who hold that the atomic bomb decision was motivated
primarily by what at the time was considered a wartime
necessity and those who contend that it was primarily a cold
war provocation.

Herbert Feis, eminent author of many diplomatic studies,
fueled the argument with his book, *The Atomic Bomb and*

the End of World War II, written in 1967. Feis took the position that the atomic bomb's effect on American relations with Russia was an important consideration in determining its use. He concluded, however, that on balance the decision to use the bomb ought not to be censured. Walter Schoenberger was eager to do so; in *Decision of Destiny,* published in 1971, he lined up squarely with Alperowitz in advancing a particularly critical viewpoint. Schoenberger sees an unsophisticated Truman swept along by a military machine whose momentum made him almost a prisoner of forces he did not set in motion. Truman, in this view, was more the captive of the bomb than a free decision-making agent.

Another major contribution to the atomic bomb controversy came from Princeton historian Martin Sherwin, who wrote *A World Destroyed: The Atomic Bomb and the Grand Alliance,* published in 1975. Both sides in the controversy have fought over Feis, and both were quick to claim support from Sherwin. He probably fits more into the "cold war provocation" camp, but Sherwin does not make Truman the chief villain. He believes that Truman, in the general transition from world war to cold war, was acting on the basis of inherited policies rather than imposing new ones of his own. Sherwin disputes the interpretation that the bomb was used above all to impress the Russians, pointing out that all policy-makers connected with the atomic bomb project had assumed all along, and had never wavered from the conviction, that the bomb would be used to win the war.

Not all those who might be lumped together as revisionist historians would appreciate the company they would be found keeping. Like all labels, it can be easier to pin on than to wear, and should not be taken to mean that all who wear it think just alike. Not all take the extreme, simplistic position that postwar U.S. foreign policy was continually satanic, that Communists were the personification of wounded innocence, and that any other version is the work of a cold warrior. Gaddis Smith, for example, is inclined to place the pendulum more in the center. He favors a more balanced look at the history of the cold war, one which recognizes that mutual fear and suspicion caused misconceptions on both sides. But Smith, too, has suggested that Vietnam resulted from Truman's response to the Berlin blockade.[18] He shares an assumption that the revisionist historians do have in common — that Harry Truman was, above all else, a general in the cold war.

One of the more recent and widely read examples of this is Charles Mee's *Meeting at Potsdam,* published in 1975. It is almost even-handed in assigning the blame for beginning the cold war, leaving the impression that it probably belongs to both sides or to neither one. Mee compares the break between Russia and the West to a divorce, with similar factors of self-esteem, a sense of moral rectitude, and hard feelings adding up to the partners' rejection of each other.[19] Whose fault was it? The author makes no judgment; he makes fools. Bent on producing a best-selling novel, Mee is at pains to tailor it to the fad inspired by Watergate revelations — that any account of momentous events must paint a caricature of the prominent figures involved. The primary concern seems to be to make the principal actors appear to be as boorish, ignoble, and altogether cloddish as possible. It is acknowledged in passing that Stalin was probably no better, but Truman bears the brunt. He is made out to be a grinning, poker-playing hick with an atomic bomb to flaunt and a reputation to make as a "tough guy." Thus Mee presents the Potsdam Conference as a farcical conspiracy. The entire episode is made out to be nothing but devious, ill-intentioned plotting by a bunch of buffoons.

The revisionist slant on Truman is generally that he was not just tough minded, but hard headed. The revisionists fault him for being — at the very least — a simple-minded believer in the morality of the American position. They criticize him for being equally stubborn about believing the enemy to be untrustworthy. If they do not dismiss Truman as an American Legionnaire who preferred force to negotiation, they condemn him for clinging to the conviction that force is the only language the enemy understands. They accuse him of benefitting from events in the cold war which he either instigated or eagerly grasped as political windfalls.

Scholars Take Stock

It is conventional wisdom that historical perspective cannot come quickly — that a certain number of years must pass before real objectivity and a proper sense of proportion are possible. What is not generally agreed upon is just how long is long enough before scholars can ply their trade dispassionately. Truman lived nearly two full decades beyond his time as President, and perhaps that provides distance enough for a reasonably accurate appraisal in light of the turbulent events of the changing times since he left office. The revisionists did not wait long before grinding their axes. And in Truman's case there is the interesting phenomenon of a monumental public urge to render a judgment. Perhaps it is because mind-boggling technological developments and the pace of change of various kinds make Truman's time seem more distant than it really was. It was less than a generation ago, not long at all in historical terms. Yet how hard it is to imagine a President going for long walks on the streets of Washington almost every day, or for that matter a President going all over the country talking to people from the back of a train.

In any event, there has been enough time — and enough interest in Truman and his times — for a great deal of writing on the Truman period. There are specialized books,

such as R. Alton Lee's useful study, *Truman and Taft-Hartley,* which zeroes in on this controversial labor law —
enacted over Truman's veto — and analyzes the struggle it
represented between business and farm groups lined up
with Congress on the one hand and, on the other, the forces
of labor aligned with the President. It was an alignment and
an issue that Truman used to advantage in the campaign of
1948, but it was a heated conflict that contributed to a
pattern of strained relations between Truman and Congress.
Susan Hartmann's *Truman and the 80th Congress* is
another useful book with a similarly narrow focus, this one
treating Truman's relationship with the particular Congress
that the Republicans controlled in the two years prior to
1948. Her study describes the evolution in Truman's approach from conciliation to combat. It shows how his leadership then succeeded in achieving a great deal by building
a foreign policy consensus despite domestic policy conflict
— conflict that built a case which enabled Truman to win
the presidency and which cost the Republicans control of
the Congress.

Although comprehensive accounts of the Truman record
are in short supply, some noteworthy observations have
been made, in any event, by some distinguished scholars
who have evaluated Truman's presidency. Clinton Rossiter
of Cornell prefaced his appraisal by making clear what a
monstrous burden any President carries, pointing out that
he is expected to fulfill no less than ten functions simultaneously. The Constitution makes him the country's chief of
state, chief executive, commander in chief, chief diplomat,
and chief legislator; the people he serves have come to
expect him also to be a world leader, protector of the peace,
chief of his party, voice of the people, and manager of
prosperity.[20] It is a classic understatement to say that it is a
big job to fill. Richard Kirkendall, the foremost scholar of
the Truman period, would doubtless agree, but also would

dispel the widely held notion that Truman came to the job wholly unprepared and without any background for it whatsoever.

"Truman was not a small man who suddenly had a very big job imposed upon him," said Kirkendall as a University of Missouri historian who had spent 15 years researching the Truman period. Truman brought to the presidency rich and varied experiences in American life and politics. He had served for eight years as the chief administrative officer of a populous county and for ten years as a U.S. senator. He had campaigned for office on local and state levels, administered and constructed courthouses, welfare agencies, roads, and other public facilities in Jackson County. He contributed significantly to the national war effort with his investigation of its economic side, and learned much about the American political and economic systems from his service in the Senate. His selection as vice-presidential candidate had enabled him to wage a national campaign. His brief time in the vice-presidency at least gave him a chance to exercise his political talents in new ways by helping organize the administration's legislative program and build support for it. Truman's career before the White House, Kirkendall contends, was not a little man's career.[21]

Rossiter's lively book on the Presidency provides one of the best across-the-board estimates of how Truman measures up to certain standards of presidential achievement. Rossiter came up with the standards after studying more than a hundred serious presidential biographies and finding the same standards repeatedly applied. He poses them as eight questions to be asked about a President:

1) In what sort of times did he live?
2) How bravely and imaginatively did he bear the burden of extraordinary responsibility?
3) What was his philosophy of presidential power?

4) How efficiently did he organize his energies, direct his lieuten-
ants, and thus exercise his powers?
5) What men did he call on for help?
6) What manner of man was he beneath the trappings of office?
7) What was his influence on the Presidency?
8) What was his influence on history?[22]

In Rossiter's view, a President cannot possibly be regarded as great unless he held office in great times. The
times must cry out for extraordinary qualities of vision and
leadership, as was the case with Washington at the nation's
birth, Jefferson in its early growing pains, Jackson during
the upsurge of democracy, Lincoln at the time of the Civil
War, Wilson during World War I, and Franklin Roosevelt
facing the great depression and World War II. Truman
qualifies on this first indispensable test. His times were
laden with nagging crises and were decisive for the American future. As to how he bore the burden, Rossiter believes
Truman studied, read, conferred, and dictated as long and
hard as any President who ever lived. He faced up to at least
a dozen decisions that shook the world with their impact,
and he made them as the people expect their President to
take such fateful steps: resolutely, solemnly, and
hopefully.[23] Rossiter asserts that not one of Truman's grave
steps in foreign and military affairs has proved to be wrong,
stupid, or contrary to the best judgment and interests of the
American people, not even the fateful decision to use the
atom bomb on live targets.

It is an assertion endorsed by the eminent historian
Samuel Eliot Morison, who observed from the vantage
point of nearly two decades after the use of atomic bombs in
the war against Japan that "certainly the war would have
gone on, and God knows for how long," if the atomic bomb
had not been used. "It simply is not true that Japan had no
military capability left," he wrote. "If the Emperor had
told them to fight to the last man, they would have fought to

the last man.''²⁴ It was a typical Truman decision. There was nothing wishy-washy about the way Truman bore the burden. He shouldered it squarely, made the hard decisions at the moment when they had to be made, and took full responsibility.

As to his philosophy of presidential power, Truman understood the strengths and obligations of his office to a degree that Rossiter believes will impress posterity more than Truman's occasional lapses from decorum. No President, he writes, ever described his job more imaginatively and accurately than Truman's folksy explanation that ''the principal power that the President has is to bring people in and try to persuade them to do what they ought to do without persuasion. That's what I spend most of my time doing. That's what the powers of the President amount to.''²⁵ While differing in their appraisals of what is the key ingredient in Truman's philosophy of power, scholars commend his grasp of it and his discerning use of it.

D. W. Brogan, a British historian and commentator on American life for 30 years, puts Truman in the line of Presidents who used their power sometimes outside, if not quite against, the letter of the Constitution — the line of Jefferson making the Louisiana Purchase, Jackson facing down the revolt of South Carolina, Lincoln deciding to open the Civil War by replying with guns to the firing on Fort Sumter. Truman was prepared to use the full powers of the office when the occasion demanded it — most notably by moving decisively when South Korea was invaded, without waiting for a congressional debate and declaration of war.

To Brogan, this power of decision was, in Truman's times, the most important power to have. It was a period when the U.S. had to be, and had to seem to be, under firm command.²⁶ Kirkendall, on the other hand, stresses Truman's sense of the limits on what the President and the

national power he directed could wisely try to do. He notes
that Truman believed the U.S. could and should play a large
role in world affairs, but that he did not believe the U.S.
could do all that it might wish or accomplish all that it might
hope. This sense of limits affected Truman's efforts in
Eastern Europe, for example, where he was distressed by
Russian behavior but believed there was little he could do to
change it. Kirkendall points out that a source of Truman's
unpopularity during his last years in office was the inability
of many Americans to accept his belief that power had
limits.[27] It was his sense of limits that prevented large-scale
American intervention in China. His sense of limits was
also at the heart of his conflict with General MacArthur.

As to efficiency in organizing his energies and directing
his aides in the exercise of his powers, Truman is cited by
Rossiter as having few equals in the long history of the
presidency. He writes that Truman learned to delegate his
authority as well as any chief executive in this century, and
that most experienced students of public administration
credit Truman with exceptional competence in organizing
and distributing his legendary energies throughout his
70-hour work weeks. Although Rossiter describes those
Truman called on for help as ranging in virtue and talent
from selfless greatness to dishonest incompetence, he managed in the areas that touch upon survival to mobilize more
talent than even Roosevelt had. Contrasting with the partisan mediocrity Truman tolerated in domestic affairs was the
nonpartisan excellence he insisted on in military and diplomatic affairs and obtained in such statesmen as Marshall
and Acheson. And as for the manner of man Truman was
beneath the trappings of the presidency, Rossiter labels him
a man whom history will delight to remember. He believes
the very lapses of dignity that brought Truman ridicule from
many Republicans will fix his place in America's memory
— his whistle stops, for example, and the angry letters,

testy press conferences, impossible sport shirts, and early-morning seminars on the streets of dozens of American cities. He won immortality in office by virtue of his Missouri wit and wisdom, by his simple dignity, and simply by remaining more "plain folks" than any other President.[28]

Summing up Truman's influence on the presidency, Rossiter gives him high marks for keeping the tools of presidential leadership intact. Roosevelt had sharpened them, and had enlarged the presidency enough to satisfy most of his countrymen for a long time to come. It was Truman's duty, in Rossiter's view, to see that the new tools of democratic leadership were not blunted or stolen by the forces of reaction. In the end, the office Truman handed over to Eisenhower was no less magnificent than the office he had inherited from Roosevelt. And that, says Rossiter — looked at in the light of what happened to every other President who succeeded a great President — may well be Truman's most remarkable achievement.[29] Brogan credits Truman with making the modern presidency a department of the nation's government in its own right. He contends that the most Roosevelt did was to make some improvement in the organization of the White House. But Truman improved markedly, and imposed discipline on, the whole organization of the executive branch. In Brogan's view, he will go down in administrative history as a great innovator and reformer who made the presidency a much more effective instrument of command.[30]

A significant example of creating executive machinery to meet modern needs is found in the way Truman organized the parts of the executive branch that deal with matters of national security. Convinced of the need for a comprehensive system for foreign intelligence, and concerned about the fact that needed intelligence information was not coordinated at any one place, Truman in 1946 established the

Central Intelligence Group. It was renamed the Central
Intelligence Agency with the enactment of the National
Security Act the next year. Among other things, this act
also created the National Security Council as an instrument
for presenting diplomatic and military policy recommendations to the President. The act replaced the former War and
Navy departments with a military establishment that had
separate Army, Navy, and Air Force departments, each
under civilian direction. The heads of each military service
together made up the joint chiefs of staff, to serve as the
President's principal military advisers. Truman drew a
clear line of authority through a single cabinet member, a
civilian secretary of defense.[31]

The influence Harry Truman had on history is seen by
Rossiter in two broad areas. Truman did not exercise much
control over either of them, but he set the direction and gave
each the full support of the presidency. The first was domestic — the real beginnings of a many-sided program to
eliminate discrimination and second-class citizenship in
American life. The second was international — the irrevoc-
able commitment of America to active cooperation with
other nations in search of world peace and prosperity.[32]
Kirkendall also calls attention to Truman's civil rights record, noting that he did more on behalf of the civil rights of
black Americans than any of his predecessors in the twen-
tieth century.[33] Brogan believes Truman's leading fault was
also his overwhelming virtue — his readiness to meet
problems head on. It sometimes meant ramming his head
against a congressional stone wall, but it also showed itself
in his bold decisiveness. On the whole, says Brogan,
Truman's legacy to the office, to the nation, and to the
world was great and beneficient.[34]

Where does Truman rank, among all the Presidents in
American history? Rossiter hazards the opinion that
Truman will win a place in the judgment of posterity along-

side Thomas Jefferson and Theodore Roosevelt. That puts him a notch below the highest level, occupied in Rossiter's mind by Washington, Lincoln, Franklin Roosevelt, Wilson, and Jackson. It puts him ahead of all the rest, including a half-dozen Presidents who, in Rossiter's opinion, may have had greater ability and intellect but who presided in less stirring times. He is a scholar who believes that wherever Truman eventually stands on the ladder of past Presidents, he will be well remembered for serving as "a lasting symbol of the noble truth that gives strength and meaning to the American experiment: plain men *can* govern themselves; democracy *does* work."[35]

The British historian who studied him agrees. He, too, in the final analysis, returns to the point that Truman showed in his brisk, man-in-the-street, man-from-the-farm way that the promise of American life for the average citizen had not been withdrawn. He notes that in an age of Presidents whose backgrounds have been very different from that of Harry Truman, the American public — rejoicing in his upset victory of 1948 — took and kept to its heart the brusque little man from Independence, Missouri.[36]

Truman's Popularity Soars

The fact is that the American public did not really take the living Truman to its heart to nearly the extent that it has exalted his memory in the few years following his death on December 26, 1972. In the brief time since his passing, his popularity has soared to unparalleled heights of public esteem. Suddenly, a quarter-century after his presidency, Harry Truman has become no less than a national folk hero. He has been memorialized in every medium available — in books and rock music, on stage, television, and in movies, on bumper stickers and T-shirts. A national magazine dubbed it "Trumania." It is an incredible phenomenon, and in a sense it represents a verdict of history of the most genuine kind. It is a verdict that comes from the hearts of the people.

The phenomenon is not without irony. Someone who was almost invariably referred to as a "little" man, revered as a giant of history. A nation trying to forget a bloody conflict in Asia, embracing the memory of a President discredited by bloody conflicts in Asia. At a time when politics has become a discredited profession, a popular idol is a man who was a politician through and through and who wanted to be nothing else. A public figure who did not waste a moment building an image, but has one built for him, larger than life.

What accounts for this strange "Trumania," and what does it mean? In part it has been no more profound than a fad. Like a "hit" song, before long the Truman T-shirts and bumper stickers and the other souvenirs and novelties lose their appeal. Much of it, too, is nostalgia, which itself has become a fad. Truman's times have an appeal as quaint, simpler times. (Never mind, the thinking goes, that they seemed anything but simple then. We got *through* them all right, didn't we? And who knows if we'll get through *these*!) Nostalgia is "in," and to an extent it is only a pleasant diversion. But to an extent it is also evidence of a yearning for simpler times and simpler solutions, and in particular for someone who could and would apply them. T-shirts have displayed not just Truman's likeness but the appeal, "America needs you." The song pleaded, "America's calling . . . Harry, you'd know what to do."

Whether or not Harry would know what to do, the recollection of Truman has been that he would be very different from the current variety of politicians. For many people, apparently, that would be enough. The Truman boom really began, in fact, because of the timing of Truman's death. It brought to national attention some characteristics of him that the public had largely forgotten or never realized but which in retrospect looked pretty good. The American public was just beginning to be wrung out by Watergate. Although the current occupant of the White House had just been overwhelmingly reelected, it was the electorate that would be overwhelmed before long. Watergate would go on and on and on, seeming to taint the whole world of Washington politics and all who dwelled within it. These were the circumstances that gave the contrasting character of Harry Truman special appeal.

The eulogies of Truman, the television specials on his presidency presented after his death, the scenes of his hometown, the reminiscences of those who had known him as President, all this had an extraordinary impact. People sat up and took notice. Truman had no corps of image-makers advising him to keep a "low profile." He did not spend his time in hideaways, shunning people and the press. Truman never engaged in double talk or deception. He did not duck the issues. His White House had no bugging devices, and no one stood between the president and an agency head — or the people, for that matter. Truman suddenly seemed to be just the kind of honest, open, candid, decision-making, straight-talking, unpretentious politician that contemporary politics seemed to lack.

It was another accident of timing that two books were almost waiting in the wings to publicize and popularize Truman even more. Plans had been set since the summer of 1972 for Margaret Truman's book about her father to be published soon after the beginning of the following year. It was to be an event of scholarly as well as publishing importance, because Margaret had exclusive access to a lot of the source material, including several hundred letters Truman had written his mother, sister, and daughter, and 50 private memoranda he had written for his own information when he sensed that important events were taking place. It was to be the January selection of the Book-of-the-Month Club, and the paperback publishing rights had been sold. When Truman died in late December, Margaret's best-seller about him was almost off the presses and ready to distribute.

The Truman boom also jarred Merle Miller into a realization that he could do something with the reams of transcripts of his interviews and conversations with Truman back in 1961 and 1962. The idea had been to do a television series on Truman, but nobody wanted to buy it and it had never materialized. Miller quickly got to work and put together a highly readable book, *Plain Speaking,* which he called an ''oral biography,'' out of the interviews. It, too, became a Book-of-the-Month choice and a best-seller. The main attraction, widely publicized in magazine and newspaper excerpts even before the book was in print, was the abundance of pithy — and often profane — observations Truman had made about a number of famous persons, including then-President Nixon.

The aging Truman had confided, in one of many informal conversations during the period when the television interviews were being taped, that Richard Nixon was one of two people during his lifetime that he came to loathe. (The other was a one-time Missouri governor.) ''Nixon,'' Truman said, ''is a shifty eyed, goddam liar and people know it.'' Truman also disclosed that he had ordered removed from Pentagon files an exchange of letters in which General Eisenhower had asked the army chief of staff, who was then George Marshall, to relieve him from duty as Allied commander in Europe so he could come back to the U.S. divorce his wife, and marry an Englishwoman. Marshall would not go along, and Truman was especially incensed some years later when Eisenhower, as President, would not stand up for Marshall when Senator Joseph McCarthy called him a traitor. Truman called Eisenhower a coward. "He hasn't got any backbone at all, and he ought to be ashamed for what he did, but I don't think there's any shame in him." Truman had some salty words about General MacArthur as well, observing that he didn't fire him for being dumb because that's not against the law for generals. "If it was," Truman said, "half to three-quarters of them would be in jail."[37]

Again, it was the contrast that was appealing, coming at a time when many politicians seemed to be made of clear, pliable plastic. It was refreshing to read of a politician saying what he really thought. Whether either best-seller — by Truman's daughter or his one-time interviewer — provides a very balanced picture is another matter. Both are entertaining and highly informative. Both have contributed greatly to Truman's popularity. But Margaret makes Truman a little too perfect and Miller makes him a little too profane. He did make mistakes, and he did not always cuss.

Miller has said he wanted his book to bring out the human quality in Truman, whom he fears may be the last human being to live in the White House. But his book is constructed, as Robert Sherrill noted in a perceptive review of it, from bull sessions, where what is said ranges widely in quality and seriousness. If the elderly Truman comes off seeming too tough and insensitive, Sherrill provides a reminder that this was also the Harry Truman who at the age of 35 picked wild daisies to decorate the church for his wedding; who, even after he was vice-president, continued to wash his own socks; who went out of his way to talk to children because "it's very lonely being a child." This was the Truman who insisted when people joked about William Jennings Bryan that "what an old man said should not be held against him as long as his record was good when he had the power" — which is good advice to keep in mind when reading parts of *Plain Speaking*."[38]

The Presidents now considered great were not always so regarded when they took office or even when they left it. Abraham Lincoln was one of them — Harry Truman is now another. When Lincoln ran for President in 1860, many Americans scorned him as a midwestern hick who was ill-prepared for the job. He was the object of critical abuse and ridicule in the presidency until he was killed, and a lot of Americans cheered the news of his murder. Small wonder that it is easy now to forget the near-panic when Truman came into the presidency, or how thoroughly he was belittled when he was in office. As in Lincoln's case, time and history have raised him.

The latter-day nostalgia for Truman naturally magnifies his good points and overlooks his faults. His use of his own postage stamps — then three cents to send a letter — when as President he could have used the mails for free is one of those myths people cherish. In Truman's case, the ''myth'' of almost perverse honesty happens to be true. Power does not always corrupt. This was the man who, as a county administrator, had sliced 11 acres off the property of his own mother for a highway project and refused to pay her a dime even though he acknowledged it would have been worth $1000 per acre.

In many ways he was indeed a man from another era. One day a presidential aide brought Truman a manila envelope found in the cabinet room after a congressional briefing. It belonged to a Republican senator and notations on the outside suggested its contents dealt with Republican congressional strategy. Did the President want to see it? The answer was an emphatic ''no.'' The envelope was returned by messenger immediately, unopened and unread. Who today would think twice about the ethics of taking a look inside? One morning Truman opened a staff meeting with reddened eyes and a catch in his throat. The secretary of the army had just told him of a widespread cheating scandal at

West Point, and Truman was saddened and disbelieving that those in whom such trust had been placed could violate a solemn oath. Who today would be moved to tears to hear that some college students had cheated?

George Elsey, who was an aide in the Truman White House, remembers Truman as serious about his job, sentimental about his family and friends, old-fashioned in personal ethics, stubborn in defense of the rights of citizens, relaxed with his small staff, and very firmly in command.[39] That just about sums up the way Truman is being remembered by history and by his people. Never mind the cuss words uttered in all-male company. It was the candor that counted, and the integrity. Never mind the lack of charisma — the verdict on Truman seems to be that he is valued for his values.

IX Summing Up

Because the Truman period is a very recent one in historical terms, it is easy to say that it is too recent for us to pass judgment on it. That is easy to say, but it is unrealistic. Perhaps historians a few generations from now will be better able to evaluate Truman objectively. But people do not wait to pass judgment. It is not our nature to defer to a future historian, wiser and more impartial though he or she may be. We draw our own conclusions. As we do, we should try, as Truman did, to be open-minded, fair, and well-informed before we reach our conclusions. If we are to be wise, we ought to recognize that we probably are not entirely open-minded, fair, and well-informed, but we should make an honest effort.

In the case of Truman's presidency, there is an abundance of information available to us. The chief problem we face in evaluating it — being historically close to the time of Truman's presidency — is one of context. To be fair, we have to realize that Truman's decisions and actions were taken in another context. They resulted from different information and different perceptions based on that information. Truman's time and our time are simply not the same, and we can judge him fairly only in the context of his time and what he knew.

Years after the fact, research was able to produce information that may convince us now, for example, that Japan might well have surrendered soon even if atomic bombs had not been used. There is, of course, no way we will ever know. The necessity for Truman's use of these horribly destructive weapons has been debated and will continue to be. That is well and good, so long as it is remembered that we have information in weighing that decision now which was not available to him in making it. Obviously, Truman could not have waited to see what several years of scholarly inquiry would turn up as to what might seem, in looking back, to have been the best decision to make. He faced the decision right then. He had to make it on the basis of the best advice he could get then. As we pass judgment on what has gone before, it is good to keep in mind that we can almost always see very clearly with hindsight, and that it is much easier to be right on the second guess. That is an advantage the student of history always has over the person who made the history, and we should not abuse the advantage.

Knowing now that everything turned out pretty well after all, it is hard to realize that when Truman became President a generation ago, the world's prospects were much more grim. It was not far-fetched to suppose in the hell of 1945 that this planet would not last this long. It had taken only two decades after World War I for the world to suffer a major economic depression and plunge into an even larger war. If history repeated itself, World War *III* would be a nuclear war and would probably destory most of human life. There was no reason to believe the world was any better equipped to handle its problems in 1945 than it had been in 1918.

We must remember that when World War II ended, much of Europe was a rubble-strewn wasteland, and it seemed likely that America would soon withdraw from it. Vast portions of the world lay prostrate, victims of unprecedented physical and psychological destruction. Millions wandered homeless, hungry, and disheartened. Desperate

people and shattered nations were tempted to submit to a
new tyranny that openly professed hostility to the very idea
of a free society and to the United States in particular.

America alone had the strength and the confidence to
provide an alternative, and Truman accepted the challenge
of doing so. He was determined that America would not be
indifferent to the world around it, but would recognize the
need and the opportunity to forge and to lead an alignment
of free and independent nations. Many years later, after a
generation of peace and undreamed-of prosperity for most
of the people in those nations — all of them still free and
independent — it is hard to imagine the courage and bold
vision which that commitment required at the time he
undertook it.

Open to Debate

Truman's record, of course, leaves many areas open to
debate. There will probably always be differences of opinion over some issues — like whether Japan would have
quickly quit fighting anyway — that can never be resolved
conclusively. Disagreement will continue over Truman's
many controversial actions such as the move to draft striking railway workers, his dismissal of MacArthur, his
strategy in Korea, and the seizure of the steel mills. There is
room for widely varying interpretations of policies and
events, and with a wealth of material for future study we can
expect to have new light shed on many aspects of Truman's
presidential performance.

The Potsdam Conference is only one example of a re-
inspected episode from the Truman period, but it illustrates
the range of opinion that can develop. Some now see in
Truman not a readiness to negotiate there in good faith, but
a bull-headed determination to be difficult. Some suggest

that he went to Potsdam to bully Stalin by figuratively shaking the atomic bomb in his face — even though the conference was already in progress when the bomb was first tested, and not until then did Truman know it would work. Others see Truman as being well-intentioned but overly assertive; as one whose confidence exceeded his intellect; as a Baptist moralist naive to the devious ways of the Soviet dictator.

Future research, or even changes in the public mood, may come to cast Truman's historic undertakings in a different light. When this happens, it is well to remember that casting new light does not always reveal new truths. Sometimes it distorts; sometimes it can be blinding. But with this note of caution in mind as one inquires, Potsdam can be only a starting point for interesting speculation. Consider the Truman Doctrine, that ringing policy declaration with such far-reaching implications. Was it a case of Truman being far tougher than he needed to be? Instead of meeting particular problems as they arose, case by case — as he had done with Trieste and was doing with Greece and Turkey — did the containment policy constitute a challenge that unnecessarily widened the cold war? Did Truman in effect invite the Soviets to test America's response by cutting U.S. military forces back so drastically to balance the federal budget? Did he encourage an armed challenge by allowing the inference that containment did not apply in all places, Korea being one of them? Did he not try to do enough in China, or in Korea? Could he have done otherwise? That, of course, is a question that can be asked of Truman's every action. Everything he did raises the question of what might have happened if he had chosen an alternative course.

What would the shape of the world be, how would the course of its history have been changed if, for example, Truman had decided against fostering the creation of the

UN? What might have resulted had he not acted with the Truman Doctrine to halt communist thrusts to the eastern Mediterranean? What if he had not launched the Marshall Plan and seen it through? Of if he had decided to give up Berlin rather than risk standing firm until the blockade was lifted? What if he had committed U.S. military forces to massive intervention in China's civil war? What if he had not intervened in Korea at all, or if he had not showed restraint when he did?

To be fair, critical inquiry should resist the temptation to take a "cheap shot." It is all too easy to magnify someone's shortcomings out of the context of the total person and the circumstances in which that person acted. It is always easy to downgrade accomplishments by saying that surely there could have been more. Within these bounds of fairness, Truman is still fair game. His foreign policy and domestic program and how he conducted them are fertile ground for further digging.

General Agreement

There is a consensus about Truman's personality, about which decisions were his toughest, and about which were his most dramatic challenges that provides a broad-brush portrait of the main features of his character and his career. Even his critics would generally concede him an impressive record of achievement. By any standard of measurement, he gave his country a triumphant presidential succession when one of its most imposing leaders died at a critical moment in history.

On the domestic front, the list of Truman's legislative victories is certainly a limited one in comparison with the size and pace of the steps Roosevelt took or that Truman took in world affairs. Truman's was not, however, a stand-pat, uncreative presidency from a domestic standpoint, despite the limitations on what he could obtain from Congress. He kept the presidency strong and decisive when strength and decisiveness mattered most. He held his own with Congress during a period when doing just that was a very tall order and a constant struggle. Where he did not succeed in winning congressional passage of measures he fought for, he deserves credit for breaking the ground and helping clear the paths for roads that were followed later. When Medicare was ready for President Johnson's signature in 1965, for example, he traveled halfway across the country to sign the bill into law at the Truman Library. Johnson was giving credit where credit was due; it was Truman who had done the spade work.

When not forced to depend on congressional initiative, Truman made significant gains on the home front. His signing of an executive order ending racial segregation in the armed services, for example, had far-reaching effect and did not require congressional action.

At his own initiative, Truman streamlined the presidency and made it function more effectively as a political institution. He created a commission to help him reorganize the executive branch and then thin out bureaucratic deadwood. He set up the first systematic table of organization for the White House staff. He increased the stature and clout of the Budget Bureau, now the Office of Management and Budget, so it could ride herd on costs and the conduct of business in the executive branch. He had it introduce modern management and accounting procedures. He balanced the budget. He began the practice of having budget briefings for reporters each January, so they could better explain the mysteries of the massive federal budget. He was the first President to ask his successor to meet with him and work out an orderly transfer of the business of the presidency.

The turbulent postwar period made Truman's a crisis presidency from beginning to end. Yet the unprecedented expansion of presidential responsibility — the relentless pressures and new dangers of a succession of challenges and conflicts — did not get him down. Each time, he rose to the occasion. "How long have we got to work this out?" he would ask a key aide like Acheson or Marshall. He would take what time was available to study the problem and weigh the alternatives. Then he would make the decisions that had to be made.

It is universally agreed that Truman grew in the job, even though he did not have as far to grow as most people thought. To a large extent, the change was less a case of Truman growing than of a growing perception of Truman in the presidency — a growing realization that it was not beyond him. Yet his depth as a cultured, intelligent person never did come across effectively. Somehow it was always easier to see him as the critics drew him, as no more than an ex-haberdasher and product of a crooked political machine, a country bumpkin with an American Legion button. It was hard to accept Truman the well-read student of history, who was fond of rereading Shakespeare's sonnets and the works of Robert Burns and Byron, and who relaxed with his extensive record collection of the music of Chopin.

He would be the first to admit that the office of President is probably too big for any one person to fill. All the same, Truman had a better background for it than almost anyone realized when he came on the scene. He had intangibles that made all the difference — his willingness to work extremely hard and to listen to good advice; his ability to make decisions and to organize well. He learned from his mistakes — except for his incurable snap response to questions at a press conference. And if he seldom admitted mistakes, at least he did not waste time bemoaning them. When a decision was made it was done with, and he went on to the next one.

In looking back at Truman's record as President, the fact that his most significant actions were as a world leader points to his wisdom in perceiving priorities. The overriding challenge of his time was to create order from chaos before the world's chaos swept everything under. There were many inconveniences at home. There were inequities; there were problems of poverty and prejudice. But to solve them it was necessary first to save a free society in which the right to dissent and to effect change could still function freely. And that meant giving primary attention to the challenges in the world of chaos beyond America's borders.

In foreign affairs, Harry Truman did no less than change the history of the world. The decade of the 1940's, during which he became the President and won election to the office on his own, shaped the world's fundamental political and military pattern for a lifetime. In that brief decade, World War II destroyed Europe as the center of world politics, made America the major world power, and extended into Central and Eastern Europe the power of Russia, which became the other world power. In that short span of time, the atomic age began; the United Nations was made into a going concern; and victory by China's Communists meant that, after centuries, China would be unified under a strong government. With Truman's hand on the helm, the critical steps were taken to check Russia's expansion and to contain its power, to assure the remarkable industrial recovery of Western Europe, to give root to European unity, and to make collective security a reality.

Was the world changed for the better? Perhaps it is enough to be able to say that life on this planet has gone on, and that the world was not changed for the worse, as surely it would have been if it had been left to chaos. Truman was not long-winded when asked once what *he* considered the most important achievements of his years in the White House. "We prevented a third world war," he said, "and kept the economy on an even keel." Actually there is much more that can be said. America's bitterest enemies of World

War II are now among its closest friends. At the same time, the prospect of another world war, a prospect that was so real in the 1940s, seems now to be remote. The enduring strength of the free world has led not to war, but detente.

A sense of the interdependence of nations has grown from a bitterly disputed premise to a generally accepted statement of the obvious. Dozens of free nations have come into being in a largely peaceful liquidation of centuries of colonial history. Atomic power has not been the uncontrollable monster many feared it would be; now the development of its peaceful uses holds the prospect of new benefits for humankind. America's singularly immense contribution to the economic recovery of the world from World War II has led to record levels of prosperity for much of the world and for the people of the United States.

These are not a string of coincidences; these are historic accomplishments. They are products of the skillful, constructive way in which President Truman coped with the forces of change in the postwar world. These gains bear witness to Truman's wisdom and courage.

Under his leadership, America showed that free nations could successfully stand together against threats of war and subversion. The fact that questions can now arise about whether NATO is still needed is the greatest tribute to its success. For that matter, Korea was a success, too, in showing that when an invasion shattered the peace, collective action under the UN Charter could be taken to turn back military aggression. The military objective in responding to Korea was to drive away the aggressor; the military objective was realized. If this is not victory, it is certainly a tolerable substitute for defeat.

Personal Legacy

It is the mark of his statesmanship that Truman made so chaotic a period into a creative one. Amid international turbulence of the most trying sort, he saw to it that a free world was built without blowing the whole world apart in the process. He distinguished himself as a political leader by perceiving the great issues of his time and facing up to them. Yet to his own people, Truman's is more of a personal legacy. One can recount all the international events and policies and decisions, but Truman's personal attributes still stand out. This in itself is remarkable, at a time when it has become rather fashionable to question America's accomplishments and even its motives in the postwar era, and to question especially mercilessly the motives of its leaders. Truman stands virtually alone as a stunning exception. Second thoughts about the cold war raise few second thoughts about Truman's role. For the most part, his motives are not questioned; his sincerity never is.

In the years before his death, Truman had come to be stereotyped as a sort of bantam rooster, often profane and pugnacious. The fact that he said what he thought, and didn't pull his verbal punches, kept him controversial. Since his death, this same kind of sterotype has almost done away with the controversy. People have come to appreciate his candor above all. In a day when cynicism about politicians runs deep, Truman the politician has etched a special place in his country's history. His openness excuses his faults, whatever they might have been. For many Americans, Truman's blunt honesty has become his overriding virtue. This is the prevailing opinion, and perhaps it will be the lasting impression. He is cheered for international dramas and grand designs, but he is loved because he was honest; because you knew he did his level best, and that he did it on the level; because he stayed close to the people, looked them in the eye, and gave them credit for good sense and good judgment; because he was willing to make enemies but not excuses.

What accounts for Truman's greatness? He was a

"common" man in the sense of lacking the stature or the kind of charisma or anything in his background and early career that would seem to mark him for greatness. How was Harry Truman different? The point is, he probably was not so different. He did not think so. He always thought less of his capabilities than did those who knew him best. But there really was nothing mysterious about those capabilities. He was willing to work hard at whatever had to be done. He was honest, with others and with himself. He was strong-willed, and would stay the course through when it was not easy or popular or fun. He would listen to others. He was a good decision maker. He had a persistent impulse to do the right thing.

Harry Truman was old-fashioned virtue personified. He had character. He was a simple person, and stayed that way. His traits were simple ones. As President, he put it all together, applied it with tireless energy, and became a potent force for good. Perhaps this "little" man from Missouri, as he was so often referred to and thought of as President, was not truly great. But one can subscribe with certainty to a remark made shortly after Harry Truman left the White House; if this was not a great man, he was the greatest little man I ever knew anything about.

Appendix

The purpose of this section is to give the reader an opportunity to read some original selections that may be helpful in forming independent judgments about Truman. Except for one commentary on him, the words are his. The selections mix samples of his private notes and memoranda with several of his key speeches and messages to Congress. The idea is twofold: to give some additional insight to Truman's character and personality; and to provide, in greater length and detail than was suitable in the body of the book, a few selections relating to important proposals and policy statements.

The reader who wishes to delve deeper need not despair for want of material. So much is available that the problem is one of selectivity. A serious study of the Truman administration would use the vast collection of his papers at the Harry S. Truman Library in Independence, Missouri. Short of that, it is essential to use his two-volume *Memoirs*, supplemented by the *Public Papers of the Presidents of the United States: Harry S. Truman* (annual volumes), which cover his public announcements, speeches, and press conferences. A Truman researcher can also usefully consult a variety of government publications such as the *Congressional Record* and congressional hearings and reports, the *Federal Register* and reports by departments and agencies, the *Department of State Bulletin, Vital Speeches,* and the Senate Foreign Relations Committee's *Decade of American Foreign Policy: Basic Documents,* Eighty-first Congress, first session, Senate Document 123.

As a starting point, it is necessary to have more than a cursory understanding of World War II and what it wrought. One cannot understand Truman's presidency without an understanding of his times. Above all, this means the war years in which he came to national prominence and which gave rise to the situations he had to deal with.

Beyond the government documents, the serious student of the Truman period should consult Richard S. Kirkendall, *The Truman Period as a Research Field;* Barton Bernstein and Allen Matusow, *The Truman Administration: A Documentary History,* which presents pertinent documentary material grouped according to major policy areas of the Truman period, and William Hillman, *Mr. President,* a rich collection of private notes and papers that Truman turned over to him near the end of his presidency.

Valuable supplements to Truman's *Memoirs* are his *Mr. Citizen,* written in retirement, and Dean Acheson's *Present at the Creation.* Valuable for reference are the yearly volumes of the Council on Foreign Relations, *The United States in World Affairs* and *Documents on American Foreign Relations.* There is not yet a comprehensive, definitive history of Truman's presidency on a par with Arthur M. Schlesinger's trilogy, *The Age of Roosevelt.* The Truman administration is dealt with as part of Alfred Steinberg's *The Man from Missouri* and is the subject of Cabell Phillips' *The Truman Presidency,* both of which are excellent books. With this brief indication of direction, the researcher is left to comb the libraries, choose a manageable amount of material, and hope that wise choices were made.

Given the overwhelming supply, it would be presumptuous to contend that the few selections that follow are perfectly representative. No such claim is made. They are a small sampling, intended as a useful supplement to this book. The hope is that they will stimulate the reader's interest in reading more on the subject.

TRUMAN'S DOMESTIC PROGRAM[1]

On September 6, 1945, Truman sent Congress a long message spelling out his domestic program. He wrote later, in his *Memoirs,* that the date symbolized for him the assumption of the office of President in his own right. He regarded the message as a combination of a first inaugural and a first State of the Union message. Although most of the proposals he made in it were ignored or defeated by Congress, it is one of the most important messages of Truman's presidency because he considered it his domestic platform. For him, it set the tone and direction of his administration, and embodied the domestic goals toward which he would try to lead the nation.

> The foundations of a healthy national economy cannot be secure so long as any large section of our working people receive substandard wages. The existence of substandard wage levels sharply curtails the national purchasing power and narrows the market for the products of our farms and factories. . . .
>
> I therefore recommend that the Congress amend the Fair Labor Standards Act by substantially increasing the minimum wage specified therein to a level which will eliminate substandards of living, and assure the maintenance of the health, efficiency, and general well-being of workers. . . .
>
> Government must do its part and assist industry and labor to get over the line from war to peace.
>
> That is why I have asked for unemployment compensation legislation.
>
> That is why I now ask for full-employment legislation.
>
> The objectives for our domestic economy which we seek in our long-range plans were summarized by the late President Franklin D. Roosevelt over a year and a half ago in the form of an economic bill of rights. Let us make the attainment of those rights the essence of postwar American economic life.
>
> I repeat the statement of President Roosevelt:
>
> > In our day these economic truths have become accepted as self-evident. We have accepted, so to speak, a second bill of rights under which a new basis of security and prosperity can be established for all — regardless of station, race, or creed.
> >
> > Among these are:
> >
> > The right to a useful and remunerative job in the industries, or shops or farms or mines of the Nation.

The right to earn enough to provide adequate food and clothing and recreation.

The right of every farmer to raise and sell his products at a return which will give him and his family a decent living.

The right of every businessman, large and small, to trade in an atmosphere of freedom from unfair competition and domination by monopolies at home or abroad.

The right of every family to a decent home.

The right to adequate medical care and the opportunity to achieve and enjoy good health.

The right to adequate protection from the economic fears of old age, sickness, accident, and unemployment.

The right to a good education.

All of these rights spell security. And after this war is won we must be prepared to move forward, in the implementation of these rights, to new goals of human happiness and well-being.

America's own rightful place in the world depends in large part upon how fully these and similar rights have been carried into practice for our citizens. For unless there is security here at home there cannot be lasting peace in the world.

I shall from time to time communicate with the Congress on some of the subjects included in this enumeration of economic rights.

Most of them, in the last analysis, depend upon full production and full employment at decent wages. . . .

To provide jobs we must look first and foremost to private enterprise — to industry, agriculture, and labor. Government must inspire enterprise with confidence. That confidence must come mainly through deeds, not words.

But it is clear that confidence will be promoted by certain assurances given by the Government:

Assurance that all the facts about full employment and opportunity will be gathered periodically for the use of all.

Assurance of stability and consistency in public policy, so that enterprise can plan better by knowing what the Government intends to do.

Assurance that every governmental policy and program will be pointed to promote maximum production and employment in private enterprise.

Assurance that priority will be given to doing those things first which stimulate normal employment most.

A national reassertion of the right to work for every American citizen able and willing to work — a declaration of the ultimate duty of Government to use its own resources if all other methods should fail and establish full employment. The prompt and firm acceptance of this bedrock public responsibility will reduce the need for its exercise.

I ask that full-employment legislation to provide these vital assurances be speedily enacted. Such legislation should also provide machinery for a continuous full-employment policy — to be developed between the Congress and the Chief Executive, between the people and their Government. . . .

During the years of war production we made substantial progress in overcoming many of the prejudices which had resulted in discriminations against minority groups.

Many of the injustices based upon considerations of race, religion, and color were removed. Many were prevented. Perfection was not reached, of course, but substantial progress was made.

In the reconversion period and thereafter, we should make every effort to continue this American ideal. It is one of the fundamentals of our political philosophy, and it should be an integral part of our economy.

The Fair Employment Practice Committee is continuing during the transition period. I have already requested that legislation be enacted placing the Fair Employment Practice Committee on a permanent basis. I repeat that recommendation.

The Government now must be prepared to carry out the Nation's responsibility to aid farmers in making their necessary readjustments from a wartime to a peacetime basis. The Congress already has provided postwar supports against price collapse for many farm products. This was a provision of wisdom and foresight. . . .

Housing is high on the list of matters calling for decisive Congressional action. . . .

I urgently recommend that the Congress, at an early date, enact broad and comprehensive housing legislation.

The cardinal principle underlying such legislation should be that house construction and financing for the overwhelming majority of our citizens should be done by private enterprise.

We should retain and improve upon the present excellent Government facilities which permit the savings of the people to be channeled voluntarily into private house construction on financing terms that will serve the needs of home owners of moderate income.

The present principles of insurance of housing investment — now tested by years of experience — should be retained and extended, so as to encourage direct investment in housing by private financing institutions. . . .

We must go on. We must widen our horizon even further. We must consider the redevelopment of large areas of the blighted and slum sections of our cities so that in the truly American way they may be remade to accommodate families not only of low-income groups as heretofore, but of every income group. We must make it impossible for private enterprise to do the major part of this job. In most cases, it is now impossible for private enterprise to contemplate rebuilding slum areas without public assistance. The land cost generally is too high.

The time has come for the Government to begin to undertake a program of Federal aid to stimulate and promote the redevelopment of these deteriorating areas. Such Federal aid should be extended only to those communities which are willing to bear a fair part of the cost of clearing their blighted city areas and preparing them for redevelopment and rebuilding.

The rebuilding of these areas should conform to broad city plans, provide adequately for displaced families and make maximum use of private capital. Here lies another road toward establishing a better standard of city living, toward increasing business activity and providing jobs.

. . .The American small business is the backbone of our free-enterprise system. The efforts of the Congress in protecting small business during the war paid high dividends, not only in protecting small business enterprise, but also in speeding victory. In spite of the fact, however, that many businesses were helped and saved, it is true that many thousands of them were obliged to close up because of lack of materials or manpower or inability to get into war production.

It is very important to the economy of the United States that these small businesses and many more of them be given opportunity to become a part of American trade and industry. To do this, assistance should be given to small businesses to enable them to obtain adequate materials, private financing, technological improvements and surplus property.

While some special facilities for small business are required, the greatest help to it will come from the maintenance of general prosperity and full employment. It is much more difficult for small business to survive the hazards which come from trade recessions and widespread unemployment. What small business needs chiefly is a steady supply of customers with stable purchasing power.

I am sure that the Congress will see to it that in its legislation adequate protection and encouragement will be given to the small businesses of the Nation. . . .

We should build and improve our roads — the arteries of commerce; we must harness our streams for the general welfare; we must rebuild and reclaim our land; we must protect and restore our forests.

This is not only to provide men and women with work, it is to assure to the Nation the very basis of its life. It is to play the part of a good businessman who insists carefully on maintaining and rebuilding his plant and machinery.

We know that by the investment of Federal funds we can, within the limits of our own Nation, provide for our citizens new frontiers — new territories for the development of industry, agriculture, and commerce.

A SERVICE MAN OF MY ACQUAINTANCE[2]

In a reflective mood, Truman wrote this memo in longhand, referring to himself in the third person as "my acquaintance." It was written during the second year of his presidency, and bears only the date, "1946."

Sept. 26, 1918, a few minutes before 4 A.M. a service man of my acquaintance was standing behind a battery of French 75s at a little town called Neuville to the right of the Argonne Forest. A barrage was to be fired by all the guns on the Allied front from Belgium to the Swiss border.

At 4 A.M. that barrage started, at 5 A.M. the infantry in front of my acquaintance's battery went over. At 8 A.M. the artillery including the 75 battery moved forward. That forward movement did not stop until Nov. 11, 1918.

My acquaintance came home, was banqueted and treated as returned soldiers are usually treated by the home people immediately after the tension of war is relieved.

The home people forgot the war. Two years later, they turned out the administration which had successfully conducted our part of the war and turned the clock back.

They began to talk of disarmament. They did disarm themselves to the point of helplessness. They became fat and rich, special privilege ran the country — ran it to a fall. In

1932 a great leader came forward and rescued the country from chaos and restored the confidence of the people in their government and their institutions.

Then another European war came along. We tried as before to keep out of it. We refused to believe that we could get into it. The great leader warned the country of the possibility. He was vilified, smeared, misrepresented but kept his courage. As was inevitable we were forced into the war. The country awoke — late, but it awoke and created the greatest war production program in history under the great leader.

The country furnished Russia, Britain, China, Australia and all the Allies, guns, tanks, planes, food in unheard of quantities, built, manned and fought with the greatest navy in history, created the most powerful and efficient air force ever heard of, and equipped an army of 8½ million men and fought them on two fronts 12,000 miles apart and from 3,000 to 7,000 miles from the home base, and created the greatest merchant marine in history in order to maintain those two battle fronts.

The collapse of the enemies of liberty came almost simultaneously, in May for the eastern front and in August for the western front.

Unfortunately, the great leader who had taken the nation through the peace-time and war-time emergencies passed to his great reward just one month before the German surrender. What a pity for this to happen after twelve long years of the hardest kind of work; three and a half of them in the most terrible of all wars.

My acquaintance who commanded the 75 battery on Sept. 26, 1918 took over.

The same elation filled the home people as filled them after the first world war. They were happy to have the fighting stop and to quit worrying about their sons and daughters in the armed forces.

Then the reaction set in. Selfishness, greed, jealousy raised their ugly heads. No wartime incentive to keep them down. The same old pacifists began to talk disarmament.

But my acquaintance tried to meet every situation and has
met them up to now. Can he continue to outface the demagogues, the chiselers, and the jealousies?

Time only will tell. The human animal and his emotions
change not much from age to age. He must change now, or
he faces absolute and complete destruction, and maybe the
insect age, or an atmosphereless planet will succeed him.

MEMO TO BYRNES[3]

Truman called Secretary of State Byrnes on the carpet on
January 3, 1946, after Byrnes returned from a foreign ministers'
meeting in Moscow. Truman did not believe he had been kept
properly informed during the meeting, and did not like the way it
had gone. He called Byrnes to the Oval Office and, to be sure he
didn't miss any of the points he wanted to make, he read to Byrnes
from the following handwritten memo. It shows the President to
be upset with the way his secretary of state was implementing the
administration's foreign policy. Its main significance, though,
was its revelation of Truman's growing impatience with the
Soviets.

> As you know, I would like to pursue a policy of delegating
> authority to the members of the Cabinet in their various
> fields and then back them up in the results. But in doing that
> and in carrying out that policy I do not intend to turn over the
> complete authority of the President nor to forgo the
> President's prerogative to make the final decision.
>
> Therefore it is absolutely necessary that the President
> should be kept fully informed on what is taking place. This is
> vitally necessary when negotiations are taking place in a
> foreign capital, or even in another city than Washington.
> This procedure is necessary in domestic affairs and it is vital
> in foreign affairs. . . .
>
> I think we ought to protest with all the vigor of which we
> are capable against the Russian program in Iran. There is no
> justification for it. It is a parallel to the program of Russia in

Latvia, Estonia and Lithuania. It is also in line with the high-handed and arbitrary manner in which Russia acted in Poland.

At Potsdam we were faced with an accomplished fact and were by circumstances almost forced to agree to Russian occupation of Eastern Poland and the occupation of that part of Germany east of the Oder River by Poland. It was high-handed outrage.

At the time we were anxious for Russian entry into the Japanese War. Of course we found later that we didn't need Russia there and that the Russians have been a headache to us ever since.

When you went to Moscow you were faced with another accomplished fact in Iran. Another outrage if I ever saw one.

Iran was our ally in the war. Iran was Russia's ally in the war. Iran agreed to the free passage of arms, ammunition and other supplies running into the millions of tons across her territory from the Persian Gulf to the Caspian Sea. Without these supplies furnished by the United States, Russia would have been ignominiously defeated. Yet now Russia stirs up rebellion and keeps troops on the soil of her friend and ally — Iran.

There isn't a doubt in my mind that Russia intends an invasion of Turkey and the seizure of the Black Sea Straits to the Mediterranean. Unless Russia is faced with an iron fist and strong language another war is in the making. Only one language do they understand — 'how many divisions have you?'

I do not think we should play compromise any longer. We should refuse to recognize Rumania and Bulgaria until they comply with our requirements; we should let our position on Iran be known in no uncertain terms and we should continue to insist on the internationalization of the Kiel Canal, the Rhine-Danube waterway and the Black Sea Straits and we should maintain complete control of Japan and the Pacific. We should rehabilitate China and create a strong central government there. We should do the same for Korea.

Then we should insist on the return of our ships from Russia and force a settlement of the Lend-Lease debt of Russia.

I'm tired of babying the Soviets.

A DAY AT THE WHITE HOUSE

Truman did not keep a day-to-day diary of his thoughts and actions as President, but he wrote informal memos from time to time — about once a week, or whenever the impulse came to him. He tucked them away as notes he might refer back to sometime. They are an incomplete record, but provide interesting insights to the kind of person he was and what was going on in his mind. Following is an example of one of these handwritten memos penned on a Sunday early in his presidency.[4]

Have been going through some very hectic days. Eyes troubling me somewhat. Too much reading 'fine print.' Nearly every memorandum has a catch in it, and it has been necessary to read at least a thousand of them and as many reports.

Most of it at night. I see the Secretaries at 9:15 after dictating personal mail for 45 minutes. Usually stop in the Map Room at 8:20 and inquire about ship sinkings, casualties, etc. Read dispatches from Stalin, Churchill, Hurley and others. . . .

Saw Herbert Hoover and had a pleasant and constructive conversation on food and the general troubles of U.S. presidents — two in particular.

We discussed our prima donnas and wondered what makes them. Some of my boys who came in with me are having trouble with their dignity and prerogatives. It's hell when a man gets in close association with the President. Something happens to him. Study Rienzi and one or two others.

Some Senators and Congressmen come in and pass the time of day and then go out and help me save the world in the press.

The publicity complex is hell and few can escape its lure. When a good man comes along who has not the bug I try to grab him.

The family left for Missouri last evening. Went to the train with them and rode to Silver Spring just as I did with my Mother and sister a week or so ago.

I am always so lonesome when the family leaves. I have no one to raise a fuss over my neckties and my haircuts, my shoes and my clothes generally. I usually put on a terrible tie which not even Bob Hannegan or Ed McKim would wear, just to get a loud protest from Bess and Margie.

When they are gone, I have to put on the right ones and it's no fun.

Went to church this morning and beat the publicity boys. Walked across . . . with no advance detail and slipped into a rear pew of St. John's Church without attracting any notice. Do not think over six people recognized me. Several soldiers and sailors stood and saluted me as I walked across the park but there were no curiosity seekers around and I enjoyed the lack of them.

Had dinner on the south porch all by myself. It is a beautiful outlook across the White House lawn to the Jefferson Memorial with the Washington Monument rising just to the left of the picture. . . .

Church was rather dull. But I had a chance to do some thinking and the time was not wasted. A lot of the world's troubles have been caused by the interpretation of the Gospels and the controversies between sects and creeds. It is all so silly and comes of the prima donna complex again.

. . . I never thought God picked any favorites. It is my studied opinion that any race, creed or color can be God's favorites if they act the part and very few of them do that.

ANSWERING MAIL

The President probably gets more mail than anyone else, and Truman received a record volume. Besides official correspondence, he got praise and criticism and letters asking for something

to be done. Truman took this very seriously and tried to answer as
many letters as possible. The number he wrote and the range of
subjects was so great that it is impossible to cite one as "typical."
The first of the following letters, which provide two examples, is
Truman's reply to a woman who had written him out of disap-
pointment because her son had been unable to get a commission in
the navy.[5] The second was written to the wife of a great concert
pianist, one of Truman's favorites.[6] They are indicative of the
kind of letters Truman wrote. They were not perfunctory. They
were thoughtful and personalized, and he usually tossed in an
observation or some free advice for good measure.

A long time ago I was refused entrance to both Annapolis
and West Point because I couldn't see. Years after that I was
instrumental in helping to organize a National Guard battery
— that was in 1905. When the First World War came along,
due to the fact that I had done a lot of studying, I was made a
first lieutenant in the 129th Field Artillery in Battery 'F.' I
attended the Fort Sill, Oklahoma, School of Fire and several
other special schools. Finally I became a battery commander
and instructor in the Field Artillery firing for the regiment
and the brigade.

After the first World War, I organized the first Reserve
Officers Association in the United States and became its
President. Luckily, or unluckily, I then got into a political
career, and you know the result. So you tell that son of yours
not to be discouraged because he can't get exactly what he
wants now. The thing to do is to take the next best, make the
most of it, and you never can tell what will happen.

*   *   *   *   *   *   *   *

Dear Mrs. Lhevinne:

Thanks very much for your good letter of October tenth,
which has just now reached me. I don't know what the cause
of the delay was.

I heard Mr. Lhevinne the first time in the early 1900s
when he made one of his first tours of the United States. He
stopped in Kansas City and I remember very distinctly that

Paderewski, Moritz Rosenthal and Joseph Lhevinne all came within about three weeks of each other and each one of them played the famous A flat Opus 42 Chopin Waltz and played Blue Danube as an encore. That was when I made up my mind that Joseph Lhevinne was the greatest of them all. After that I heard him every time he came to town — I expect as much as half a dozen times. I think he had a touch and interpretation that has never been equaled. I have as many of his records as I have been able to obtain and I have almost worn out the Blue Danube I've played it so much.

I also have a Polonaise of Chopin's and I have the same Polonaise played by Iturbi. It is most interesting to compare the technique of the two men.

I certainly appreciate hearing from you, and I know that you are doing a great work at the Juilliard School of Music.

THE TRUMAN DOCTRINE[7]

The President's dramatic address to a joint session of Congress on March 12, 1947, proposed a bold response to the news that Great Britain could no longer provide aid to meet the threatened collapse of Greece and Turkey. The Truman Doctrine, as the response was called, embodied the concept of containing the expansion of Soviet power and influence, and represented the essence of Truman's foreign policy.

I believe that it must be the policy of the United States to support free peoples who are resisting attempted subjugation by armed minorities or by outside pressures.

I believe that we must assist free peoples to work out their own destinies in their own way.

I believe that our help should be primarily through economic and financial aid, which is essential to economic stability and orderly political processes.

The world is not static and the status quo is not sacred. But we cannot allow changes in the status quo in violation of the Charter of the United Nations by such methods as coercion, or by such subterfuges as political infiltration. In helping free and independent nations to maintain their freedom, the United States will be giving effect to the principles of the Charter of the United Nations.

It is necessary only to glance at a map to realize that the survival and integrity of the Greek nation are of grave importance in a much wider situation. If Greece should fall under the control of an armed minority, the effect upon its neighbor, Turkey, would be immediate and serious. Confusion and disorder might well spread throughout the entire Middle East.

Moreover, the disappearance of Greece as an independent state would have a profound effect on those countries in Europe whose peoples are struggling against great difficulties to maintain their freedoms and their independence while they repair the damages of war.

It would be an unspeakable tragedy if these countries, which have struggled so long against overwhelming odds, should lose that victory for which they sacrificed so much. Collapse of free institutions and loss of independence would be disastrous not only for them but for the world. Discouragement and possibly failure would quickly be the lot of neighboring peoples striving to maintain their freedom and independence.

Should we fail to aid Greece and Turkey in this fateful hour, the effect will be far reaching to the West as well as the East.

We must take immediate and resolute action.

I therefore ask the Congress to provide authority for assistance to Greece and Turkey in the amount of $400,000,000 for the period ending June 30, 1948. In requesting these funds, I have taken into consideration the maximum amount of relief assistance which would be furnished to Greece out of the $350,000,000 which I recently requested that the Congress authorize for the prevention of starvation and suffering in countries devastated by the war.

In addition to funds, I ask the Congress to authorize the detail of American civilian and military personnel to Greece and Turkey, at the request of those countries, to assist in the tasks of reconstruction, and for the purpose of supervising the use of such financial and material assistance as may be furnished. I recommend that authority also be provided for the instruction and training of selected Greek and Turkish personnel. . . .

The seeds of totalitarian regimes are nurtured by misery and want. They spread and grow in the evil soil of poverty and strife. They reach their full growth when the hope of a people for a better life has died.

We must keep the hope alive.

The free peoples of the world look to us for support in maintaining their freedoms.

If we falter in our leadership, we may endanger the peace of the world — and we shall endanger the welfare of our own Nation.

Great responsibilities have been placed upon us by the swift movement of events.

I am confident that the Congree will face these responsibilities squarely.

CIVIL RIGHTS MESSAGE[8]

On February 2, 1948, Truman sent this special message to Congress on civil rights. His strong stand split the Democratic Party, causing a revolt that culminated after the national convention in the formation of the States' Rights Party, or Dixiecrats. Although congressional action was slow in coming, Truman's commitment gave impetus to the civil rights movement that later won judicial and, ultimately, legislative victories to help secure these goals.

The Federal Government has a clear duty to see that Constitutional guarantees of individual liberties and of equal protection under the laws are not denied or abridged anywhere in our Union. That duty is shared by all three branches of the Government, but it can be fulfilled only if the Congress enacts modern, comprehensive civil rights laws, adequate to the needs of the day, and demonstrating our continuing faith in the free way of life.

I recommend, therefore, that the Congress enact legislation at this session directed toward the following specific objectives:

1. Establishing a permanent Commission on Civil Rights, a Joint Congressional Committee on Civil Rights, and a Civil Rights Division in the Department of Justice.

2. Strengthening existing civil rights statutes.

3. Providing Federal protection against lynching.

4. Protecting more adequately the right to vote.

5. Establishing a Fair Employment Practice Commission to prevent unfair discrimination in employment.

6. Prohibiting discrimination in interstate transportation facilities.

7. Providing home-rule and suffrage in Presidential elections for the residents of the District of Columbia.

8. Providing Statehood for Hawaii and Alaska and a greater measure of self-government for our island possessions.

9. Equalizing the opportunities for residents of the United States to become naturalized citizens.

10. Settling the evacuation claims of Japanese-Americans.

Strengthening the Government Organization

As a first step, we must strengthen the organization of the Federal Government in order to enforce civil rights legislation more adequately and to watch over the state of our traditional liberties.

I recommend that the Congress establish a permanent Commission on Civil Rights reporting to the President. The Commission should continuously review our civil rights policies and practices, study specific problems, and make recommendations to the President at frequent intervals. It should work with other agencies of the Federal Government, with state and local governments, and with private organizations.

I also suggest that the Congress establish a Joint Congressional Committee on Civil Rights. This Committee should make a continuing study of legislative matters relating to civil rights and should consider means of improving respect for and enforcement of those rights. . . .

A specific Federal measure is needed to deal with the crime of lynching — against which I cannot speak too strongly. It is a principle of our democracy, written into our Constitution, that every person accused of an offense against the law shall have a fair, orderly trial in an impartial court. We have made great progress toward this end, but I regret to say that lynching has not yet finally disappeared from our land. So long as one person walks in fear of lynching, we shall not have achieved equal justice under law. I call upon the Congress to take decisive action against this crime.

Protecting the Right to Vote

We need stronger statutory protection of the right to vote. I urge the Congress to enact legislation forbidding interference by public officers or private persons with the right of qualified citizens to participate in primary, special and general elections in which Federal officers are to be chosen. This legislation should extend to elections for state as well as Federal officers insofar as interference with the right to vote results from discriminatory action by public officers based on race, color, or other unreasonable classification.

Requirements for the payment of poll taxes also interfere with the right to vote. There are still seven states which, by their constitutions, place this barrier between their citizens and the ballot box. The American people would welcome voluntary action on the part of these states to remove this barrier. Nevertheless, I believe the Congress should enact measures insuring that the right to vote in elections for Federal officers shall not be contingent upon the payment of taxes. . . .

Fair Employment Practice Commission

Once more I repeat my request that the Congress enact fair employment practice legislation prohibiting discrimination in employment based on race, color, religion or national origin. The legislation should create a Fair Employment Practice Commission with authority to prevent discrimination by employers and labor unions, trade and professional associations, and government agencies and employment bureaus. The degree of effectiveness which the wartime Fair Employment Practice Committee attained shows that it is possible to equalize job opportunity by government action and thus to eliminate the influence of prejudice in employment.

Interstate Transportation

The channels of interstate commerce should be open to all Americans on a basis of complete equality. The Supreme Court has recently declared unconstitutional state laws requiring segregation on public carriers in interstate travel. Company regulations must not be allowed to replace unconstitutional state laws. I urge the Congress to prohibit discrimination and segregation, in the use of interstate transportation facilities, by both public officers and the employees of private companies. . . .

The position of the United States in the world today makes it especially urgent that we adopt these measures to secure for all our people their essential rights.

The people of the world are faced with the choice of freedom or enslavement, a choice between a form of government which harnesses the state in the service of the individual and a form of government which claims the individual to the needs of the state. . . .

We know that our democracy is not perfect. But we do know that it offers a fuller, freer, happier life to our people than any totalitarian nation has ever offered.

If we wish to inspire the peoples of the world whose freedom is in jeopardy, if we wish to restore hope to those who have already lost their civil liberties, if we wish to fulfill the promise that is ours, we must correct the remaining imperfections in our practice of democracy.

We know the way. We need only the will.

EXECUTIVE ORDER[9]

Since Congress failed to enact his civil rights program, Truman took a significant stride that did not require congressional action. Using the President's constitutional power as commander in chief, he issued Executive Order 9981 on July 26, 1948, to end racial segregation in the armed services.

WHEREAS it is essential that there be maintained in the armed services of the United States the highest standards of democracy, with equality of treatment and opportunity for all those who serve in our country's defense:

NOW, THEREFORE, by virtue of the authority vested in me as President of the United States, by the Constitution and the statutes of the United States, and as Commander in Chief of the armed services, it is hereby ordered as follows:

1. It is hereby declared to be the policy of the President that there shall be equality of treatment and opportunity for all persons in the armed services without regard to race, color, religion or national origin. This policy shall be put into effect as rapidly as possible, having due regard to the time required to effectuate any necessary changes without impairing efficiency or morale.

2. There shall be created in the National Military Establishment an advisory committee to be known as the President's Committee on Equality of Treatment and Opportunity in the Armed Services, which shall be composed of seven members to be designated by the President.

3. The Committee is authorized on behalf of the President to examine into the rules, procedures and practices of the armed services in order to determine in what respect such rules, procedures and practices may be altered or improved with a view to carrying out the policy of this order. The Committee shall confer and advise with the Secretary of

Defense, the Secretary of the Army, the Secretary of the
Navy, and the Secretary of the Air Force, and shall make
such recommendations to the President and to said Secretaries as in the judgment of the Committee will effectuate
the policy hereof.

4. All executive departments and agencies of the Federal
Government are authorized and directed to cooperate with
the Committee in its work, and to furnish the Committee
such information or the services of such persons as the
Committee may require in the performance of its duties.

INAUGURAL ADDRESS[10]

On January 20, 1949, Truman delivered the inaugural address
that followed his upset election victory the previous fall. In his
state of the union message to Congress two weeks earlier, he had
called again for passage of virtually the same domestic program
he had proposed in September of 1945. The inaugural speech
concentrates on foreign affairs, and contains "Point Four," the
technical assistance program through which Truman had high
hopes for helping people in developing nations to help themselves.

I accept with humility the honor which the American people
have conferred upon me. I accept it with a deep resolve to do
all that I can for the welfare of this nation and for the peace of
the world.

In performing the duties of my office, I need the help and
the prayers of every one of you. I ask for your encouragement and for your support. The tasks we face are difficult,
and we can accomplish them only if we work together.

Each period of our national history has had its special
challenges. Those that confront us now are as momentous as
any in the past. Today marks the beginning not only of a new
Administration, but of a period that will be eventful, perhaps
decisive, for us and for the world.

It may be our lot to experience, and in a large measure to
bring about, a major turning point in the long history of the

human race. The first half of this century has been marked by unprecedented and brutal attacks on the rights of man, and by the two most frightful wars in history. The supreme need of our time is for men to learn to live together in peace and harmony.

The peoples of the earth face the future with grave uncertainty, composed almost equally of great hopes and great fears. In this time of doubt, they will look to the United States as never before for good will, strength, and wise leadership.

It is fitting, therefore, that we take this occasion to proclaim to the world the essential principles of faith by which we live, and to declare our aims to all peoples. . . .

Since the end of hostilities, the United States has invested its substance and its energy in a great constructive effort to restore peace, stability, and freedom to the world. In the coming years, our program for peace and freedom will emphasize four major courses of action.

First, we will continue to give unfaltering support to the United Nations and related agencies, and we will continue to search for ways to strengthen their authority and increase their effectiveness. We believe that the United Nations will be strengthened by the new nations which are being formed in lands now advancing toward self-government under democratic principles.

Second, we will continue our programs for world economic recovery. This means that we must keep our full weight behind the European Recovery Program. We are confident of the success of this major venture in world recovery. We believe that our partners in this effort will achieve the status of self-supporting nations once again. In addition, we must carry out our plans for reducing the barriers to world trade and increasing its volume. Economic recovery and peace itself depend on increasing world trade.

Third, we will strengthen freedom-loving nations against the dangers of aggression. We are working out with a number of countries a joint agreement designed to strengthen the security of the North Atlantic area. If we can make it sufficiently clear, in advance, that any armed attack affecting our national security would be met with over-whelming force, the armed attack might never occur.

Fourth, we must embark on a bold new program for making the benefits of our scientific advances and industrial progress available for the improvement and growth of underdeveloped areas. Our aim should be to help the free peoples of the world through their own efforts, to produce more food, more clothing, more materials for housing, and more mechanical power to lighten their burdens. We invite other countries to pool their technological resources in this undertaking. Their contributions will be warmly welcomed. This should be a cooperative enterprise in which all nations work together through the United Nations and its specialized agencies whenever practicable. It must be a world-wide effort for the achievement of peace, plenty, and freedom.

Our allies are the millions who hunger and thirst after righteousness.

In due time, as our stability becomes manifest, as more and more nations come to know the benefits of democracy and to participate in growing abundance, I believe that those countries which now oppose us will abandon their delusions and join with the free nations of the world in a just settlement of international differences.

Events have brought our American democracy to new influence and new responsibilities. They will test our cour-age, our devotion to duty, and our concept of liberty. But I say to all men, what we have achieved in liberty, we will surpass in greater liberty.

Steadfast in our faith in the Almighty, we will advance toward a world where man's freedom is secure. To that end we will devote our strength, our resources, and our firmness of resolve. With God's help, the future of mankind will be assured in a world of justice, harmony, and peace.

LIFE IN THE PRESIDENCY

The pomp and elegance that surrounds the presidency were not

Truman's cup of tea. The other side — the lonely side — of the seemingly glamorous life-style comes through in this example of one of the informal memos Truman liked to dash off.[11] It also reveals the humor and unpretentiousness he retained in the presidency.

> Had dinner by myself tonight. Worked in the Lee House office until dinner time. A butler came in very formally and said 'Mr. President, dinner is served.' I walk into the dining room in the Blair House. Barnett in tails and white tie pulls out my chair, pushes me up to the table. John in tails and white tie brings me a fruit cup, Barnett takes away the empty cup. John brings me a plate, Barnett brings me a tenderloin, John brings me asparagus, Barnett brings me carrots and beets. I have to eat alone and in silence in a candlelit room. I ring. Barnett takes the plate and butter plates. John comes in with a napkin and silver crumb tray — there are no crumbs but John has to brush them off the table anyway. Barnett brings me a plate with a finger bowl and doily on it. I remove the finger bowl and doily and John puts a glass saucer and a little bowl on the plate. Barnett brings me some chocolate custard. John brings me a demitasse (at home a little cup of coffee — about two gulps) and my dinner is over. I take a hand bath in the finger bowl and go back to work. What a life!

LAW ENFORCEMENT PROBLEMS

One could dismiss as platitudes — as cynics often did — the homespun sentiments Truman was inclined to express. He would connect almost any subject to the importance of the family, education, doing right, and having a proper frame of reference — which he regarded as one based on religion and sound moral principles. But he really thought that way, and meant what he said. He put great stock in fundamental values, and would relate them to a wide range of current issues. An example is this brief speech given on February 15, 1950, to the attorney general's conference on law enforcement, which reflects much of Truman's basic philosophy and outlook.[12]

. . . It is important, therefore, that we work together in combating organized crime in all its forms. We must use our courts and our law enforcement agencies, and the moral forces of our people, to put down organized crime whenever it appears.

At the same time, we must aid and encourage gentler forces to do their work of prevention and cure. These forces include education, religion, and home training, family and child guidance, and wholesome recreation.

The most important business in this nation — or any other nation, for that matter — is raising and training children. If those children have the proper environment at home, and educationally, very, very few of them ever turn out wrong. I don't think we put enough stress on the necessity of implanting in the child's mind the moral code under which we live.

The fundamental basis of this nation's law was given to Moses on the Mount. The fundamental basis of our Bill of Rights comes from the teachings which we get from Exodus and St. Matthew, from Isaiah and St. Paul. I don't think we emphasize that enough these days.

If we don't have the proper fundamental moral background, we will finally wind up with a totalitarian government which does not believe in rights for anybody except the state.

Above all, we must recognize that human misery breeds most of our crime. We must wipe out our slums, improve the health of our citizens, and eliminate the inequalities of opportunity which embitter men and women and turn them toward lawlessness. In the long run, these programs represent the greatest of all anti-crime measures.

And I want to emphasize particularly equality of opportunity. I think every child in the nation, regardless of his race, creed or color, should have the right to a proper education. And when he has finished that education, he ought to have the right in industry to fair treatment in employment. If he is able and willing to do the job, he ought to be given a chance to do that job, no matter what his religious connections are, or what his color is.

POLICY IN KOREA[13]

Firing General MacArthur set off a public outcry that burst forth with explosive force. As the storm of protest erupted, Truman felt obliged to make a radio address to restate to the nation the policy he was pursuing in Korea. The speech does not emphasize the negative; it does not catalogue MacArthur's sins of insubordination or state the very solid case for dismissing him. Instead, Truman attempts to give a reasoned explanation of just what the American objective is and why a policy of restraint is in order.

Truman gave the speech on April 11, 1951, the day after firing MacArthur. Having thus gone on record with this statement of his position, Truman gave the floor to MacArthur and his partisans, who staged a long and emotional outburst.

The whole Communist imperialism is back of the attack on peace in the Far East. It was the Soviet Union that trained and equipped the North Koreans for aggression. The Chinese Communists massed 44 well-trained and well-equipped divisions on the Korean frontier. These were the troops they threw into battle when the North Korean Communists were beaten.

The question we have had to face is whether the Communist plan of conquest can be stopped without general war. Our Government and other countries associated with us in the United Nations believe that the best chance of stopping it without general war is to meet the attack in Korea and defeat it there.

That is what we have been doing. It is a difficult and bitter task.

But so far it has been successful.

So far, we have prevented World War III.

So far, by fighting a limited war in Korea, we have prevented aggression from succeeding, and bringing on a general war. And the ability of the whole free world to resist Communist aggression has been greatly improved.

We have taught the enemy a lesson. He has found out that

aggression is not cheap or easy. Moreover, men all over the world who want to remain free have been given new courage and new hope. They know now that the champions of freedom can stand up and fight and that they will stand up and fight. . . .

We do not want to see the conflict in Korea extended. We are trying to prevent a world war — not to start one. The best way to do that is to make it plain that we and the other free countries will continue to resist the attack.

But you may ask why can't we take other steps to punish the aggressor. Why don't we bomb Manchuria and China itself? Why don't we assist Chinese Nationalist troops to land on the mainland of China?

If we were to do these things we would be running a very grave risk of starting a general war. If that were to happen, we would have brought about the exact situation we are trying to prevent.

If we were to do these things, we would become entangled in a vast conflict on the continent of Asia and our task would become immeasurably more difficult all over the world.

What would suit the ambitions of the Kremlin better than for our military forces to be committed to a full scale war with Red China?

It may well be that, in spite of our best efforts, the Communists may spread the war. But it would be wrong — tragically wrong — for us to take the initiative in extending the war.

The dangers are great. Make no mistake about it. Behind the North Koreans and Chinese Communists in the front lines stand additional millions of Chinese soldiers. And behind the Chinese stand the tanks, the planes, the submarines, the soldiers, and the scheming rulers of the Soviet Union.

Our aim is to avoid the spread of the conflict.

The course we have been following is the one best calculated to avoid an all-out war. It is the course consistent with our obligation to do all we can to maintain international peace and security. Our experience in Greece and Berlin shows that it is the most effective course of action we can follow. . . .

If the Communist authorities realize that they cannot defeat us in Korea, if they realize it would be foolhardy to widen the hostilities beyond Korea, then they may recognize the folly of continuing their aggression. A peaceful settlement may then be possible. The door is always open.

Then we may achieve a settlement in Korea which will not compromise the principles and purposes of the United Nations.

I have thought long and hard about this question of extending the war in Asia. I have discussed it many times with the ablest military advisers in the country. I believe with all my heart that the course we are following is the best course.

I believe that we must try to limit the war to Korea for these vital reasons: To make sure that the precious lives of our fighting men are not wasted, to see that the security of our country and the free world is not needlessly jeopardized and to prevent a third world war.

A number of events have made it evident that General MacArthur did not agree with that policy. I have, therefore, considered it essential to relieve General MacArthur so that there would be no doubt or confusion as to the real purpose and aim of our policy.

It was with the deepest personal regret that I found myself compelled to take this action. General MacArthur is one of our greatest military commanders. But the cause of world peace is more important than any individual.

The change in commands in the Far East means no change whatever in the policy of the United States. We will carry on the fight in Korea with vigor and determination in an effort to bring the war to a speedy and successful conclusion.

The new commander, Lieut. Gen. Matthew Ridgway, has already demonstrated that he has the great qualities of leadership needed for this task.

We are ready, at any time, to negotiate for a restoration of peace in the area. But we will not engage in appeasement. We are only interested in real peace.

Real peace can be achieved through a settlement based on the following factors:

One: The fighting must stop.

Two: Concrete steps must be taken to insure that the fighting will not break out again.

Three: There must be an end to the aggression.

A settlement founded upon these elements would open the way for the unification of Korea and the withdrawal of all foreign forces.

In the meantime, I want to be clear about our military objective. We are fighting to resist an outrageous aggression in Korea. We are trying to keep the Korean conflict from spreading to other areas. But at the same time we must conduct our military activities so as to insure the security of our forces. This is essential if they are to continue the fight until the enemy abandons its ruthless attempt to destroy the Republic of Korea.

That is our military objective — to repel attack and to restore peace.

THOUGHTS IN MEMOS

The random thoughts Truman would jot down in private memos provide a unique source of his ideas and attitudes on a variety of subjects. Sometimes the memos reflect his mood and feelings of the moment — one time highlighting his humor, another time his irritation, still another revealing him troubled about certain difficult problems. Many of these memos give us a significant glimpse of his outlook, and record his views and thinking on subjects not connected to a particular issue of the day or current event. Following are two brief examples of these private memos. In the first, Truman jots down views ranging from constitutional matters — the proper role of the courts, legislative procedure, and making impeachment simpler — to the need for better schools.[14] The second one gives his opinion on a broader problem he perceived.[15]

The courts, I think, should be strictly judicial and not dabble in policy — except interpretation of the Constitution. It is not at all proper for courts to try to make laws or to read law school theories into the law and policy as laid down by the Congress. We want no Gestapo or Secret Police. . . . I should like to see the Constitution amended to do away with all two-thirds rules. This means treaty ratification and presidential vetoes. These two matters should be accomplished by requiring a majority of those present. Every legislator should be required to express his opinion by vote on these two most important legislative responsibilities. They should never be accomplished by unanimous consent. Impeachment should be made simpler. And an impeachment court should be set up or the Supreme Court should conduct the trial. The result to be ratified by a majority of Senate and House — same sort of majority as before stated. School system needs overhauling. Kids should learn more fundamental 'reading, writing and arithmetic.'

* * * * * * * * * * * * * * *

One of the difficulties from which this country is likely to suffer is that some seem to think that everything ought to be handed to them on a silver platter without any effort on their part. When a nation ceases to have something to struggle for it usually gets fat and dies of a heart ailment just like a human being does.

AN UNKNOWN SIDE OF TRUMAN[16]

The following is an editorial view that Eric Sevareid wrote in the *Washington Evening Star* on February 4, 1964. It is a tribute to Truman, but also a significant assessment of him by a perceptive reporter. It describes Truman's sensitivity, and discerns in this quality an unseen measure of the depth and substance of his character.

The devoted students of Sherlock Holmes are as divisive as they are numerous, but they must surely agree that there was a certain respect as well as affection implicit in Holmes' exclamation, 'Good old Watson, you are the one fixed point in a changing age!'

This must be the sentiment of many Americans, at least those of middle age or more, as they see the news films of Harry Truman striding out on his morning walk, each foot firmly planted, each crisp pronouncement — on Panama, Lyndon Johnson, Barry Goldwater — delivered with the finality of a man who has no regrets, who relishes his enemies as much as his friends, and who enjoys the final freedom: contentment with life and no fear of death.

It is a good and inspiring thing to witness, this evening of a life that was full to the brim and never seriously marred. A man's character is his fate, said the ancient Greeks. Chance, in good part, took Harry Truman to the presidency, but it was his character that kept him there and determined his historical fate: He is, without any doubt, destined to live in the books as one of the strongest and most decisive of the American Presidents.

It was Dean Acheson, Mr. Truman's Secretary of State, who said once, in musing about the presidency: 'If a President will make decisions, you're in luck. That is the essential quality. And if he has a high batting average in the correctness of his decisions, then you're in clover.'

About this quality of Truman's there was never any doubt from the beginning, in the minds of those of us who covered his presidency all the way through. His simplicity, his honesty and his self-discipline were so obvious as to be non-arguable, however much we disagreed about some of his actions and appointments. We were aware of his sensitivity about the institution of the presidency — 'This is the most honorable office a man can hold,' he used to say — and aware of his relative lack of sensitivity to criticism of himself. What we were not aware of, at least not I, was his sensitivity about the feelings of other people.

This has been a sadly belated discovery of recent days for this reporter. It was made during private and therefore, privileged conversations, but I think he will not mind if I extract the small portion of the talk that illustrates my theme. The talk had wandered back a dozen years or so, and an aide remarked that Mr. Truman should have fired so and so. The man who had occupied the most powerful office in the world immediately said, 'No, no. That would not have been right. There were other ways to do it. What you don't understand is the power of a President to hurt.'

An American President has the power to build, to set fateful events in motion, to destroy an enemy civilization, to win or lose a vast personal following. But the power of a President to hurt the feelings of another human being — this, I think, had scarcely occurred to me, and still less had it occurred to me that a President in office would have the time and the need to be aware of this particular power among so many others.

Mr. Truman went on to observe that a word, a harsh glance, a peremptory motion by a President of the United States could so injure another man's pride that it would remain a scar in his emotional system all his life.

He recalled a painful episode during one of the lectures he loves to make to student audiences about the story and the art of governing America. A college boy stood up to ask the former President what he thought of the State's Governor, whom he described as 'our local yokel.' Mr. Truman told the boy he should be ashamed of himself for his lack of respect toward the high office of Governor. The boy turned pale and sat down. Later, Mr. Truman made it a point to seek out the shaken, apologetic lad and to reassure him. He did much more. He had the boy's dean send him frequent reports on the lad's progress in school and followed his later career with the interest of a friend. What this interest by a former President must have done for the boy's pride and self-respect may be imagined.

The simple point here is that Mr. Truman had instantly

realized how a public scolding by a former President could
mark and mar the boy's inner life and his standing in the
community.

I feel gratified to have heard this story. It has given me an
insight to the responsibilities of a President that I did not
have, and it has immeasurably added to my own residue of
memories about the man from Missouri. He is nearly 80
now. He may live to be 100 — his is strong stock — but this,
I know, is the specific memory that will return to me when
his time does come.

A PRAYER[17]

Truman had written this prayer in pencil on White House
stationery, dated August 15, 1950. He later described the prayer
as one he had said since his high school days in Independence,
Missouri — during his days as timekeeper for a railroad gang, as a
bank clerk, as a farmer behind a plow, through his many years as a
public official, and as President of the United States.

Oh! Almighty and Everlasting God, Creator of Heaven,
Earth and the Universe:

Help me to be, to think, to act what is right, because it is
right; make me truthful, honest and honorable in all things;
make me intellectually honest for the sake of right and honor
and without thought of reward to me. Give me the ability to
be charitable, forgiving and patient with my fellow men —
help me to understand their motives and their shortcomings
— even as Thou understandest mine!

Amen, Amen, Amen.

Footnotes

Chapter I

[1]Harry S. Truman, *Memoirs,* Vol. I, p. 146. Cited hereafter as *Memoirs* with appropriate volume number.

[2]*Ibid.,* p. 165.

[3]Margaret Truman, *Harry S. Truman,* pp. 150–151.

[4]Cabell Phillips, *The Truman Presidency,* pp. 34–35.

[5]*The Congressional Digest,* Vol. I, No. 2 (February 1942), p. 43. Author's italics.

[6]Phillips, *Truman Presidency,* p. 37.

[7]*Memoirs,* I, p. 190.

[8]*The New York Times,* July 18, 1944.

[9]*Memoirs,* I, pp. 192–193.

[10]*The New York Times,* July 21, 1944.

[11]*Ibid.,* July 22, 1944.

[12]*Memoirs,* I., p. 193.

[13]*Ibid.,* pp. 2–4

[14]*Ibid.,* p. 57.

[15]*The New York Times,* April 1, 1945.

[16]*Ibid.,* April 8, 1945.

[17]*Ibid.*

[18]Margaret Truman, *Harry S. Truman,* pp. 225–227.

[19]*Memoirs,* I, p. 5.

[20]*Ibid.,* pp. 9–10.

[21]*Ibid.,* p. 17.

[22]*Ibid.,* p. 19.

[23]*Ibid.*

[24]*Ibid.,* p. 43.

Chapter II

[1]Alfred Steinberg, *The Man from Missouri,* p. 109.

[2]Merle Miller, *Plain Speaking,* pp. 31–32.

[3]*Ibid.,* p. 19.

[4]Steinberg, *Man from Missouri,* p. 26.

[5]*Ibid.,* pp. 23, 27–28.

[6]*Ibid.*, pp. 41–42.
[7]William Hillman, *Mr. President*, p. 171.
[8]Steinberg, *Man from Missouri*, p. 46.
[9]*Ibid.*, p. 62.
[10]*Kansas City Star*, August 3, 1924.
[11]Margaret Truman, *Harry S. Truman*, p. 76.
[12]*Ibid.*, p. 77.
[13]Steinberg, *Man from Missouri*, pp. 86–89.
[14]Margaret Truman, *Harry S. Truman*, pp. 79–80.
[15]Steinberg, *Man from Missouri*, pp. 107–108.
[16]*Ibid.*, p. 123.
[17]*The New York Times*, December 18, 1934.
[18]Phillips, *Truman Presidency*, pp. 29–30.
[19]*Ibid.*, p. 30.
[20]*Ibid.*, pp. 31–32.
[21]*The New York Times*, April 14, 1945.
[22]William S. White, *The Responsibles*, p. 30.

Chapter III

[1]*Memoirs*, I, p. 23.
[2]*Ibid.*, p. 327.
[3]Winston Churchill, *Triumph and Tragedy*, p. 497.
[4]*Ibid.*, p. 502.
[5]*Memoirs*, I, p. 214.
[6]Churchill, *Triumph and Tragedy*, p. 502.
[7]*Memoirs*, I, p. 212.
[8]*Ibid.*, pp. 265, 416.
[9]*Ibid.*, p. 314.
[10]Bill Lawrence, *Six Presidents, Too Many Wars*, p. 125.
[11]*Memoirs*, I, p. 416.
[12]*Ibid.*, p. 419.
[13]Official Japanese statistics released six months after the war and quoted in Len Giovannitti and Fred Freed, *The Decision to Drop the Bomb*, p. 269.
[14]*Memoirs*, I, p. 419.
[15]*Ibid.*, p. 412.

Chapter IV

[1]Hillman, *Mr. President*, p. 23.
[2]Quoted in George F. Kennan, *Memoirs, 1925-1950*, Appendix C, pp. 547–559.
[3]Joseph M. Jones, *The Fifteen Weeks*, p. 133.
[4]*Department of State Bulletin*, XIV (March 10, 1946), pp. 355–358.

[5]*The President's Speeches,* 1946, Original (Harry S. Truman Library). Cited hereafter as *Speeches* with appropriate year.

[6]American Institute of Public Opinion poll of March 13, 1946, cited in Cantril and Strunk (eds.) *Public Opinion,* pp. 963, 1060.

[7]Arthur Krock, *Memoirs,* pp. 224–231 and Appendix A.

[8]Interview with Harry S. Truman, November 18, 1959.

[9]Quoted in Jones, *Fifteen Weeks,* p. 142.

[10]*Memoirs,* II, p. 105.

[11]*Speeches,* 1947 (Truman Library).

[12]*Memoirs,* II, p. 113, and Jones, *Fifteen Weeks,* pp. 25–27 and 276–280.

[13]Harry Bayard Price, *The Marshall Plan and Its Meaning,* p. 22.

[14]W. Phillips Davison, *The Berlin Blockade,* pp. 109–110.

Chapter V

[1]Quoted in Steinberg, *Man from Missouri,* p. 268.

[2]*Ibid.,* pp. 302–303.

[3]*Ibid.,* p. 304.

[4]Krock, *Memoirs,* pp. 240–241.

[5]*Memoirs,* II, p. 186.

[6]*Ibid.,* pp. 207–208.

[7]Margaret Truman, *Harry S. Truman,* p. 5.

[8]*Ibid.,* p. 19.

[9]*Ibid.,* p. 25.

[10]Lawrence, *Six Presidents,* p. 166.

Chapter VI

[1]Herbert Feis, *The China Tangle,* p. 410.

[2]United States Department of State, *United States Relations with China,* pp. 131–132. Cited hereafter as *Relations.*

[3]White House Central Files, OF 150, Truman Papers, Harry S. Truman Library. Cited hereafter as *Central Files.*

[4]*Relations,* p. 652.

[5]*Ibid.*

[6]*Ibid.,* pp. 209–211.

[7]Statement by the President, December 18, 1946, *Central Files* (Truman Library).

[8]*Relations,* pp. 255, 763–864.

[9]*Ibid.,* pp. 260, 774.

[10]United States Congress, *House Document No. 536,* 80th Congress, 2nd Session, p. 2.

[11]*Ibid.,* p. 4.

[12]Memorandum, Robert A. Lovett to the President, October 11, 1948, *Central Files* (Truman Library).
[13]*Relations*, p. 885.
[14]*Ibid.*, p. 887.
[15]*Ibid.*, p. 279.
[16]*Ibid.*, p. 280.
[17]Statement by the President, August 5, 1949, *Central Files* (Truman Library).
[18]Statement by the President, January 5, 1950, *Central Files* (Truman Library).

Chapter VII

[1]Truman, *Memoirs,* II, pp. 236–237.
[2]*Ibid.*, p. 230.
[3]*The New York Times*, March 2, 1949.
[4]Memorandum to the President from the joint chiefs — then made up of Admirals Leahy and Nimitz and Generals Spaatz and Eisenhower — quoted in *Memoirs,* II, p. 325.
[5]*Ibid.*, p. 331.
[6]*Ibid.*, pp. 334–335.
[7]Transcript of Press Conference, June 29, 1950, Records of the White House Official Reporter, Truman Papers, Harry S. Truman Library. Cited hereafter as *Transcript* with appropriate date.
[8]Dean Acheson, *Present at the Creation*, p. 518.
[9]Senate Committees on Armed Services and Foreign Relations, 82nd Congress, 1st Session, *Hearings to Conduct an Inquiry into the Military Situation in the Far East and the Facts Surrounding the Relief of General of the Army Douglas MacArthur from His Assignments in That Area*, pp. 3541–3542. Cited hereafter as *Hearings, Military Situation in the Far East.*
[10]*Ibid.*, p. 3544.
[11]Hillman, *Mr. President*, p. 33.
[12]Steinberg, *Man from Missouri*, p. 401.
[13]*Memoirs,* II, p. 492.
[14]*Transcript,* April 16, 1952 (Truman Library).
[15]David S. Thompson, *HST*, p. 120.
[16]*Transcript,* December 22, 1952 (Truman Library).
[17]*The New York Times*, January 20, 1953.
[18]Thompson, *HST*, p. 125.

Chapter VIII

[1]S. J. Woolf, "President Truman: A Portrait and Interview," *The New York Times Magazine*, October 14, 1945, pp. 5, 48.

[2]*Ibid.,* pp. 47, 49.

[3]Acheson, *Present at the Creation,* p. 730.

[4]*Ibid.,* p. 731.

[5]Arthur Krock, writing in *The New York Times Magazine,* April 7, 1946.

[6]Edward T. Folliard, reporting in *The Washington Post,* October 23, 1945.

[7]Jonathan Daniels, *The Man of Independence,* p. 25.

[8]Thompson, *HST,* p. 123.

[9]Acheson, *Present at the Creation,* pp. 732–733.

[10]Steinberg, *Man from Missouri,* p. 429.

[11]*Ibid.*

[12]Phillips, *Truman Presidency,* pp. 399–400.

[13]*Ibid.,* p. 401.

[14]William S. White, *The Responsibles,* pp. 43, 28–29.

[15]*Ibid.,* pp. 11–17.

[16]Press conference of July 27, 1972.

[17]Letter to columnist Vic Gold, quoted in *The Washington Star,* March 5, 1974.

[18]Gaddis Smith, "Visions and Revisions of the Cold War," *The New York Times Magazine,* April 29, 1973, p. 55.

[19]Charles L. Mee, *Meeting at Potsdam,* p. 135.

[20]Clinton Rossiter, *The American Presidency,* pp. 16–43.

[21]Address by Richard S. Kirkendall at Columbia, Missouri, January 17, 1973, published in *Harry S. Truman: Memorial Tributes Delivered in Congress,* pp. 70–71. Cited hereafter as *Tributes.*

[22]Rossiter, *American Presidency,* pp. 143–144.

[23]*Ibid.,* pp. 153–154.

[24]Samuel Eliot Morison, *The Two-Ocean War,* p. 572.

[25]Rossiter, *American Presidency,* p. 154.

[26]D. W. Brogan, "An Historian's View of Harry Truman's Presidency," in Thompson, *HST,* p. 138. Brogan's article is also reproduced in *Tributes,* pp. 108–111.

[27]Kirkendall, *Tributes,* p. 71.

[28]Rossiter, *American Presidency,* pp. 155–157.

[29]*Ibid.,* pp. 157–158.

[30]Brogan, "Historian's View," p. 139.

[31]*Memoirs,* II, pp. 59–64.

[32]Rossiter, *American Presidency,* p. 158.

[33]Kirkendall, *Tributes,* p. 71.

[34]Brogan, "Historian's View," p. 141.

[35]Rossiter, *American Presidency,* p. 159.

[36]Brogan, "Historian's View," p. 141.

[37]Miller, *Plain Speaking,* pp. 134, 188, 308.

[38]*The New York Times Magazine,* February 10, 1974.

[39]George M. Elsey, "Truman's White House," in *The Washington Post,* June 5, 1974.

Appendix

[1]Excerpts from *Public Papers of the Presidents of the United States: Harry S. Truman,* 1945, pp. 263–309.

[2]Hillman, *Mr. President,* pp. 7–8.

[3]Excerpts from *Memoirs,* I, pp. 551–552.

[4]Excerpts from Hillman, *Mr. President,* pp. 117–118.

[5]*Ibid.,* pp. 34–35.

[6]*Ibid., p. 43.*

[7]*Speeches,* 1947 (Truman Library). Also in the *Congressional Record,* 80th Congress, 1st Session, pp. 1980–1981.

[8]Excerpts from *Public Papers: Truman,* 1948, pp. 121–126.

[9]*Federal Register,* XVIII, p. 722.

[10]Excerpts from *Speeches,* 1949 (Truman Library). Also in Lewis Copeland (ed.), *The World's Great Speeches,* pp. 589–591.

[11]Hillman, *Mr. President,* p. 143.

[12]*Ibid.,* pp. 71–72.

[13]Excerpts from *Speeches,* 1951 (Truman Library). Also in *Hearings, Military Situation in the Far East,* pp. 3547–3551.

[14]Hillman, *Mr. President,* p. 114.

[15]*Ibid.,* p. 232.

[16]Reprinted in Phillips, *Truman Presidency,* pp. 433–434.

[17]Hillman, *Mr. President,* unnumbered page preceding the Foreword.

Bibliography

PRIMARY SOURCES

Acheson, Dean. *Present at the Creation: My Years in the State Department*. New York: W.W. Norton, 1969.

Bernstein, Barton J. and Allen J. Matusow. *The Truman Administration: A Documentary History*. New York: Harper and Row, 1966. (Available in paperback, Har-Row CN120.)

Bohlen, Charles E. *Witness to History*. New York: W.W. Norton, 1973.

Byrnes, James F. *All in One Lifetime*. New York: Harper, 1958.

———. *Speaking Frankly*. New York: Harper, 1947.

Clemons, Cyril (ed.). *Truman Speaks*. Webster Groves, Missouri: International Mark Twain Society, 1946.

Congressional Digest.

Congressional Record.

Copeland, Lewis (ed.). *The World's Great Speeches*. New York: Dover, 1958.

Council on Foreign Relations. *Documents on American Foreign Relations*.

Dennett, Raymond and Robert K. Turner (eds.). *Documents on American Foreign Relations*. Vol. IX, 1947. Princeton, New Jersey: Princeton University Press, 1949.

——— — ———. *Documents on American Foreign Relations*. Vol. X, 1948. Princeton, New Jersey: Princeton University Press, 1950.

Department of State Bulletin.

Harry S. Truman: Memorial Tributes Delivered in Congress. Washington: U.S. Government Printing Office, 1973.

Hillman, William. *Mr. President: The First Publication from the Personal Diaries, Private Letters, Papers and Revealing*

Interviews of Harry S. Truman. New York: Farrar, Straus and Young, 1952.

Kennan, George F. *Memoirs.* Boston: Little, Brown, 1967.

Krock, Arthur. *Memoirs.* New York: Funk and Wagnalls, 1968.

Miller, Merle. *Plain Speaking: An Oral Biography of Harry S. Truman.* New York: Berkley, 1973. (Available in paperback, Berkley Medallion T2664.)

Millis, Walter (ed.). *The Forrestal Diaries.* New York: Viking Press, 1951.

Public Papers of the Presidents of the United States.

The New York Times.

Transcripts of Press Conferences. Records of the White House Official Reporter. Truman Papers, Harry S. Truman Library, Independence, Missouri.

Truman, Harry S. *Memoirs.* 2 vols.; New York: Doubleday, 1956.

———. *Mr. Citizen.* New York: Bernard Geis Associates, 1953.

———. "Public Opinion and American Foreign Policy," *Department of State Bulletin,* XXI (August 1, 1949), 145–147.

Truman, Margaret. *Harry S. Truman.* New York: William Morrow, 1973. (Available in paperback, Pocket Books 78647.)

U.S. Congress, *House Document No. 536,* 80th Congress, 2nd Session.

U.S. Congress, Senate Committees on Armed Services and Foreign Relations, 82nd Congress, 1st Session. *Hearings to Conduct an Inquiry into the Military Situation in the Far East and the Facts Surrounding the Relief of General of the Army Douglas MacArthur from His Assignments in That Area.* Washington: U.S. Government Printing Office, 1952.

U.S. Department of Commerce, Bureau of Foreign and Domestic Commerce, Office of Business Economics. *Foreign Aid by the United States Government, 1940–1951.* Washington: U.S. Government Printing Office, 1952.

U.S. Department of State. *American Foreign Policy, 1950–1955*. 2 vols.; Washington: U.S. Government Printing Office, 1956.

U.S. Department of State. *American Opinion Report*. (1940–1949)

U.S. Department of State. *NATO, 1949–1959, The First Ten Years*. Publication No. 6783, March, 1959.

U.S. Department of State. *Point 4*. Publication No. 4868, February, 1953.

U.S. Department of State, *The Conference of Berlin (The Potsdam Conference)*. 2 vols.; Washington: U.S. Government Printing Office, 1960.

U.S. Department of State. *United States Relations with China*. Washington: U.S. Government Printing Office, 1949.

U.S. International Cooperation Administration, Office of Public Reports. *NATO, Its Development and Significance*. Washington: U.S. Government Printing Office, 1955.

Vandenberg, Arthur H. Jr. (ed.). *The Private Papers of Senator Vandenberg*. Cambridge, Massachusetts: Houghton Mifflin, 1952.

Vital Speeches.

Washington Post.

Washington Star-News.

White House Central Files, OF 150, 1945–1952. Truman Papers, Harry S. Truman Library, Independence, Missouri.

White House General Files (China — 1948, 1949). Truman Papers, Harry S. Truman Library, Independence, Missouri.

Wilcox, Francis O. and Thorsten V. Kalijarvi. *Recent American Foreign Policy: Basic Documents, 1941–1951*. New York: Appleton-Century-Crofts, 1952.

SECONDARY SOURCES

Almond, Gabriel A. *The American People and Foreign Policy*. New York: Harcourt, Brace, 1950.

Alperovitz, Gar. *Atomic Diplomacy*. New York: Simon and Schuster, 1965.

Beloff, Max. *Foreign Policy and the Democratic Process.* Baltimore: Johns Hopkins University Press, 1955.

Berman, William C. *The Politics of Civil Rights in the Truman Administration.* Columbus, Ohio: Ohio State University Press, 1970.

Bernstein, Barton J. (ed.). *Politics and Policies of the Truman Administration.* New York: Watts, 1970. (Available in paperback, Quadrangle, QP72.)

Brown, Seyom. *The Faces of Power: Constancy and Change in U.S. Foreign Policy from Truman to Johnson.* New York: Columbia University Press, 1968. (Available in paperback, Columbia C97.)

Brown, William Adams, Jr. and Redaers Opie. *American Foreign Assistance.* Washington: The Brookings Institution, 1953.

Carleton, William G. *The Revolution in American Foreign Policy, 1945–1954.* New York: Doubleday, 1954.

Churchill, Winston S. *Triumph and Tragedy.* Boston: Houghton Mifflin, 1953.

Council on Foreign Relations. *The United States in World Affairs, 1945–1947.* New York: Harper, 1947.

———. *The United States in World Affairs, 1947–1948.* New York: Harper, 1948.

———. *The United States in World Affairs, 1949.* New York: Harper, 1950.

———. *The United States in World Affairs, 1950.* New York: Harper, 1951.

———. *The United States in World Affairs, 1951.* New York: Harper, 1952.

———. *The United States in World Affairs, 1952.* New York: Harper, 1953.

Cochran, Bert. *Harry Truman and the Crisis Presidency.* New York: Thomas Y. Crowell, 1973.

Daniels, Jonathan. *Man of Independence.* Port Washington, New York: Kennikat, 1971.

Davies, Richard O. *Housing Reform During the Truman Administration.* Columbia, Missouri: University of Missouri Press, 1966.

Davison, W. Phillips. *The Berlin Blockade*. Princeton, New Jersey: Princeton University Press, 1958.

Dayton, Eldorous L. *Give 'em Hell Harry*. Old Greenwich, Connecticut: Devin, 1956.

Dean, Vera M. *Foreign Policy Without Fear*. New York: McGraw-Hill, 1953.

Druks, Herbert. *Harry S. Truman and the Russians*. New York: Robert Speller and Sons, 1967.

Elder, Robert Ellsworth. *The Policy Machine: The Department of State and American Foreign Policy*. Syracuse, New York: Syracuse University Press, 1960.

Fairbank, John K. *The United States and China*. Cambridge, Massachusetts: Harvard University Press, 1948.

Feis, Herbert. *The Atomic Bomb and the End of World War II*. Princeton, New Jersey: Princeton University Press, 1966.

————. *Between War and Peace*. Princeton, New Jersey: Princeton University Press, 1960.

Freeland, Richard. *The Truman Doctrine and the Origins of McCarthyism*. New York: Alfred A. Knopf, 1972.

Gaddis, John Lewis. *The United States and the Origins of the Cold War*. New York: Columbia University Press, 1972. (Available in paperback, Columbia C133.)

Giovannitti, Len and Fred Freed, *The Decision to Drop The Bomb*. New York: Coward-McCann, 1965.

Gordon, Morton and Kenneth N. Vines. *Theory and Practice of American Foreign Policy*. New York: Thomas Y. Crowell, 1955.

Halle, Louis J. *The Cold War as History*. New York: Harper and Row, 1967. (Available in paperback, Har-Row, CN202.)

Hamby, Alonzo L. *Beyond the New Deal: Harry S. Truman and American Liberalism*. New York: Columbia University Press, 1973.

Hartmann, Susan. *Truman and the 80th Congress*. Columbia, Missouri: University of Missouri Press, 1971.

Haynes, Richard F. *The Awesome Power: Harry S. Truman as Commander in Chief*. Baton Rouge, Louisiana: Louisiana State University Press, 1973.

Hehmeyer, Walter and Frank McNaughton. *This Man Truman*.

New York: Whittlesey House, 1945.

Helm, William P. *Harry Truman, A Political Biography*. New York: Duell, Sloan and Pearce, 1947.

Jones, Joseph M. *The Fifteen Weeks*. New York: Viking Press, 1955.

Kennan, George F. *American Diplomacy, 1900–1950*. Chicago: The University of Chicago Press, 1951.

Koenig, Louis W. (ed.). *The Truman Administration: Its Principles and Practice*. Washington Square, New York: New York University Press, 1956.

Kolko, Joyce and Gabriel. *The Limits of Power*. New York: Harper and Row, 1972.

Latourette, Kenneth S. *The American Record in the Far East, 1945–1951*. New York: Macmillan, 1952.

Lawrence, Bill. *Six Presidents, Too Many Wars*. New York: Saturday Review Press, 1972.

Lee, R. Alton. *Truman and Taft-Hartley*. Lexington, Kentucky: University Press of Kentucky, 1966.

Lenczowski, George. *Russia and the West in Iran, 1918–1948: A Study in Big-Power Rivalry*. Ithaca, New York: Cornell University Press, 1949.

Lerche, Charles O., Jr. *Foreign Policy of the American People*. Englewood Cliffs, New Jersey: Prentice-Hall, 1958.

Lippmann, Walter. *The Cold War*. New York: Harper, 1947.

Markei, Lester *et al. Public Opinion and Foreign Policy*. New York: Harper and Brothers, 1949.

Mee, Charles L., Jr. *Meeting at Potsdam*. New York: Evans, 1975.

Morison, Samuel Eliot. *The Two-Ocean War*. Boston: Little, Brown, 1963.

Morley, Felix. *The Foreign Policy of the United States*. New York: Alfred A. Knopf, 1951.

Mosteller, Frederick. *The Pre-Election Polls of 1948*. New York: Social Science Research Council, 1949.

Notter, Harley A. *Post-War Foreign Policy Preparation, 1939–1945*. Department of State Publication No. 3580, February, 1950.

Osgood, Robert E. and Robert W. Tucker *et al. America and the World, From the Truman Doctrine to Vietnam*. Baltimore: Johns Hopkins University Press, 1969.

Phillips, Cabell. *The Truman Presidency*. New York: Macmillan, 1966. (Available in paperback, Pelican A1140.)

Platig, E. Raymond. *The United States and the Soviet Challenge*. Chicago: Science Research Associates, 1960.

Price, Harry Bayard. *The Marshall Plan and Its Meaning*. Ithaca, New York: Cornell University Press, 1955.

Rosenau, James N. *Public Opinion and Foreign Policy*. New York: Random House, 1961.

Rossiter, Clinton. *The American Presidency*. New York: Harcourt, Brace, Jovanovich, 1956. (Available in paperback, Harvest HB 35.)

Schnapper, M.B. (ed.). *The Truman Program*. Washington: Public Affairs Press, 1948.

Schoenberger, Walter. *Decision of Destiny*. Athens, Ohio: Ohio University Press, 1970.

Sherwin, Martin. *A World Destroyed: The Atomic Bomb and the Grand Alliance*. New York: Alfred A. Knopf, 1975.

Spanier, John W. *The Truman-MacArthur Controversy and the Korean War*. Cambridge, Massachusetts: Belknap Press, 1959.

Steinberg, Alfred. *The Man from Missouri*. New York: G.P. Putnam's Sons, 1962.

Stone, Isidor F. *The Truman Era*. London: Turnstile Press, 1953.

Thompson, Danicl S. *HST*. New York: Grosset and Dunlap, 1973.

Westerfield, H. Bradford. *Foreign Policy and Party Politics, Pearl Harbor to Korea*. New Haven, Connecticut: Yale University Press, 1955.

White, Theodore H. and Annalee Jacoby. *Thunder Out of China*. New York: William Sloane Associates, 1946.

White, William S. *The Responsibles*. New York: Harper and Row, 1972.

Williams, William Appelman. *American-Russian Relations, 1781–1947*. New York: Rinehart, 1952.

————. (ed.). *From Colony to Empire: Essays in the History of American Foreign Relations*. New York: Wiley, 1972.

————. (ed.). *The Shaping of American Diplomacy*. Chicago: Rand McNally, 1956.

————. *The Tragedy of American Diplomacy*. New York: World, 1959. (Available in paperback, Delta 9007-5.)

Wriston, Henry M. *Diplomacy in a Democracy*. New York: Harper and Brothers, 1956.

Index

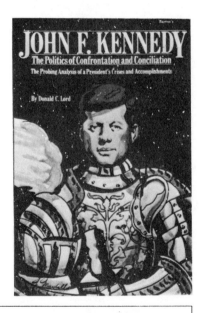

A serious attempt to deal with Jimmy Carter and what he stands for, with emphasis on his past record as state senator and Governor of Georgia, his campaign for the presidency and a look at his administration. $2.95

With information on Indian nationalism, the political scene in Gandhi's time, his own religious evolution, his ethics and economics, and his attitudes toward war and untouchablility. $2.95

The dual biographies in the series present a contrastive view. They offer fresh, previously unexplored perspectives and reveal surprising similarities and differences. $3.95

Thomas Wendel presents the reader with the varied — sometimes conflicting aspects of Franklin's life as a printer, inventor, politician, land speculator, statesman, and philosopher. $3.50

Jefferson & Hamilton presents history as it was lived by two young men. The problems they faced and the controversies that divided them are presented through a balanced treatment. $4.95

Cowboy, hunter, soldier, author, politician: our 26th President held the attention and enthusiasm of the nation perhaps as no other President has since. I. E. Cadenhead, Jr., presents an objective but vivid account of Roosevelt's controversial career. $3.95

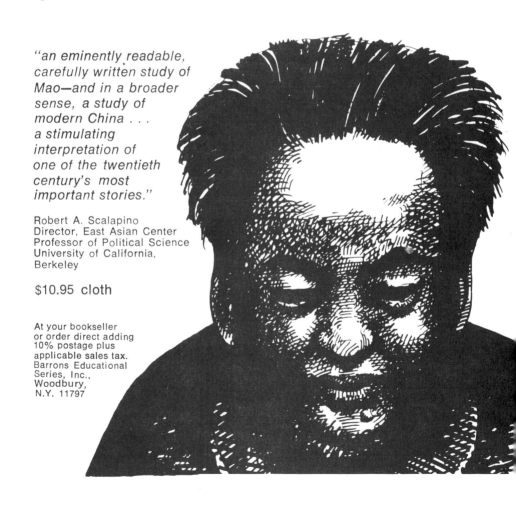

WRITING THE HISTORY PAPER

**How to Select,
Collect, Interpret,
Organize, and
Write Your
Term Paper**

By David Sanderlin

Use the methods of
historical scholarship
to produce a profes-
sional paper. With
extensive discussion of
the reasons for research
and suggestions for
applying the topic to
the contemporary
world. Also develops
the ability to use the
tools of research and
sharpens the historical
thinking process. With
a lengthy bibliography
of standard historical
references and outlines
of Dewey Decimal and
Library of Congress
classification systems.

Barron's Educational
Series, Inc. $2.50